Nothing to Declare: A Guide to the Flash Sequence

D1557318

Nothing to Declare
A Guide to the Flash Sequence

Edited by
Robert Alexander, Eric Braun, and Debra Marquart

WHITE PINE PRESS / BUFFALO, NEW YORK

WHITE PINE PRESS
P.O. Box 236 Buffalo, New York 14201
www.whitepine.org

Copyright © 2016 by White Pine Press

All rights reserved. This work, or portions thereof, may not be reproduced in any form without the written permission of the publisher.

Acknowledgments:

Acknowledgments for the individual pieces are included in the Contributors' Notes.

Publication of this book was made possible, in part, with public funds from the New York State Council on the Arts, a State Agency.

Cover photograph: Rocky Acosta. *IBM Automatic Sequence Controlled Calculator Sequence Indicators.* Copyright © 2015 Rocky Acosta. Used by permission.

Marie Alexander Poetry Series, No. 20

First Edition

ISBN: 978-1-935210-81-8

Printed and bound in the United States of America.
.
Library of Congress Control Number: 2015943680

Contents

A NOTE FROM THE SERIES EDITOR

Nickole Brown

Here, then, is the Marie Alexander Series' fourth anthology, a continuation of our mission to promote the appreciation, enjoyment, and understanding of American prose poetry and to demonstrate the broader literary context within which this elusive form exists. With *Nothing to Declare: A Guide to the Flash Sequence*, our mission takes on a unique focus— the flash sequence, defined in our call to writers as an "accumulation of two or more prose pieces, with each segment not to exceed 500 words." Those vague terms—*accumulation*, not *series*; *pieces* and *segments*, not *prose poems* or *flash prose*—were intentional, inviting the wide range of what the form has to offer and embracing the possibilities of cross-genre work. What you will find here represents the diverse assortment of work we received: linked prose poems, narrative sequences, lyrical essays, and many surprises in between, such as groupings of koans and fairy tales and epistolary addresses. For this reason, the selections are simply presented alphabetically; any other order imposed on these wild variations seemed forced. But what they have in common is that each sequence in its entirety stands alone as a fully realized and crafted piece of writing, and we'll leave it up to you to decide how to categorize them if you so desire.

Of course, what makes the idea of the sequence—or any literature, for that matter—compelling is not how you define it but how you experience it. The title, *Nothing to Declare*, suggests a reader at home both everywhere and nowhere, traveling with little burden and no need to be defined. For us, witnessing the originality of each author's approach to the task—gathering various short pieces together under the auspices of a single work—was something we enjoyed tremendously. With a close look at what happens *between* the segments, the white space often crackles with its own energy, acting sometimes as connective tissue, sometimes as the gravity between two discrete but related planets of prose. Much like the gutter between panels in a comic book, the gap between one given illustration and the next is where the reader does the good work of imagination and juxtaposition, exploring the transitions, filling in what's left unsaid. This exercise is what creates both the propulsion and tension that gives the flash sequence its unique flavor. Even the different ways authors chose to separate their fragments on the page—with simple line breaks or numbers or subtitles—creates a certain frisson.

Since 1996, the Marie Alexander Series has been a safe harbor for the much misunderstood (and often neglected) prose poem. For two decades, we've published one or two books annually. These titles are usually by a single author, but occasionally we muster up the gumption to take on an anthology. In fact, our first anthology appeared even before the series had a name, a collection of contemporary prose poems titled *The Party Train*, published by New Rivers Press. Since then, we've also taken on an anthology of international prose poetry—*The House of Your Dream*, published in 2008—and, in 2012, we investigated the history of the form with *Family Portrait: American Prose Poetry, 1900-1950*.

With *Nothing to Declare*, we're happy to continue our exploration of this important though hard-to-define form. This collection of flash sequences is testament to the simple pleasure of continuity, of seeing what comes before and what comes after, fulfilling that basic human urge to answer the question, *What next?* And although there are several selections here that move along the smooth trajectory of linear short stories, most make up their own rules for what defines a sequence. Some are braided, others collaged together by subject matter or writing style; still others fractal outwards, taking an intuitive and internal logic of their own. Moreover, all these sequences gain a certain momentum by gathering together into a chorus of sorts to make a layered and deepening song. We hope you enjoy the complexities of their music and appreciate this surprising collection as much as we do.

Nothing to Declare

Robert Alexander

Richmond Burning

When I met her she was wearing on the lapel of her vest, where a carnation or a political button might go in election years, a two-inch image of Jupiter. This was a Halloween party but the button and vest were her only costume, unless you count her chicory-blue eyes and the purple leotard she had on beneath her vest.

"What's with Jupiter," I asked the woman whose name I had not yet learned.

"Abundance," she said. "Jupiter signifies abundance."

"I could use some of that," I told her. Her blue eyes were abundance enough for me. Shortly after that, a couple of beers beneath our belts, we went back to my apartment, the upstairs of a small story-and-a-half, to walk my dog around the block and get to know each other better, to set our costumes aside.

*　　*　　*

The couple leaving the Richmond airport looked from a distance like many at this time of year, dressed for Christmas vacation, a casual but slightly dressy air that signifies dinner with family and, a day later, an hour spent opening presents beside a well-lit tree. She wore an alpaca scarf which lay lightly on her leather coat, and he an overcoat that looked as though it could have come off one of the Confederate statues on Monument Avenue. Which is to say it appeared an even shade of gray, the sparse colored threads of the Harris Tweed blending into the gray warp and weft.

After picking up their rental car, they drove from the airport, by the old Confederate fortifications (only a few cannon and mounds of earth remaining from the fifty-mile dike which, for nearly four years, held back the Yankee tide)—and headed on the empty expressway to their hotel downtown, on the south side of Capitol Square. This being Christmas Eve, all the politicians had gone back to their wives and families, leaving their mistresses for the more tedious distractions of home: wrapping Christmas presents, trimming the tree, attending the seasonal caroling at the local school or church. Hence there were suites available at a heavily-discounted rate, less than the usual cost of a single room, which the husband appreciated, his wife having expensive and not-often-satisfied tastes. The trade-off was this: for the cost of a single room facing the Capitol, you could have a suite of back rooms with no view at all.

It was the only hotel that he had ever been in where—instead of a mini-bar stocking those tiny bottles of booze that airlines sell their passengers—the bottom drawer of the customary hotel dresser was filled with an assortment of pints and half-pints of whiskey. Here he saw an eminent example of traditional Virginia smoking-room politics, played out over a deck of cards.

*   *   *

That year I spent most afternoons in the rare book reading room of the University library, paging through brittle copies of literary magazines dating from the early years of the twentieth century. In the early evening I'd leave the library and return to my sorrowful dog in my upstairs apartment, and then after dinner she of the purple leotard would show up with a bottle of wine, climb the back stairs of the house and knock on my door. I will spare myself the pain of voyeuristi-

cally reliving the sweet details, from a time so long gone, and leave the erotica to the reader's imagination.

*   *   *

A short time later darkness had fallen and the couple left the hotel and walked across the street to their rental car parked alongside Capitol Square, which was enclosed by a dark iron fence. Inside was the massive form of Jefferson's white Capitol, façade lit by spotlights, surrounded by oaks whose fallen leaves lay in the gutter by the car. The temperature was around freezing and there were spots of ice among the leaves. In normal times there wouldn't have been a parking place for blocks around, but this Christmas Eve all was quiet as they stepped gingerly across the fallen oak leaves.

It was, given the empty streets, a shorter drive than usual to her adoptive mother's house in Henrico County. It is a peculiarity of Virginia that certain "independent" cities lie like separate islands within their surrounding counties. Thus there were no sheriffs patrolling the city streets and it was unusual, in certain neighborhoods, to see a traffic cop at all. The police had their hands full elsewhere, Richmond being one hub of a bustling trade in which drugs from New York City were brought south and exchanged for firearms where gun laws were more lax.

*   *   *

We shared our stories with each other. Dropping out of college, she'd left for California years before. Now she was back and planned to spend the winter living in a friend's apartment on the East Side, studying astrology with a guy who had a slot on a local radio show. She told me she had fallen in love

19

with her voice instructor in college—who was, as I recall, al-
ready married—and had become pregnant with his child. He
never learned that she gave birth to a baby girl. In California
she had put their child up for adoption.

*   *   *

Later, he would look back at that dinner as the opening scene
in the final act of his marriage. His mother-in-law was there,
and her sister—and the neighbor from across the street, a
woman twenty-some years younger who drove the van when
they all went on excursions to Charlottesville. "I miss the
summers here," his wife said, "when you lie in bed at night
and your body's covered by a thin layer of sweat." He re-
membered cicadas and honeysuckle, a slight breeze through
the willow oak out back.

*   *   *

Like all such things this couldn't last, and didn't. By January
we had burned each other out and she left for California. The
winter in Wisconsin and the memories of her home above the
Russian River had sent her westward once again.

I followed her out there on my spring break—I remember
flying over the snow-covered Sierras shining beneath a full
moon—and for a couple of weeks we lived together in an old
wine vat with a roof of sliding Plexiglass panels, perched on
the side of a mountain. We opened the panels to the madroño
trees and redwoods, to cloudless sky. I began investigating
the possibility of teaching at a local college.

One morning my lover told me it was her daughter's
birthday. She carried that sadness within her—probably one
thing that so attracted me to her—and each year, on that par-
ticular day, it rose and nearly swamped her.

At the college they told me they could have their choice of any poet they wanted in the Bay Area—so why would they choose me? I returned to my apartment and my little magazines, while the Wisconsin spring began in its slow way to flower the landscape. Soon I finished my degree and quit teaching altogether. And my California friend I saw only once again, a few years later, when she was back for a brief visit and we went out for breakfast. Her eyes were as blue as I remembered.

*   *   *

Back in their hotel room the first thing she did, after taking off her coat, was to pour herself a drink from the half-filled pint of Maker's Mark.

"So where is it?" she asked him.

He had worried about it all through both airports, going through security in Madison and then again walking through the airport in Richmond. He always worried when he carried weed on a plane, though in those far off days before 9/11 security was a spotty affair at best. But there was always the chance a butterfly could flap its wings in Mexico and his suitcase would fall off the conveyor belt and split open on the tarmac, and his rolled-up socks fall out for all to view.

"I'm saving it for Christmas," he said. "Something special for Santa."

She slapped him hard across the mouth. His lips stung, and he tasted blood from where her wedding ring had caught him.

"Fuck you," he told her. "You can wait until tomorrow."

She slapped him again. And then she closed her fist and hit him in the face.

*   *   *

In the meantime the father of her child had become a public figure. The local chamber music society, which he conducted, began playing a series of public concerts downtown during the summer months. Every Wednesday evening at these "Concerts on the Green" a local French restaurant provided box picnics for people drinking wine out on the lawn.

*   *   *

It wasn't the first time she'd gotten violent. He'd been advised to stay away until the rage subsided. But this time it was a suite they were in, and there was a second bedroom— so he went into the second room, closed the door and put the little hook through the loop on the doorjamb. He took his shoes off and lay down on the bed fully dressed. She broke the door open, the eye-bolt flying off the splintered doorjamb, and the door swept open and there she was in the room. He stood up from the bed and she threw the heavy cocktail glass at his head and it smashed against the wall and glass suddenly covered the floor. She was hitting him in the face. He pushed her away and backed out into the main room of the suite and went to the telephone.

Trying to fend her off with one hand and hold the receiver in the other, he called the front desk and told the guy his wife had flipped out and he needed another room. All the time his wife is yelling, "Where's the goddamn pot, just tell me where's the goddamn pot."

He took his suitcase from the closet and started trying to stuff his clothes in—shirts, pants, jacket, shoes—and then there was a knock at the door and a young guy stood there waiting. His wife, calming down in a hurry as she could when she wanted to, started telling the guy that things were really just fine and her husband was acting crazy. She remained behind while he dragged the suitcase down the hall to the elevator. He hadn't managed to zip the suitcase all the way up and there were pieces of clothing sticking out through the open zipper.

*   *   *

One summer afternoon I flew to New York to visit my mother, who was still living there after the death of my father. That particular flight I sat by chance next to the conductor of the chamber music society, who had a score laid out on his lap for the entire trip. He was a middle-aged paunchy guy a few years older than me, by no means the handsome young man I'd imagined when my lover told me he'd been the love of her life. By way of the forced intimacy of airline flights, we introduced ourselves—he told me he was a composer, on the way to see his publisher. I toyed with the thought of mentioning our mutual acquaintance. I imagined telling him he had a child he knew nothing about. With a few words I could change his life, and I had no idea what effect that change would have on him. The guy seemed so content, reading his score. Just who did I think I was? So as the plane touched down, and we went our separate ways, I remained silent.

*   *   *

Standing in the doorway of his new room, two floors up, facing the Capitol, he asked the night clerk not to tell his wife what room he was in.

"Don't worry," he said, "I heard her over the phone."

"I'm a little worried she'll call the cops."

"Don't worry about that. They know me. And anyway they have other things to think about tonight—there's some guy with a gun running around the Capitol." And then he

23

said, incredibly, "If you need a little smoke, 1 have some I could share."

*   *   *

Some years later I had begun to spend my summers up north, and only by chance did I learn one day that the conductor had been found dead of a heart attack in a parked car on a downtown street. The coroner surmised that he had suddenly felt sick, driving to his Wednesday gig, and he'd pulled over to wait for the feeling to pass.

*   *   *

Alone in the new room, he rummaged through his suitcase. He had a single joint. It was by then well after midnight, and as he lit up he told himself, *Merry Christmas.* He stood looking out at the spotlit Capitol. He remembered the descriptions he'd read of Capitol Square the night before the Yankees arrived in 1865. Where the hotel now stood there'd been a building that housed the Confederate secret service. When the order to evacuate arrived that afternoon, they started burning all their files, right out there in the street. As darkness fell the sparks from the burning files rose into the night sky. Before they departed, the Confederate troops smashed all the barrels of liquor in the storehouses, so the mobs wouldn't get them, and lit off the stored ammunition so the Yankees wouldn't get it, and the fires spread and by midnight the whole downtown was ablaze.

All that night, refugees from the burning buildings had huddled on the square, watching as their world went up in smoke.

Nin Andrews

Snow Magic

The Year Prayer Wasn't Enough

Gil

Whatever you want, you just pray for it, my nanny, Lila May, used to say. But by the year I turned eleven, I knew. Prayer wasn't enough. That year everyone in my school turned mean, and my mama developed a conscience, as she put it, which meant she was always out. If she wasn't at a meeting for the citizens of Gordon County, or delivering cans of Dinty Moore Stew to the local soup kitchen, or going horseback riding with her Hunt Club friends, she was checking on old Mrs. Mellinger, our widow-neighbor who had a habit of getting lost in her own home. *Your mother,* my daddy said, as he poured himself another whiskey, *is always trying to save lost souls.*

Does she ever save them? I asked.

He didn't answer me. He just rattled the ice in his cocktail glass. I could tell by his sad eyes that he missed her as much as I did. My mama and daddy had stopped talking to each other that year, so even when she was home, our house went so quiet it felt like the inside of a funeral parlor before the mourners arrive. On the nights when we sat down to the supper table together, I felt a hush in the air and a chill. As if snow were falling inside each one of us, and no one would make it stop.

Confederate Gil

Sarah

In the town where I grew up, folks were still fighting the Civil War. They blamed the North for all their problems, including taxes, old age, the economy, the rising murder rate, even the tomato wilt and the raspberry blight. My friend, Gil Simmons, bragged that his great-grandpa was wounded in the Battle of Cedar Run. The Simmons lived on the outskirts of town in one of those old plantation homes with white pillars and lace curtains on the windows and acres and acres of green fields with thoroughbreds grazing in them. Gil was an only child, and whenever I visited, he gave me a tour of the bathrooms. All nine of them, not counting the servants' bathrooms. Rumor had it that Mrs. Simmons, or Violet, as my father called her, planned to have an ample family, but Gil was the only child she carried to term. Gil, my daddy said, never looked fully here. He was so pale and thin, he was almost see-through. The town doctor, Dr. Repolt, said Gil was bitten by a spider when he was a bitty thing, and he barely survived. My daddy said Gil looked like he'd been dipped in Clorox. Rumor had it Mr. Simmons wasn't even his daddy. People joked that he was the son of a Confederate soldier, so he was part-ghost. On Halloween Gil's mama dressed him like a ghost in a gray suit with a Confederate flag in one hand, a trick-or-treat bag in the other. *Ghosts aren't gray,* I told him, *and they don't wear uniforms.*

Yes, they do, too, he said. *In the South, they do. Casper is a Yankee ghost.*

Any Place Else

Gil

My parents wouldn't let me visit my best friend Sarah Parker's house very often because she lived on the wrong side of town, and I missed her all the time since Sarah and I were what we called twin souls. Which meant we both liked crustless grilled cheese sandwiches cut in triangles (squares never did taste right), and our favorite other things were magic, the numbers 2 and 9, and snow. But we always argued about the color of 9. I said it was blue, but she was sure it was white. How could 9 be white? I'd still like to know. But Sarah said it was simple as a fact, just like pink is a 2. I had to take her word for it because she was the only person I could talk to about things like that. She was the only one who knew the color of numbers and music. How it was scary to feel too good or taste something too sweet like ice cream, which is why I never ate ice cream or Boston cream pies or caramels. I said I didn't care for them, thank you very much. So did Sarah. Back then we even shared lies. But the best part was when she stayed overnight when her folks were out of town, and I couldn't sleep. Neither could she. We snuck into the kitchen and ate bowl after bowl of ice cream. The taste so cold, so sweet, so light.

Hide and Seek

Sarah

My friend Gil's favorite game was hide and seek. We would play it for hours in his huge house that always smelled of Pine-Sol and Old English furniture polish. His house was so big, I never could find him. I was always distracted by the china bowls of chocolates in every room. *Give me a hint,* I'd say, my mouth full of bonbons. Gil would promise to hide in a bathroom next time. But there were so many bathrooms, and some were the size of living rooms. Every one of them had a vanity with a peach-colored marble top and a wooden cabinet full of monogrammed towels. And some of the bathrooms were for the servants. *We don't go in those*, Gil said, his arms on his hips, giving me the stink eye. *But where are the servants?* I asked. I didn't see them. Or hear them. But one day Gil's mama rang a bell for them. And there they were, servants, like a tide rising up from the shadows. *Yes'm, Miz Violet. Yes'm.* Then the servants receded again, vanishing like smoke into the shadows and hallways and basement rooms.

Hair Spray and God's Minions

Gil

My father hated unusual things, and he especially hated my nanny, Lila May, because she was *too damned peculiar. Isn't it strange,* he said, *that a pretty lady like Lila May never married in the first place?* That was the first time I ever looked at her and decided she was pretty, even if she was old. Lila May was the only white woman that ever worked inside our house. Only Mama said she wasn't really white. She was what they called high yeller, but she looked white to me. And she must have been forty years old at least. Her face didn't have any wrinkles or spots, and her waist and ankles were so thin she would have looked girlish if she didn't have a behind the size of two watermelons side by side. Daddy said she had been a beauty contestant once and had been the peach blossom or orange blossom or some kind of blossom queen. He never did ask what kind of blossom she was. He knew she'd say she was God's blossom, and he hated to hear her talk of God and miracles and virgin saints who got the stigmata, and how even their blood smelled like roses and attracted bees in the summertime. The bees always did like Lila May, but I think it was her hairspray that drew them. They'd hover around her, buzzing and buzzing, and she'd say they were all just God's minions. Then she'd glare at me as if to ask, *Who was I to say otherwise?*

Mr. Simmons

Sarah

Gil's daddy, Mr. Simmons, was almost never home when I played at Gil's house. When I asked what his daddy did and where he was, Gil said he was a historian, and that was why he was away. *History,* he explained, *is something you have to search for.* And you have to search not once, but many times. That's what the word, *research,* means. Searching over and over again. His daddy hadn't found it yet, but when he did, he'd be real famous. And everyone would agree at last that the South should have won the War. And the North was to blame. I imagined his daddy coming home with a Confederate soldier in hand who could tell us things we didn't already know. Gil said there were loads of Confederate ghosts around because many of the dead were never buried. He said he could hear them at night. And their ghost dogs, too. Howling for everything they lost. And everything they wanted back again.

Practicing Snow

Gil

The year everything went wrong in my life, Lila May taught me magic. She said all I had to do was sit for a spell. Close my

29

eyes and bring one wish into focus. She said everything else in my mind had to leave. And she meant everything. *It's best to start simple,* she said. *Start with something like the weather. Like a day of sunshine. Or rain.* So I started with snow, even if we did live in the South. I practiced snow at breakfast and at lunch and in the school cafeteria when I was eating my bologna sandwich and Wise Owl potato chips all by myself. I practiced snow after school when Sarah Parker didn't call because she wasn't my friend that day. Sometimes I could touch that snow and taste it. Sometimes I rolled imaginary snow balls and built imaginary snowmen. If I did it right, my toes turned blue, my breath foggy, and a chill ran up my arms and legs. Even my nose ran. Nights I pretended I was falling asleep in snow banks. I kept the windows open, even if the rain gusted in, even if the curtains looked like ghosts flying in the wind. I dreamt I was walking in deep snow, calling out, *Sarah, Sarah!* The snow was falling so thick, like it was answering me with giant white flakes. And I knew, I just knew it would snow soon. One day in early November, it did snow, the heavy flakes falling so fast they covered the ground in a thick, wet blanket. When I told Lila May that I made that snow, she just smiled. *Of course you did. But don't you tell another soul now. You hear me?*

Snow

Sarah

One snowy day in fifth grade, my friend Gil Simmons bet me five bucks we'd get over a foot of snow. He bet we wouldn't have school the next day. Or the day after that. I bet him we would too have school. But the next day there was so much snow the roof on our tool shed caved in. Two trees toppled over on the power line. I didn't want to get out of bed because we didn't have any heat or electricity, and the house was cold as an ice cube. Mama had to cook over the wood stove, and my daddy couldn't get out of the driveway. Mrs. Mellinger, Gil's crazy old neighbor—we learned later that day—had died in a car wreck. Her tan Ford Falcon slid over to the wrong side of the road, right into oncoming traffic. Two teenagers were in intensive care over at the Martha Jefferson Hospital. My mother said Mrs. Mellinger was drunk and British, and she always did drive on the wrong side of the road, but I blamed Gil. Especially when he phoned all happy, and asked me to pay up. I couldn't believe he would do a thing like that. Neither did my mama. She said she didn't want me playing with Gil Simmons. She said that all the time, but that day I nodded, *Yes ma'am. Gil Simmons isn't even my friend no more.*

Magic

Gil

One day I told Lila May that Sarah Parker was the girl I loved. The next day Sarah Parker gave Timmy Preston, my archenemy, a sweet tart the size of a baseball at recess, so I didn't love her anymore. I told Lila May I didn't care one lick if I ever laid eyes on Sarah Parker again. *Not one lick,* she nodded. *Not one lick.* And when she said it, I knew it was true.

John Azrak

The DH

1. #1, Keith Jarrett, ss

We were playing the game you introduced us to, subbing jazz greats for all-star authors. I said Jarrett would be good leading off because he could improvise at the plate, fake the bunt, use his primal moan when a pitch grazes his uniform. Hannah laughed. She seemed relaxed, and told me that she was glad to have taken on the Student Service job, that she could see herself pursuing a doctorate in educational administration, and that it was more than just keeping busy. Working with kids who want to help others seems a perfect fit, and a doctorate, wow, I said, avoiding eye contact, afraid of catching a glimpse of you.

2. #10, Billie Holiday, 2nd base

Hannah said that we needed a woman up next. I agreed. Billie Holiday, she said, in a surprising nod to your poem: Billie on the jazz station, you and I on the Williamsburg Bridge, the confidence you exuded, the joy I felt that you and Hannah were considering marriage against the odds. You were wedded in spirit, and the image of the full moon rising over the Chrysler Building seemed an affirmation. Hannah's cut her waterfall of hair, which startled me at first. That signature auburn mane is now a blond-streaked Peter Pan. Hard for you to imagine, I know. Her freckled, pale Irish beauty looks polished. Her cheekbones are more prominent, eyes electric blue, and she sports a runner's blush. After a summer of hibernation, she's training rigorously for a half-marathon, eight miles this morning. She looks sleek in black jeans—called *super skinny,* I'm serious, she laughed—and a stretch, white T-shirt. It came to me then that her oversized outfits, and layers of muted colors, befitted the space she'd made for the two of us, and are probably now gone for good.

3. #7, Miles Davis, cf

Hannah graciously offered me the heart of the order. I slid my hand over the worn corduroy in the familiar groove on the brim of your couch, the only piece of furniture Hannah has kept. The walls are bare, but I assume you left her the treasure of literary and sports memorabilia the two of you had collected. I was missing your old place, for sure. Miles, I said, and Hannah gave me a thumbs up. After you left she painted your apartment despite having signed a lease to move to this studio in Fort Greene. When I asked why, she said: "I like watching pain dry."

4. #5, John Coltrane, 1st base

Like I didn't know you were going to say that . . . as Lou Gehrig is to Ruth, as Shakespeare is to Dante, Coltrane is to Miles, she said with an impish grin. She swung her legs around, propping herself up against the arm of the couch in a lotus position that stole my breath. I never hid my physical attraction to Hannah from you, but it feels like cheating somehow, telling you without you here. We were often painfully honest with one another, and I see no reason to stop now. When you first professed your love, something opened up in me that I knew—no, felt—I would never be able to close. Not if I wanted a place in your interior world, not if I hoped to realize whatever it was that you saw in me. You were rescuing me from perpetual frat boyhood, three years of college sleep, my dire need to wake up in perfect collusion with meeting you. When I rode your coattails into a teaching position, happily caught up in your whirlwind of energy, what mattered most was the chance to work with you every day. The tutorials were invaluable, but they didn't make me feel alive. You did. I can't pass your classroom without feeling . . . well . . . you know. I remember the night we met Al Foster at the bar in the Vanguard, and he told us between sets how hard it was some nights to take the stage and see the ghost of his beloved Miles playing in front of him. I'm glad the American school in Paris is going well for you so far. I read your email several times to hear your voice.

5. #12 Charlie Parker, rf

I asked Hannah if she thought Bird had the arm for right. She said that's where he would do the least damage. How about using him as the designated hitter, see how the rest plays out, I suggested. DH? she said, and frowned. The DH is an artificial construct that spoils the purity of the game. Whoa, listen to you, a regular George Will, I said. She rolled her eyes and tried to stifle a smile. When she looked directly at me, I held her gaze, and for that brief moment I thought I might be shaking you off, like a pitcher dismissing a sign. Try Bob Costas, she said, he has better hair, and I couldn't hold back my laugh, the pebble of an ache forming behind my heart. My face felt flush with the two of you.

6. #8, Thelonious Monk, c

It's time for another woman, right, I said, the urgency in my voice misleading. What I needed was to keep playing. I got that covered, Hannah said. Ella is the manager! Nina Simone coaches first; Sara Vaughn, third. Brilliant, I said. Reid would be proud. She pinned back her shoulders, sat erectly, her flat torso and narrow waist, the center of my peripheral vision. To keep you at bay, we decided not to see each other this summer. I stopped by once with the excuse of returning books you had given me and her weight loss frightened me. I knew she didn't want to talk so I left after a tense hug. What she has restored looks expertly sculpted. I'm glad you mentioned him, she said. Her eyes brightened, and my chest tightened. I couldn't stand the suspense, she added wryly. I said I didn't mean to, that it was probably a reflex. She pulled up her legs, tucked her knees to her chest. He got me to love myself, she said. That I get to keep, and the person living inside of me who learned how to take an emotional risk. She took a deep breath. After that leap, things that used to terrify me just don't. I jumped at the opportunity to head up Student Service, before Reid I wouldn't have had the nerve. I plan to follow up on the dream we had to go to China, and I'm going alone. She rocked her head back and forth. I'm learning how to live with him as a piece of me. You should too. I talk to him in my head all the time. Now? I wondered, and guessed your ears must be ringing. Just let the mentor die. You could look at it as if he's done that for you, she said without a trace of irony. I reached for my beer on the coffee table, left it there. You can look at me, you know, she said. I turned, stiff-shouldered, to face her straight on. Don't ever think he left easily. The last year was miserable. God knows we'd been soul searching since our first night together so there was little left to say, but it's not like he *wanted* to stop making love. I knew what I was getting into when we married, probably more than you think. And even if you had been able to do for him what he needed—she dug her fingers into her kneecaps—he wouldn't have, not here . . . hell, not even in this country, it turns out. She loosened her grip. Her eyes began to brim with tears. I reached over and put my hand on her knee. I never resented you, she said. I think you know that. I couldn't have faked the closeness I've felt with you any more than I could have faked an orgasm with Reid, to be blunt about it. We loved the same man and he loved us back equally. It was intoxicating for me, former Miss Catholic Conventionality. She smiled, put her hand on mine. The charge was electric. How to explain, Reid? I had no desire to defuse it. As much as I loved Hannah, inside and out, the high that was our triangle of kindred spirits, three beautiful years, I didn't want to end— I'd never even fantasized a moment like this. She removed her hand from mine. Does Monk sound like a catcher's name, or what, she said.

7. #6, Charles Mingus, 3rd base

Well, I like the sound of Mingus following Monk in the order, what do think? Hannah nodded, her eyes beginning to clear. I wanted nothing more than to get you out of my head, off your couch, to hold Hannah, and when she stretched out her legs and rested one bare foot on my thigh, I did just that, held it, like an anchor, before caressing her ankle, and she lowered her eyes, and the sound of our breathing in the near empty room had a pulse of its own.

8. #23, Sonny Rollins, lf

I ran my finger up the side of her jeans. You've come a long

36

way in a short time, I said. She crossed her arms over her chest. I let myself grieve, took the cure, she said, and then whispered, I think we need to finish. My voice caught in my throat. Saxophone Colossus, I managed. She bent over from the waist, collapsing her body in two, and I let my hand slip into the fold. She grabbed her toes, face down, held a runner's stretch, and I withdrew my hand slowly and palmed the back of her neck, a wave of heat rushing through me. I traced a line down to the base of her spine with my forefinger and she sighed. I lowered my head and brushed my lips behind her ear. She shook her head slowly before pulling herself up until we met face to face. I'm right there with you, she said, and my heart beat wildly, the exultation that had been clearly missing with every woman in my life. We breathed each other in as she held my face in her hands. It's been a long abstinence and I do love you, she said gently, but I can't let you use me to let go of him . . . or get to him, for that matter . . . or become. . . . Her voice trailed off. My body went cold. The room that had fallen away returned in a heart beat. She kissed my forehead and spun around on the couch, her back to me. No substitutions for either of us, please, she said, not tonight . . . not ever, the ache palpable in her muffled voice. I'm not trying to be him, I said, less forcefully than I'd intended, and I squeezed my eyes closed, as if to shut out the possibility. Hannah got up from the couch. I don't know where we are, or should be, only where we shouldn't, she said. She extended her hand and I grabbed it and pulled myself up abruptly from the couch, my legs wobbly, the room in a nasty spin. Hannah leaned in and wrapped her hands around my forearms. She asked me if I was okay, and I made a feeble joke about being put on the disabled list. We're going to be good, she said, and we hugged, holding each other tightly as we hadn't been able to since you left. Hannah took a step back. How about I text you later with a pitcher, she said.

9. #37, Dizzy Gillespie, p

I texted back: *Good one, thinking Dizzy Dean!*

Wendy Barker

from *Nothing Between Us:*
The Berkeley Years

Teaching *Uncle Tom's Children*

He was the only other honky in the room. But wasn't. Blond
natural. Was his mother or his dad white or black? Kid played
the best sax in town and only fourteen. Sax so sweet and cool
the moon rose cream over the hills and stars broke the fog.
He didn't talk much. Neither did I, that first Black Lit class
any of us taught. I didn't know what to put on the board.
Erased everything I'd written before, but the erasers were full
of dust from the chalk. The blackboard turned powdery, a
blur, clouded. We moved on through *Nigger, Black Boy, Na-
tive Son.* Not a kid caused trouble. Small sounds, fingers flip-
ping the white pages of the paperbacks I collected and
stacked in the corner cupboard after class. Slap of gum
stretching in and out of a mouth, hard sole of a shoe on the
floor, scraping the surface, an emery board. And the train,
track barely a block away, the train running the whole length
of San Francisco Bay, cry moving ahead of it, toward us, that
wail.

After School

The way the halls loosened, softened. You couldn't call what
the coaches did walking. Even the metal lockers seemed to
move. Those jogging suits with zippers down their chests and

straight up the sides of their calves. Colors of candy, lol-
lipops, suckers, lime, cherry, orange. Didn't make a sound
with their feet, the way they walked as if they were running
but in slow motion, all the parts of their bodies moving to-
gether. Mmmm. You new here? Where you from? What do
you teach? Voices like insides of M&M's. Halls cleared of
kids, they moved through like syrup through a snow cone.

Seven periods of trying to keep ninth-graders from shrieking,
tearing at each other. Somebody thrown into a locker, Pepsi
and sudden ice sticky all over the floor, slippery. All day I'd
picked up trash, books, ragged spiral papers.

The tallest coach would hang back from the others, stand at
my door, basketball nestled in the crook of his arm, talk direct
as a shot clean through the net. When the Home Ec teacher
had a party where the air hung thick and milky from the great
dope somebody'd gotten out of Nam, I went ahead and close-
danced in the corner to Roberta Flack until four. Seven peri-
ods a day, five days a week, telling the kids to calm down, sit
still, keep their hands to themselves, and I didn't move his
hand away when his fingers found my nipple and began to
pull as if it were soft, sweet taffy.

Stitchery

In one package you got the yarn, cloth for the pillow cover,
and directions with a picture—a knight and his spear on a
white horse clip-clopping along a green road lined with pink
daisies toward a gray castle. I piled the papers that needed
grading on the dining room table. French knots for the horse's
eye and the flowers. Chain stitch for the leaves. I bought a
half yard of linen, a book on American embroidery, made a
sampler of stitches: stem, feather, star, cross, herringbone,

40

running, and New England laid. Fewer weeks when the table was cleared. I began to work a remnant of burlap with thick wool. Stretched uneven petals zigzag across the weave. I'd been having the students do free-writing. Anything they wanted to say, the way they'd talk to a friend. Centers of flowers like eggs, spirals, like cocoons, leaves like wings. The flowers exploded in colors that shouldn't have mixed. Harder and harder to spot spelling errors, comma faults. The strands hurled across to each other. I stopped embroidering. Tired of prickings, the little stabs.

Remedial Reading

The smallest classroom in the ninth grade school. Yellow walls, and the ceiling seemed too high. Boxes lined up in bright colors on the tables, each a different level. This class for retards? This a toony class? The kids swaggered and straggled through the door, unwilling. To be seen here. Laminated cards, one at a time. Second, third grade skills for fourteen year olds. Mostly boys. I'd been assigned to help the reading teacher, her long gray hair bunched and slipping along with hairpins and combs. Ruth organized field trips, took her own beat-up station wagon. Once she drove us up the coast to the great blue herons' nesting grounds. We walked up and up until we could look straight down into the tops of the big trees. She showed us how to spot the saucers of nests resting in the branches.

I never got the kids to move beyond a level or two. Nobody stayed on task. Once I was pronouncing vowels with Lester Sims, light-skinned, freckled, a skinny little dude. O: okra, Oakland, Coke. And o: butter, supper, dove. His eyes shone. He was standing beside me. "Doves," he said. "We can talk about birds?" "Sure," I said, and told him about the finches I was raising at home in as big a cage as I could afford. "Man, why didn't you say you wanted us to talk about birds?" and he was out the door. Before the bell rang for the next class he was back. I was putting cards away in their boxes, red tipped ones in the red box, brown in brown, folding the lids closed. "You like pigeons?" he grinned. "I do, I do," I said. He unzipped his jacket. I don't know how many wings flapped out from him, ruffled my hair and fluttered all through that yellow room, a sound only feathers can make, as Lester told me every one of their names.

On the Bay

It was the art teacher Norm who had the doctor friend who was leasing the twenty-seven foot sailboat we took out onto the Bay that Saturday before Margie the history teacher's party, and we smoked dope all day out on the water. There for a while we drifted on out beyond the Golden Gate into the open sea before we knew what we were doing, so it took about three hours just to get back under the bridge, everybody laughing except the one guy who'd had the six sailing lessons so he knew what was maybe about to happen. Norm was getting it on with Nini on the foam mattress under the prow and everybody else was sopping from the spray that was everywhere over us. That whole day no fog at all, even after we docked back at the Marina and stopped at the Safeway to pick up some Cribari red for the party, where Margie had put out candles on the tables, all sizes and shapes burning down into little puddles of different colors of hot wax around their flames, like the lights of the city we'd just spent the whole day sailing past, turned on.

Macramé

I never got into it. Too many knots. Rope or string, mostly
white, or that pale yellowy color, twisted in on itself, maybe
a few beads. All that work just to hold a house plant off the
floor. I was weaving. Different yarns. Crinkly silk like hair
from an unraveled braid. Silver. A fat wool, furry, the shade
of lichen under a pine. And blue, a deep teal, turquoise, the
way you remember an inland high sky in winter. Purple, fuch-
sia, orange, sunsets. Dawn. Sometimes I thought of the stu-
dents I liked while I worked. Frances, her low voice, her
cello. Jennifer's little giggles. Charles, his wide smile, giant
Afro. Andrew, trying to get me to read *Dune*. The warp
strands sturdy, brown. Backstrap loom tied to the window
latch. I pushed the weft threads down, a soft thud. Over and
under. One color showing more now, another the next time.
I gathered eucalyptus bells that fell under the tall trees in the
hills. Clean smelling, a good medicine. I liked working the
dark seeds into the pattern. I wanted to make something big,
fill a space, soften a wall.

Freed Up

He said I had nice ones, even though I'd always thought they
were so little, but why did I bind them up? One day I left my
bra in the drawer. All day could feel the feel of them.
Couldn't forget they were there. Felt good just leaning down
to throw a wad of paper in the trash. And standing up, nipples
like third and fourth eyes, looking straight out at whoever
was coming toward me in the long hall. Looking clear inside.
Into secrets, hiding places. Until they were out for good, out
of the muffled fiber-filled shells, elastic tightenings, hard-
wire frames. Like bare green leaves unfolding in April,
swelling as they opened. Leisurely, soft, brushing into a hand.

Teacher's Lounge

Ken always sat in the pink high-backed chair. He'd started selling real estate on the side, just residential, he didn't want to get into apartment buildings, not with all the riff-raff moving in these days. The whole place had changed so much he felt he was living on Mars. The trash on the streets now, and he meant human. Why the hair. He wanted me to know, because, he said, he could tell I was a nice person, not one of these wandering bums the school district was hiring, and he wanted me to understand this city had been the Athens of the West until the hippies started running it. Even just a couple of years ago the kids had manners. He thumped his pipe into the ashtray already filled with butts, cellophane strips from cigarette packs, paper clips and razor blades for correcting dittos.

I should have been grading papers. Or preparing. Compound sentences. Conjunctions. And, but, or. I was pouring water over a two-day-old tea bag when Ardis Baine the Latin teacher walked in, black eyes snapping, and slid her ditto master into the machine. Ardis had three degrees from Howard University. She glanced into my cup. "What on earth are you drinking, honey," she said. After she left with the fresh damp stack of purplish paper in her hands, the room turned silent. My tea tasted like polluted water. The next day I brought in a jar of instant coffee. Made it strong and drank it black. That was before I stopped coming to the lounge at all, unless I had to use the machine to run something off.

Audio-Visual

One of the boys would help if the film broke. Some of them

even knew how to fix the oldest projector, the one that sputtered and cluttered and moaned to a stop in the middle of the story. Like when Ulysses had himself bound up, so he could sail past the Sirens, or when he was barely making it through between Scylla and Charybdis. A couple of the girls would stay and talk over their sandwiches at lunchtime about Mr. Taylor who always asked for help in the auditorium's projection booth whenever they showed movies for all the history classes at once. He'd accidentally brush against them in the dark, then take his time feeling them up. They laughed about it. Everybody thought he was pretty cute. The administrators had their eye on him to get his credential, be a principal in a year or two. Movie days were a relief. The sound drowned out the traffic on University Avenue, and late in the afternoon, with the blinds down the pimps didn't bother to hassle their girls through the windows, hollering in, "Inetta, you get your black ass out on this street, Yvonne, you hear me girl." Even with the volume turned up high, the soundtrack distorted, everything seemed just that much quieter.

Oil Spill

Karla talked me into going over that night, said they'd been working around the clock, they needed everybody they could get. Thousands of birds. Cages. Mostly grebes. Feathers clotted in thick crude so they couldn't fly. The warehouse a hive, a make-do hospital, everybody working in twos and threes—pony tails, headbands, long sweeps of straight hair fanning down over pairs of hands. One to press the wings—with the thumbs—close to the body, keep the bones of the wings from spreading out, and, with the fingers, hold the cold webbed feet immobile. Another to hold the beak shut, everyone had been bitten. One moment of relaxing the pressure and— panic, flapping, out of control. Hundreds of lean backs bent

45

together in small groups over birds, swabbing with detergent. The grebes' red eyes. No one knew the detergent removed the birds' natural oils. Nobody knew that when the birds were released, their feathers would absorb the water they had always surfaced on, to rest. It wouldn't take long for them to drown.

Eric Braun

My Beard

I look great in this beard, lots of people say so, like an author or czar. A brand new man. Even my sister says so, and she doesn't usually talk much, so when she does speak up you have to listen, and you can mark it down what she says is for real. She says: You could weave a nice cardigan from that thing.

Ha ha ha. We have a good laugh at that, because you probably can't. But it's funny to think about.

My Beard at the Game

My sister Gina made the varsity softball team even though she's only a sophomore. She hits for power and plays catcher, the hardest position. She carries authority with pitchers, rapport with umpires. She runs the bases slapdashedly. (I use words like that now.) I sit in the front row of the bleachers. Sometimes I bring a lawn chair and curl my fingers in the backstop. Strangers say: What a beard. When Gina flings off her mask and helmet to chase a pop-up, her hair wavers like a wild sea plant. When she takes practice cuts on deck, the only word to describe her is *ferocious*. Think of a crocodile, eyes above the dark water. Then think of its vicious, sudden strike, unleashed on some preppy old flamingo in an explosion of water.

Feathers everywhere.

My Beard at Work

Things are changing and the reason is my beard. You know about washers, how important they are. When objects vibrate, shift, or jerk, washers keep the screws from falling out. Bed frames and clocks. Tables, trains, and toilets. So many things owe their stability to washers. Most washers used in the Upper Midwest are made at the Washer Company, where I have worked for four years. That chair that supports you. The yield sign that helps us take turns. Since I was fifteen I have helped the world keep it all together. I felt satisfied.

But then my beard.

John Ruiz! Galen says. He wears his goggles on top of his head and finger streaks of Cheeto dust on his smock. He has been here for seventeen years. He says: You spec those Bellevilles yet?

Not yet, I say.

John, that order's got to fly. What's bugging you?

Nothing. Why?

I'm concerned. We all are.

About what?

You. The thing with—you know.

I dig my fingers in my beard, give it a good tug. Usually Galen is grumpy and doesn't ask what's bugging you, just complains. Plus, he isn't very smart. He says *in this damn age* when he means *in this day and age*.

Don't take this the wrong way, Galen says, but some people are wondering . . . well, maybe you should get some rest.

I'm not tired.

I mean take some time off. Visit your dad in the hospital. Have you seen him since he fell?

Before the beard, I would have done what Galen said. I would have gone home to my apartment, and I would have visited Dad. Waited for "some people" to tell me what to do. What they think is best for me. But instead I spec the

48

Bellevilles, which are heading for an amusement park in Ohio, and I find that one box is infected with a few cup washers: they look similar, but their load capacity is nowhere near as high. Normally, I'd check a couple other boxes to make sure they're filled with Bellevilles, but what I do is I have the entire shipment unloaded and each box re-checked. Everyone grumbles; they slam boxes and pallets, *bang!, ka-bap!;* shipping is set back several hours. They give me glares like the black eyes of geese.

My Beard on a Date

When not playing softball, my sister usually wears jeans and black t-shirts with band names on them. Some people think she's a lesbian, even though she isn't. I tell Nancy this. I say: She wears this black leather jacket.

I know, Nancy says.

You know?

I'm just saying it's okay, she says.

This is our third date, dinner on a weeknight. Nancy's ex-husband used to hit her with closed fists, which I know because she talked about it at a retreat during her "Obstacles" talk, so we are taking things slow. The first date was coffee, the second lunch. The fourth, should we choose to have it, will be a weekend dinner. Soon she will want to meet my sister Gina.

It's okay, Nancy says again. We're seated at a sidewalk table. She reaches her hand across and I touch it. It feels vulnerable but not like a kid's hand, like you could wrench it and make her do what you want. Her hand feels like a bar of soap, like I could scrape up a ribbon with my fingernail.

What's okay? I say.

Wearing a black leather jacket. Jeans and t-shirts.

I know that, I say.

49

A car in the street plays rock you like a hurricane. My beard flutters bravely in the breeze.

My Beard: A Brief History

What happened was I went on a one-week retreat at a lake up north with this church group I'm in. I've always kept my face shaved clean and my hair "high and tight," as they say, which is a military expression, except I've never been in the military. Men of my generation are lucky, that's what my dad says, we've grown up mostly in peace times with no draft. We have a volunteer military.

Anyway we were up there, doing trust-me drills and talking about our obstacles, and some of the guys were letting their beards grow and so did I. When I went into the decrepit little bathroom by the beach, and I saw myself in the cracked piece of mirror hanging on the wall, it was like I was a different person. Imagine looking in the mirror and seeing a stranger. Someone with *charisma*. Someone who, who knows, might be brave.

I almost had sex that week too, I won't go into the details, and this is not to say that sex is a good reason to make life decisions like whether to have a beard, but, you know. Who could blame me for liking my beard after that?

Well, maybe not "almost." But anyway Nancy held my hand.

I got into a fight about it, though. This guy said it was not the place for "scamming chicks," and I was like *bam! Fookya!* Right in the face! He sure was surprised. So was I.

And I thought: That's some beard.

And I couldn't talk about my obstacle, even though I wanted to. When my turn came, all I did was cry. Nancy was there, sitting close like she had been all week, and she gave me a hug.

50

When I got home I kept letting it go. The beard. You can keep letting something go and it can be good. It's not always bad to let something go.

My Beard at Church

My sister Gina doesn't like to go because she says it's full of hypocrites, but one time I brought her. People kept turning toward us. I could tell they were looking at my beard because it tingled. Also, we were talking, which people don't like you to do at church. Gina said: No. No. She shook her head, her wild hair swaying.

This woman down the pew leaned in front of her husband, her fancy silk scarf dangling in her lap. *Shhh,* she said. Not once, Gina said. Talking to me.

And I felt pretty good about that, pretty satisfied, because I knew she meant it. But at the same time I felt terrible because what had I ever done for her? Nothing.

But maybe with this beard.

My Beard and My Dad

I wasn't going to bring up my dad but since I did already I might as well say: He does not have a beard. My beard is an original. He shaves with a wet razor everyday, twice a day if he goes out to dinner. He wears "the finest" shirts and dress shoes and stands really tall and imperious so everyone will think he's stately. He said I'm a retard and I don't know what's right, and as long as I lived under his roof I had to do what he said, everything, even the stuff I didn't like, like when he'd just come out of the shower.

Gina said when he stands all uppity he looks like a cold,

dumb water bird with long legs. We were younger then, and she said it really quietly in her room. She had a book about herons that she pointed to, and after that we'd bring home books to show each other: ibis, egret, curlew, crane, stork. Ha ha ha, we laughed and laughed even though it was barely even true that he looked like that. And we kept our laughing quiet.

I moved out four months ago. At first Gina said things were not so bad, but she was just trying to make me feel better since I left her alone. She is like that. Like she's the older sibling. Dad bought her a used Honda and said those things go until 300,000 miles.

My Beard at Work Again

Someone left a home-baked chocolate cake in the break room, one of those three-layer deals that are so moist and delightful. Even though it's only 9:00 a.m., I have a slice. If I wait until a more reasonable time for cake, like after lunch, it will be gone. I eat standing up and leaning a little forward when I take bites so no crumbs drop into my beard, and nearby on the window sill I have a little Styrofoam cup of milk, which somebody also brought in because it goes well with chocolate cake.

That's when Galen enters the break room. He snaps his fingers and points at me. Good cake, huh?

I nod and stuff another big bite into my mouth so there's no way I can be expected to talk. My mouth is full and it would be rude.

Wife made it, Galen says, then adds, just to make sure I get the message, I brought it in.

Mmm, I say.

Good for the troops' morale, right? Little chocolate?

I drop the rest of my cake in the trash, gulp the last of my milk. Well thanks, I say, and wipe my lips on a napkin. I have to kind of scrub right in there.

Hey, you're welcome. You're welcome.

Thanks.

No problem.

Okay, then.

I make for the doorway, but Galen steps in front of me.

Hey, how's your dad? I heard he woke up.

He and my dad are friends. That's how I got this job in the first place.

Just great, I say.

You want to bring him some cake?

No.

How about you? You doing okay?

I'm great too.

You sure? It must be hard to think about someone doing that to him.

Doing that?

He didn't just *fall* off that ladder.

Galen's tongue flicks out and mops his lips, which are stained brown from coffee or cake or both. He has no beard. He could not pull it off. But he has a little stubble and by God there are crumbs stuck in it. My eyes begin to well, suddenly, I don't know why, who can understand these things, but I can see the future, just a bit into the future, like a few seconds, and I will be sobbing on the floor like a terrified little kid if I don't do something, and Galen will be standing smugly above me.

So I poke Galen hard in the left eye. He leaps back as if he's witnessed something awful and the only thing he can do is recoil from the very sight of it, as if that would make it go away, even though it won't.

Christ, Ruiz! What the hell?

He holds both his hands over his eye, still stumbling backwards.

53

Mind your own business, I say to him.

Ow! God!

I bury both my hands in my beard and go home.

My Beard at the Game Again

The ball pops into Gina's glove, puffing dust into the air. Ball three—full count. Gina says something to the ump and runs the ball back to the pitcher, a girl with a red ponytail. I focus my gaze through one diamond-shaped opening in the chainlink backstop. The pitcher is distressed. Gina puts a hand on her shoulder. She tips her mitt so the ball rolls over the edge and into the pitcher's glove.

Behind me, a woman says: She's so good with the pitchers.

Nancy leans forward in her lawn chair as if to hear what Gina says.

In the high school's parking lot I see two cop cars by the gate. At first I think the cops are looking at my beard, but then I realize I'm wrong. My beard is not as big as I thought it was.

I put my hand on Nancy's knee.

For the first time I try to imagine what Dad was thinking when he was on the ladder all the way up at the second story, cleaning out the gutters, when Gina rammed into it. Like a charging rhino, Gina said. That's what she told me in church, and the question I asked her after that is if she ever wishes she was born into a different family. It's a question I've thought about a lot, even though it's pointless. You can't change your family. And anyway she said no, and the reason is because of me.

Gina jogs back to her spot behind home plate, crouches, and beats her glove twice with her fist. The sound of the beating is so big. Like the sound of God dusting off his hands because He's done with something.

Amy Knox Brown

Four Episodes in the Life of the Sheridan Boulevard Troll

1. After Drinking Two Bottles of Night Train, the Troll beneath the Sheridan Boulevard Bridge in Lincoln, Nebraska, Awakens to the Sounds of Goats

The troll opens his eyes. He lies next to a culvert. Rocks rattle in his head, the taste of sulfur fills his mouth.

Overhead, a bell rings again and again.

The troll curls his fingers around the spindly trunks of volunteer trees to haul himself up the incline and onto the bridge.

He sees a goat—so young that his horns are only tiny mounds on his skull—riding an old Schwinn. Screwed to the handlebars is one of those little bells the goat strikes his hoof against again and again. The sound penetrates the troll's skull like a blade.

The sound must stop.

The troll lurches toward the bicycle. The goat's eyes widen and he veers around the troll, looking back as he rides away, still ringing the godforsaken bell.

In the park on the other side of the bridge, children scream.

The troll has an intimation that things will get worse before they get better. He sinks down against the bridge's railings and rests his head in his hands.

Along comes a second goat, this one larger and older than the little one, riding a cream-colored Vespa.

The thought of cream nauseates the troll. He stands. The clouds overhead part and a spear of sunlight cuts into the troll's face. The goat is singing, loudly and off key, a song about not getting any satisfaction.

The troll thinks he needs to kill the goat. He'll kill the goat, stop the singing, and sell the scooter for Mad Dog.

He heads toward the Vespa, his hairy hands outstretched to grab.

The goat—the insolent, adolescent goat—looks right at the troll and sneers. He yells out, "And I try, and I try—" and then shoots away along Sheridan Boulevard, leaving the troll in a puff of exhaust.

The troll coughs. He doubles over. He thinks of the phrase "coughing up a lung." That's what it feels like he's doing. He wonders if he's going to die.

Maybe this is the *worst* part. Black dots swim in front of his eyes.

From the park comes a noise that sounds as if one of the children is hitting the pole of a swing set with a crowbar. And then, a moment of reprieve: the crowbar sound stops, a cloud covers the sun, the troll finds himself able to breathe again.

He straightens. In the gutter, he sees a half-smoked Marlboro someone tossed from a passing car. He lifts the cigarette to his lips. He tastes the lipstick of the previous smoker. He thinks of the phrase "hair of the dog."

But then, from the west, a police car rolls up and parks. The driver is a goat in an officer's uniform. He wears sunglasses, so you can't see his eyes, but the troll expects they hold no mercy.

The police goat steps out of the car. He taps his billy club against his palm. Sounds bleat from the scanner, a jumble of words that might be in a foreign language, because the troll doesn't understand a single one of them. The police goat smiles, showing yellow teeth, and the troll understands that the worst is yet to come.

2. Friendly Bearers of Salvation A and B

A. The troll lies under the Sheridan Boulevard bridge, beaten—badly beaten—but not dead. His eyes are closed. His fingers twitch, long nails digging divots in the earth. A hot wind washes over him.

In the distance, the bells toll from the Cathedral of the Risen Christ. It must be Sunday. Or it might be Saturday, or some Holy Day. The troll opens his eyes to see—or does he open his eyes to see?—a nun approaching. Wind swirls the skirt of her seersucker habit and curls the edges of her wimple. Her pupils are vertical lines in her golden eyes. Her face appears to be covered with soft gray fur. In one hand she holds a chalice, in the other a round wafer the size of a quarter.

She places the wafer in the troll's mouth. She tells him to raise his head. Can't, he says.

Yes, you can. You have to try.

He lifts his head. She places one hand against the back of his neck to hold him steady, tips the chalice against his lips, and fills his mouth with blood.

B. The troll lies under the bridge, staring at the vertical lines of the concrete pillars. From a nearby tree, a squirrel drops acorns that smack into the troll's open palms.

Who are you? asks the squirrel.

The troll considers. *Trip trap*, he replies.

Trip, trap, whispers the bridge. *Trip, trap.*

3. Forgive Us the Trespassers

Sister Mary Frances was walking across the Sheridan Boulevard bridge at 11:50 p.m. on Monday, June 21, 1981, when she heard glass shatter against the joists beneath her feet. Bursts of light rose from under the bridge.

At the scene, officers found tracks leading down the embankment: sole prints from Converse tennis shoes, as well as small divots that appeared to have been made by hooves.

Against the west bridge abutment lay shards of glass from mercury bulbs that, according to a janitor at Lincoln Southeast High School (three blocks east), had been deposited in the outdoor trash bin on the afternoon of Monday, June 21.

The railroad tracks under the bridge still held some heat from the Burlington Northern, which passed through at 11:30 p.m.

On the ground by the east bridge abutment lay five empty Falstaff cans.

A homeless man nearby was drinking from a can of Falstaff. He claimed he'd seen nothing unusual; he'd found the Falstaff on the ground; the can was still cold.

Approximately fifty yards from the bridge, three billy goats grazed. Animal Control was called, but the goats absconded, running south, before Animal Control officers arrived.

The janitor explained that, when the mercury bulbs were broken, the small amount of gas inside them ignited and produced a burst of fire.

Sister Mary Frances believed she'd seen the work of the Devil.

A trail of Falstaff cans (some still containing beer, which officers poured on the railroad tracks) led south along the tracks and up the incline toward 33rd Street.

Questioned again, the homeless man repeated that he'd seen nothing unusual. He said he wanted to clarify that he wasn't homeless, that he was a troll, and that the bridge was his home.

One officer explained that the bridge, in fact, belonged to the city of Lincoln. The troll shrugged.

Another officer followed the trail of Falstaff cans, which ended at 33rd Street. He reported hearing laughter in the distance (the laughter, he thought, of teenage boys), as well as bleating that sounded like goats.

4. A Christmas Story

December arrives, that month of blood and ice. Snow coats the streets, piles on the pillars of the Sheridan Boulevard bridge, melts on the lashes of carolers whose words of Holy Nights and King Wenceslas freeze when leaving their mouths and drop like teeth into the snow.

Under the bridge, the troll builds a fire. Flames glint cheerfully on the broken shards of Night Train bottles around him. He can barely hear the carolers. He is warm enough.

A trio of goats has been seen around town, as far away as Havelock, where they trip-trap past the window of Arnold's Bar, startling the railway workers who've stopped for beer after work. There are three goats: a little one, a middle-sized one, and a big one with evil-looking horns. For years, the men who see the goats will argue about the size of the horns, the order in which the goats passed the window, what each goat meant. Over the years, the stories change. The stories grow. In the stories, the goats live on, forever.

The nuns outside the Cathedral of the Risen Christ wear their black winter habits under their black winter coats.

On the snowy park ground, a black squirrel slices through the whiteness like an exclamation point. It is said that black squirrels mean change. We want to know what kind of change is coming. We lock our doors.

The smell of wood smoke and meat rises from under the Sheridan Boulevard Bridge. O my pretty ones, let us step closer and see what the troll is roasting over his little fire. As we descend the incline, our feet leave no tracks in the snow. Our breath does not cloud in the air as the carolers' does when they pass overhead, singing.

The troll sits on his haunches, sheltered from the inclement weather by the bridge, which stretches overhead like the sky. He wears a plush Santa hat, a gift from one of those boys who goes under the bridge to drink Falstaff and break things. The troll radiates the kind of contentment you see in someone fishing; he's transfixed by his yellow flames, the quiet sound of falling snow that will not touch him. He nudges the object he is roasting with a stick.

We see that the roasting object is an animal. It is, in fact, a goat. But which goat? We step closer. The troll adjusts his rudimentary spit and prods again to see if the meat is done, and we can tell, now, that he's roasting the largest of the three goats once seen running around town, the goat some gullible children had mistaken for a reindeer because of its horns.

Nickole Brown

Ten Postcards from a Plane, 2004

1.

Fanny, every day I worry: will I have enough water to swallow that pill? Big as a bee's head and Pepto pink, silly that it could keep you from a baby. But think: jazz, swimmers, spoo, invisible tadpoles smelling of a Bradford Pear, a suburban cheap-tree blooming, nauseating April again with petals that bruise brown as soon as they hit the ground.

I don't mean to embarrass you; I know grandmothers don't want to hear such things. But who wants to carry a baby through security? It's one shoe off, then the other, and the belt too, the bobby pins always sounding the alarm anyway— *I need a female check!* and off I go to the glass partition, barefoot and wishing I'd worn socks. *Stand on the designated spot, ma'am. Raise your arms palm up, ma'am. Now, I'm going to check you here with the back of my hand. . . .*

2.

The Turkish woman with her two babies. Twins, boys. One light, one dark, both bawling. *This seat is empty,* I tell her, hoping I can hold one, especially the darker one—*brown as a berry,* you'd say—in doll-sized denim overalls and a white shirt, brows grown into a V down his nose. *Sit here,* I say

again, patting the seat, moving the in-flight magazine and pil-
low. He pulls at her shirt—fierce little hands, yearning.

3.

I pray when the wheels go up, Fanny. You've never flown,
but it's true: nothing but air sustains. Then, an impossible
breaking, a climb through the gray film to light, a light you
wouldn't believe exists, not on a rainy day like today.

I try to believe in this; I try to forget my spider-bitten, aching
left knee, the dinge of spring, Kentucky a greenbrown mun-
dane below.

4.

10,000 feet. 30,000. Limited beverage service. Red line on
the screen, moving south. Two hours closer to your body,
your body dying 32,000 feet below. Two hours away from
my mother, your youngest daughter, clicking around J. C.
Penney's hair salon with three screaming telephone lines.
Two hours from my sky-blue bike lonely against the wall and
a painting I can't finish. Fanny, I will fly over you soon; I
will be a contrail dirtying your sky. I distract myself with the
island names ahead, syllables curved like a woman's inner
thigh: Patrai, Athena, Santorini.

5.

Within four hours: darkness, the exploding star of some city
below, then light again—the plane chasing the sun, making

it rise too soon, forcing the bloom. In front of me, a girl from Alabama, her *O*'s round as peaches, her vowels crisp iced tea with lemon. She's gone to the bathroom to brush her teeth in a tiny metal sink. If I were a better person, I'd be in Florida now, with you, but instead I lean forward into the empty between seats and to no one whisper, *I told you I would come.*

6.

Fanny, the trip ahead is too planned, one wake-up call after the next, air-conditioned sedans with admissions fees prepaid, the Acropolis (The Acropolis!) with mouse ears included. I am bit and my left leg never quits aching. At home, the tulip magnolia quietly drops her pink panties to the grass. A raccoon pads over the dry garden wondering what things might grow, but for now rummages the trash, breaks his teeth into the yolks of a nest's first eggs. A sparrow furrows under one wing, and in the morning he'll make his way to my window again. You always told me birds trying to get into the house meant death was coming; every day, he taps the glass with his black, black beak.

7.

Fanny, it's not like the movies. Marilyn Monroe is not reading her book upside down, and there is no *hey-tall-n-handsome* flashing pilot wings. People aren't pretty on planes. We are a bloat of pretzel salt and breathe air still warm from another's lungs. A lady across the aisle has skin stretched to a shimmering flawlessness, her cheekbones cheetah-taut. I want to tell her, *I know, I can tell. You were beautiful once.*

63

8.

Yesterday, when I called home, Mama answered with an exhausted *yes. Stop calling me,* she didn't say. *Just have a good time.*

Not like your oldest girl though, no, not like my aunt. *If you were mine,* she said. *If you were mine, you wouldn't go. But you ain't mine; you're my sister's. You got to do what your mother tells you to do, because you belong to her.*

I belong to Mama, Mama belongs to you, a mama that won't be here for long. Then who will she belong to? Me? Can I reverse these charges? Stay. Go. Stay. Go. *Your Mama loves you and your sister loves you and your daddy loves you and you've planned this trip to Greece for a long time. You need to go. We all think you should go.* A sky blue bike against the wall, an unfinished painting.

9.

You are trying to sleep now, too. Dehydrated, you dream of sage that won't turn the Thanksgiving dressing gourd-green. You aren't dreaming of diarrhea slick and dark as engine oil, the broken footboard of your bed rigged together with picture wire, the chandelier crooked over your kitchen table, each prism glazed with nicotine. A cereal bowl next to your bed is full of hair rollers and years of nerve pills, saved for what, I don't know. Your skin, smooth and thin as a Bible page. Not too long ago, I held your hand and remarked how soft it was, meaning it as a compliment. *Don't be silly,* you said. *That ain't no lotion and you know it. Grandma's just gotten old and thin-skinned. That's all there is to it.*

10.

What's under that white smog? A city, I suppose. Athens, ready to celebrate Easter, lambs speared on spits and eggs colored red. Or maybe these wings will slice into something else entirely—a cloud, a cloud like this cloud, a cloud as veil, as caul, a scrim between this life and .

Leah Browning

Little Signs

1. Because I Didn't Notice the Little Signs

The day after my mother's birthday, I take her to the premiere of a film. It is a local, low-budget production. My friend Lori helped with the lighting, and she gave me the tickets.

I am sitting in the auditorium. It is dark. We are about ten minutes into the film. It is a documentary about a woman whose mother was dying, whose mother died during the course of the filming.

We arrived early, and we're in the front row. My mother is sitting to my right, and the woman who is the subject of the documentary is on her right. Lori is somewhere in the darkness behind us, probably holding hands with her boyfriend, the director.

On the screen in front of us, the dying mother retches into a plastic trash can before raising her head weakly and asking for water.

Leaning close to me, my mother twists her mouth into a frown. "I don't like this," she says in a loud voice.

I try to shush her. I am too embarrassed to look in the direction of the woman sitting on her other side. I hope she didn't hear.

"The acting is terrible," my mother complains.

"Shhh! It's not acting," I whisper. "This is a documentary."

My mother clicks her tongue. "Well, it's awful."

I hiss, "Mom, please—she's sitting right next to you."

The woman on her right stands up, sharply, and her seat swings back and forth before coming to rest. She doesn't look back at us as she walks up the aisle and through the doors at the back of the auditorium.

Sighing, my mother says, "This is the worst thing I've ever seen."

I no longer bother whispering. "You know, she was sitting right next to you."

My mother shrugs. "Well, she's not anymore, is she."

My mother has always been difficult, but not like this. She stares at me defiantly, a teenager in the body of a seventy-something woman, waiting to see what I will do. Her eyes glitter in the dark.

2. Allegiance

My mother accuses her new housekeeper of stealing.

"One of the forks is missing," she says. "I wanted to polish the good silver, and when I got it out, there were only eleven forks."

She is scowling, looking pointedly at the housekeeper's pale pink smock with its pattern of tiny rosebuds and its roomy pockets.

"Where is my sewing machine?" she asks suddenly. Suspiciously. Her eyes narrow.

Her ancient sewing machine is in its usual spot, on a tiny wooden table in the guest bedroom. But when I point it out, she seems unmollified. If anything, she seems more suspicious than ever, but now her focus has shifted to me.

For the rest of the visit, every time I look up, I catch her studying me. I'm in the same boat as the housekeeper, now; I can tell. When she catches my eye, I try to smile but it comes out wrong and I can tell she knows it. I have to look away because now I'm questioning myself, wondering what I have done, how many things I am guilty of.

3. A Little Luck

My friend Lori meets me for lunch. We sit outside on the patio and drink lemonade while we wait for our food.

Her children are in college; her oldest son is already in his first year of med school.

I waited until I was almost forty to have my children. They are both in elementary school. In fact, they need to be picked up at 2 o'clock, so the whole time I am at the restaurant with Lori, I am checking my watch.

I can't help thinking that if I had just had my kids earlier, I could really focus on my mother right now. I could be at her house, taking care of her, instead of hiring a housekeeper to do it for me.

But she's turned mean.

If I am completely honest, I have to admit that I am grateful for the housekeeper, with her pale pink smock and her seemingly endless well of patience.

In all likelihood, there are many years of this ahead of me: a downward slide of doctor's appointments, assisted care, maybe a nursing home. After the kids go to bed, I sit next to my husband on the couch and Google "symptoms of Alzheimer's" on the laptop while he watches reruns of *Frasier*. This is where we are right now.

Across the table, Lori is smiling. She is fifty years old, with a beautiful face. Good bone structure, as my mother would have said at one time.

Lori's children have left home, and on nights and weekends, she has become increasingly involved in local theatre. She has been dating the film director for almost a year, and they are still infatuated with each other. We didn't know each other as girls, but sometimes when she talks about him, I can imagine what she must have been like.

"What do you think we'll be doing a year from now?" Lori asks.

It's almost fall, and here and there, leaves are scattered on the sidewalk near our table. The sky is blue, though, and it's not cold enough yet to need a sweater in the middle of the day. We are both healthy. Lori is in love. The children will stay occupied for almost another hour.

She stretches happily, looking up. "With a little luck," she says, "we'll be sitting here, having lunch."

And maybe that is the answer, when so much is uncertain: to plan and prepare and fix things as much as possible, and then to sit outside in the sun and drink lemonade with Lori for as long as possible, until the hands of my watch shift ahead and point me in the next direction.

Cathleen Calbert

When Death Took a Holiday

When Death took a holiday, he picked her for his summer girl, glad to have a slab of flesh against his femur at the seaside. Cold waves rolled over her toes, whirling them into seashells. A meringue of foam creamed her lips. He liked her. She felt delicious. Death flew a fancy Japanese kite: dip and return, dip and return. Sand crabs crawled inside a blue bathing suit. Sad arms weakened into jellyfish. Death placed sand dollars on the closed eyes and stroked the seaweed ringlets. "Sylph, selkie, siren," he grinned. If he'd had lips, he would have pressed them to her sinking breasts and the new, translucent fins. "My mother died," Death's girlfriend thought she said. "Now I am dying." "I don't want you to see anyone else," Death told her. "I need a commitment." She thought she nodded in agreement. "My mother died in June," she thought she said. "Now I'll live with you." "Until the fall," Death promised. He lifted her long body into the sea, and they swam all the way to the moon.

God's mistake was not loving them enough. These tricksters, blue-black as ink drops, ambivalent as midnight, are the color of in-between. They name the sadness of living, the tedium of phone wires. Crows pose, picturesque, in the artist's wheat fields. Crows, like Time, are thieves. Don't scorn them. Let their cries ignite your own loneliness. Welcome the murder of crows that descends when one has fallen. If you're lucky and pure of heart, some day a crow may lengthen its wings and invite you to nestle within the deathly feathers, then fly your body, small ant that you are, into the blue-black sky, into its forever dream.

Death's girlfriend is depressed because no one is sad anymore. People grieve but not longer than three weeks. Then they perform "personal rituals" for "closure" before they get back to "the business of living." They have people to do and things to see. Death's girlfriend doesn't want to see. She places cucumber slices on her eyelids and sinks into yet another tepid bath. Death can do nothing with her. She won't listen to reason. She won't mourn in moderation. She only lets him hold the soles of her wet feet as he swoons her into another afternoon. Finally, he pulls three envelopes from his vest pocket. It's against the rules, but what can he do? He's crazy about her. She opens the first letter. *Mock apple pie*, she reads, *will never taste like the real thing.* She rips into the second. *Please pick up my dry cleaning.* Slowly, she unfolds the third. *Dear Daughter,* she reads but can't go on: the words swim away from her. Death looks at the single sheet. "Ah," he says. "An idiolect I don't speak."

Death's daughter lives in Dingle. Her flaxen braids unravel in the breeze. She's the dream, green-eyed. She has dug a tunnel to China. She's nothing but firm lines and honesty. She lives upside down in Australia. She's as thin as a ghost and as sweet. She lives in the mirror, just out of sight. She sings, *Cockles and mussels, alive, alive oh.* She sings of the high road and the low and *Where oh where can my baby be?* She loosens the pollen from store-bought flowers, fills the bed with leaves, and fingers half a heart on a frosted window. She's the perfect one, of which Death will not speak.

My precious dead are a little tired in the beginning of their dreams, so I sing them to sleep. I kiss their blue-white bellies and stroke their fox-like faces. They are safe. They are with me. I crack a window in case they decide to breathe. If they're thirsty, I shed three drops of pearly tears, a milk that pleases me to see them drink. If they're hungry, I break my heart into pieces: chips of rubies, or is it pomegranate seeds?

When Death naps, he dreams of Kool-Aid ice cubes and your mother's glad hands. The kittens survive. Not one drowns. Look, there's your perverted dachshund. The car sails by, chrome-plated, complete. Your father watches the moon-landing but doesn't pour himself another drink. Your mother isn't wailing over his body. His third wife doesn't pull her away. Your mom still has a body. She's not bone and ash sealed in an urn on your brother's mantle. This newly beautiful brother is traveling across the country on a spiritual journey. His VW bus has been refurbished. He hasn't sold it. No one's died in it. His fist doesn't cave in the plaster next to his girlfriend's face. The life inside her curls into a pearl before disappearing in a shower of rubies. There you are, a mermaid in ivy, swimming in the usual fantasies. Your mother's voice draws you from the heart-shaped leaves. Your mother has made biscuits to accompany the Sunday chicken. When she gives you one, warm from the oven, you kick your feet up on the lawn—now you are a pony—and eat the floury thing as evening comes on. There's no humidity. There are no possibilities. You have no idea why a man and woman would choose to do what your brother says it takes to make a baby. When Death wakes, you're weeping.

Once upon a time, in a land as far away as Sylvia's health, my mother sang, "Too ra loo, ra loo ral, hush, little baby, don't you cry, this mockingbird will never die." I giggled like an idiot, afloat on waves light with salt, my little penis my only rudder. I was her prize, her piglet. She nursed me with black milk as thick as molasses, as strong as rum. I think she laid my sister on a rock for the vultures or whatever: what did she care about the girl? I was the one who drank in the night of her hair and the sadness of her sex. Minnows, quick ribbons, fled. Roses, a glorious gold, wilted. The lamb, the tiger, even the pit bull: all dead. She said I was unlucky. She said I was just clumsy. She said that she loved me. Her end-

less pull, the call to lose my body in her waters, was too much for me. I pointed out the loads of debris, the yellow foam, and oil-slicked seabirds. The tide receded, leaving me a man. I guess she's glad I'm a success, but she doesn't understand who I am.

Death says, "Don't listen to them. Don't invite them in. Blow out those black candles, put away your high school Ouija board, unclasp your hands, and throw open the curtains when you catch the scent of oranges or roses, feel a heaviness on the bed, see a solid silhouette, find your milk drunk or soured, jewelry and shoes moved, wine turned to vinegar, mind to the afterlife. Even face-to-face with a manifestation, don't acknowledge its nonexistence. Spirits feed on courtesies. They will stumble, confused, about your floral bedroom. They'll linger on the basement stairs, pulsing with electricity. They'll lie down in the iridescent green pooling under pedestrian bridges. They won't mean to harm you, but they will: a big wind to your mobile home of a body. Don't believe their stories. Like the demimonde, they can't help lying." His girlfriend won't listen to him. She throws out his sprigs of rosemary and his pepper spray to plead with her dead mother, "Mama, do anything. Torment me. Terrify me. Just don't leave me with nothing." Death says, "Dearest, don't you know the toughest ghosts to get rid of are those that won't visit?"

It began with little things: sparrows whispered secrets into his invisible ear: how vile they found earthworms and how their songs were screams. Then came the bit with the shoes. Left was right, right left. His own breath smelled like a donkey's ass: shit, shit, shit everywhere he went in this world. Death checked himself into Our Lady of Mercy, where shrinks said, "Borderline Personality"; he became fused, they claimed, with every new partner. Was Death psychotic? Just another neurotic? In love with his mother? Enraged with his father? It's always difficult to say in these matters, so they jolted his brain with bolts of blue juice and gave him milk toast in whitewashed mornings. He might be left, they said, with a wet noodle. But Death always could get a hard-on. That was never his problem. They asked if he had any hobbies. "Hobbies?" Death said. Before his release, he stenciled stars and a crescent moon all over the hospital walls. Then, shaken and bruised, he lay off the sauce, sticking to a regimen of barley water and vitamin supplements. His feet fell into the right right, the right left. And the birds no longer said anything he thought worth hearing.

Her mother was gone. Alas and alack. Siblings dissolved into sarcasm and dinners in family restaurants. This was an ending. This was the beginning of her end. She could barely speak. She wrote death poems instead. Friends said, "I hope you feel better soon." But she didn't feel better soon. Friends said, "I don't know how to respond to this level of grief." Their babies burned the phone wires. Their jobs put them to sleep. Mouse shit littered her cupboards. She tried live-catch traps, then poison. The house quaked and creaked. The house told her she owned nothing. The dogs said, "Don't look to me, Goddess of Love. I too am dying." Her husband coughed up, "I love you, hon, but I'm on deadline." Death tapped at her window like a dapper Dracula. He said, "Illicit sex is all that's left of romance." He bought her soft-serve and rowed them out to sea, where porpoises laughed and promised a kind of immortality or at least the suburban version of Lethe: cheese, wine, and movies. Death kissed her fingers into ice, ran his cold tongue down her chest until her heart froze, blue topaz: the maiden encased in ice. Nothing felt good to her. So why did she break up with him? His icicle penis? His one-track mind? The fact that, at core, he was a man of business? Was it something he said? "Disintegration"? "Final Solution"? Something he hadn't done? Killed the mice? Changed the light bulbs? Yes and yes. Mostly, it was September. New England is gorgeous in October. In November, she'd need to rake the leaves. Come December, gifts for nieces. As much as she loved death, she wasn't dead yet.

Michael Campagnoli

from *Dispatches: Beirut (1982-84)*

September 16

Pink leaflets dropped by fighter jets littered the streets. Arafat and his men were gone. With assurances from Sharon and American Ambassador Habib. Wives and children left behind. Old fathers and mothers.

Then fell the leaflets.

Gaby, an Armenian who owned a barber shop in the Commodore's basement, was close to hysteria. *"What does this mean?"* he cried. He was one who believed Sharon when he said it was only the Katyusha rockets he wanted. Forty-three kilometers. Nothing more. He believed when American Ambassador Habib guaranteed the safety of the women and children. But here we were, Kittredge breathing hard from the climb, on top of a high-rise on the Rue Assi, watching the Israeli advance. Then came the cluster bombs.

And everything changed.

The Druse

We were cutting through a stand of cedar, when the scouts found a Druse sniper who had fallen from the crotch of a tree. The first dead I'd ever seen. The sniper rested on one side, head propped against a rock, lips slightly parted. Camel flies swarmed over his body and climbed in his mouth where the blood had pooled and dried.

Saadi checked him. "Hit in the spine," was all he said.

77

The Bar of the Commodore

The shelling had gone on for 24 hours, but Fouad was smiling. Coco, the parrot, was skilled at imitating the incoming. She whistled and everyone ducked.

"At least they're not aiming at us," I said (I was still young then).

"That's precisely what does worry me," Kittredge, the Englishman, answered.

We couldn't get our dispatches out. We couldn't get anything in or out. We couldn't get food or mail or those Turkish cigarettes Kittredge loved. But, somehow, the bar of the Commodore was always stocked and Fouad always smiled. "Tonight," he said in his broken, unctuous English, "we 'ave *Bar-r-r-Bee-Kew,*" and smiled broadly (a mouth full of yellowed teeth like fat golden corn). And Coco did her act.

She was very good. And we all ducked.

The Beards

He was Hezbollah. But very young. The Christians waited until he got over the retaining wall then shot him. He was carrying a grenade launcher and it was heavy, clumsy, and he was all alone and having trouble getting over. "Ooou-ah!" he cried and fell head-first, then sat up and kicked the launcher, which snapped back and hit him in the head. It stunned him and he began to weep, violently, like a child. It was embarrassing. That's when they shot him.

"I hate the beards," the shooter said smiling. That's what they called Hezbollah, the "beards."

But he was just a kid, really.

It Happened All the Time

Haji was drunk. Very drunk. A few days before, his brother (a civilian, home for the holidays, studying medicine at Ohio State) was shot by a Christian sniper somewhere along the Green Line. The brother was unarmed, moving supplies for the Red Cross to the refugee camps. This was shortly before the massacres at Sabra and Chatilla during the Israeli occupation.

And now the brother was dead and Haji was drunk. Muslims were forbidden to drink, but Haji was drunk. He was holding the muzzle of an old Kalashnikov in the face of a liquor store owner who had complained after Haji cracked open a bottle of rum. Haji thrust the barrel of the Russian weapon into the man's nose and mouth and laughed maniacally.

The owner, his nostrils shoved close to his eyes, decided, after all, it was Haji's rum, several cases of it.

It happened all the time. People shot each other over traffic jams on the Mar Elias. The police were powerless. They'd distribute a press release, saying, "A warrant has been issued for assailants unknown," and that would be the end of it.

"Wake up, Jake my boy," Kittredge told me. "It's every man for himself, now. Click, click, click. A simple errand, a trip to the market, you wind up dead."

So Haji sat on the curb drinking. Weeping, appealing to Allah. He'd always been the wild one, the crazy one, the one who didn't care, who believed in nothing but his body's length. The brother was the "smart one," the "Good One," the "gentle one," the one with a *future*. Baby brother. Liquor never touched his lips. Haji wailed. He pounded his chest, ripped handfuls of hair from his head and beard. And I stood on the sidewalk, watching, still trying to be young.

Puissant and Ready to Prove

"Sanctuary!" Kittredge howled, "Sanctuary!"

A plaintive cry, deep-bellied and over-wrought. He raised his arms, stumbled, and nearly fell. "Sanctuary!!!" he howled again and pulled his long black actor's cape over his huge bloated actor's head. Standing near the clock tower on the campus of American University, he performed a hunchback worthy of Laughton: drunk, loud, delusional, bathos and lunacy mixed. I tried to quiet him, but he hammed it up for the benefit of a passing patrol. Maronite militia. Teenagers, most of them, puissant and ready to prove.

"Hold thy bloody hand!" Kittredge boomed, as the guard converged. Men had been shot for less. They lined us against College Hall at gunpoint, made us strip (smirking at Kittredge's white spindly legs, his ample gut, his puckered diminished ass and shriveled privates). Relieved of our cash, they departed (tires screeching, weapons firing in the air) while Kittredge and I scrambled to retrieve our soiled jockies and torn-up shirts.

Humane Interests

When Kittredge returned from the Iraqi border, all morning and all afternoon, he drank. But he wasn't drunk. He just sat staring straight ahead. A slim young man with a pretty mouth sat next to him, but they didn't speak. I waited for his friend to leave and went over.

"They're using children to clear mine fields," Kittredge told me.

"What?"

"Kids." He shook his head. "Iraqi mines are decimating Khomeini's tanks, personnel carriers. So he's using 9- and

10-year-olds to clear the fields. Lines them up at arm's length, wide enough to move an armored column. Three waves are usually enough. You think I'm kidding? They can't wait to volunteer, to die for the Ayatollah."

I was skeptical.

Kittredge laughed. But it was hollow and soundless.

"You can't imagine the carnage," he whispered, looking down at his hands, the fingernails chewed to a nub. "Blown apart. The Iraqis are eager, positively gleeful, to provide proof. Purely 'humane' interests, of course."

He raised both eyebrows in unison.

"They actually have 'child' POW camps. Isn't that extraordinary?"

The Stump

In the building opposite, a wall had blown away and everything was in view like the back of a doll's house. The shell had hit in the street just moments before and there must have been a tunnel beneath because it all caved in, creating a kind of escarpment. The sun was high and it was hot and in the dust and heat was a little girl on one of the floors hanging out toward the street—naked, shaking, scared stiff—watching the Amal militia shooting their guns off as they drove by in their Range Rovers.

They sat him against the wall of a Mosque. His face was sweaty and caked with dirt. His eyes were black dots in wide open whites. They darted around wildly. He couldn't say anything, but you could tell that he wanted to know if he was going to die. A grenade had ripped out his belly and they had dragged him from the street to be clear of the AK-47s. His legs were splayed and lifeless and his blood was all in a puddle. He kept looking up, but they ignored him.

In a few minutes, it was over.

81

"A body's just a 'thing,' Jake," Kittredge said. "Unaspirated. A 'thing.' A leaf. A shard."

"A human stump."

On the Esplanade

One morning, down by the esplanade, Kittredge saw a group of young boys tormenting a kitten, tossing it in the air, throwing it back and forth. When he yelled at them to stop, they hurled it into the sea. Broken-down and out of shape, he lumbered over the sand and into the water. The boys were furious. They mocked and jeered him. When he returned empty-handed, they were jubilant.

"Little bastards!" he roared.

Heartless and superior, they taunted and sneered.

Kittredge had to throw rocks to chase them away. But his anger soon broke against the hard malice of their insolence. Though he tried to hide it, you could see tears in his eyes. Thereafter, whenever one of the boys saw him, they'd yell, *"Hey Meester, the kitten, she swimming!"*

The Song of Zokat Blatt

On the last day of the siege, Kittredge and I were walking behind a caravan of carts and cars and trucks and ragged people when shells began exploding around us. He got hit and was bleeding badly. "Christ," I yelled and Kittredge smiled, pale blue eyes in blasted face. We scrambled, me lugging him over my shoulder through the smoke and debris. There were several close calls.

When we finally got to Zokat Blatt, corpses lined the streets and Kittredge was dead in my arms. People were weeping and I began to weep, too. Openly and without shame. But it was not for Kittredge, not yet. It was for the terrible relief of knowing this was not the day I was going to die.

Christopher Citro

The Little Book of Monsters

Happy Birthday to Me

"The last thing I need is a zombie with a replica of my own face," said Willy. "So you don't like your birthday present then," replied Bianca. "It isn't that," said Willy, "but what is he for, anyway? What am I supposed to do with one around the house?" "He could help with the cleaning," suggested Bianca as she waved a hand, palm open, towards the rumpus room. Willy followed her gesture: entertainment center (cobwebbed), sunken conversation pit (filled with alligators and musty water), one of those giant egg chairs you sit in while smooth music plays on the hi-fi (spikes all along the inside, a cobra coiled on the cushion). Without saying a word, Willy looked Bianca right in the eye. His birthday present stepped to his side and, with the same eyes (only clouded over and crusty at the edges), did the same. Willy had to stop himself putting an arm across his own shoulder.

Martin Swerves

Earlier that night, he'd picked her up from her parents' two-story house near the country club—her mother at the door waving, her father at an upper window not waving. Burgers. Malts. A drive-in double feature: boy meets girl, goes to war, returns to girl married to a sheep farmer and has to deal with it; followed by creature crawls from a festering pit and feasts on cheerleaders until some hero stops him—and along a lonely country road, down which they'd driven many times, Martin turns to Jenny who's staring wide-eyed out the window beside her. She knows Martin has turned to her. Martin opens his mouth and, at that moment, a creature crawls from the forest into their path. Or a hero.

Happiness, in a Way

Once upon a time, a door slammed somewhere in the house. Evie looked up from her crossword puzzle—a Danish reputation, in a way—and the light from her bedside lamp flickered. Who could that be, she thought? A seven letter word for bump in the night. It can't be Steven. He's just six letters and he said he's never coming back. Richie, the same. Six letters again and he even tore his name from the little white card the mailman slipped into the mailbox window. It must be Johnny. My first love, fifth grade—he let me sit in his lap while he showed me his scratch 'n' sniff sticker album. Or the other Johnny, the boy from the cornfield next to the senior parking lot, the corn already harvested, just stalks halfway up and shredded silk in the autumn light. Two Johnnys. That's seven letters. J-o-h-n-n-y-s. Now a nine letter word for joy in the middle of the night when my Johnnys come marching home, slamming the door.

Something Awful, Autumn Nights

The sound of Linda's chattering teeth is the greatest sound in the world to me. It's as if the stars climb down the tree trunks and dance around us clapping. They have claws for hands. "They have claws for hands, Linda!" I cry. Linda turns to me, says, "I know they do. Now can we please go inside. My knees are beginning to knock." "The gods of the underworld have coconut feet!" I yell. I have to yell. Linda's heading for the back door. Suddenly I am sitting here alone. Wishing I had a hot cup of tea. Trying to recall the greatest sound in the world. The stars twinkle in the black sky. I miss them.

Be My Guest

Walking through the house just a few minutes ago, I felt the monsters welling up inside me, pouring into my throat, tapping at the inside of my two big front teeth with their claws. Elbowing one another to get out, bellowing that incomprehensible yell-language they use when I deny them air, keeping my mouth shut. The time wasn't right. You were not here. It wasn't twelve-thirty yet. And now it is. I'm sitting next to you here at the picnic table. Answering the expectancy in your eyes, I lean to you, tilt my head and open my chompers. Nothing. The monsters have departed. They do not like to be kept waiting. It's not my fault. You're welcome to go in looking for them, I say. You look me right in the eyes and do so.

Jennifer Kwon Dobbs

Myths to Have a Good Time*

FSH 76. I'm thirty-five years old. To avoid osteoporosis and some forms of cancer, I'll need to wear a patch and take progesterone every day until I'm fifty.

While listening to my doctor, I'm looking through my kitchen window to the backyard. The lilacs and day lilies are blooming. When my husband and I bought this ranch-style house four years ago, we loved its brick patio where we imagined abendbrot with our child. *Do you want to eat inside or outside?* The back porch's roof provides just enough shade for gochujang to ripen inside clay onggi during the summer.

My doctor says she's sorry.

Last year in Seoul, my mother and I reunited after she read my story in an online newspaper. For seven years, Omma searched for me after finding out through family gossip the name of the orphanage where my great-aunt had taken me without her permission. I was two weeks old.

My name is Jennifer Kwon Dobbs. My name is Jennifer Synobia. My name is Kwon Young Mee. My name is case #1314. My name is Sujin. Omma named me for the monsoon rain, a northern pine mountain facing her window overlooking summer cornfields. She wasn't a prostitute who my adoptive mother said had fallen in love with a G.I. and who loved me so much that she chose for me "a better life." Instead, she belonged to the high school traditional dance troupe, and after graduation she moved to Seoul to work in Namdaemun Market while her older brother attended basic training. She sent money home to her parents, and three younger sisters and brother. Her hair fell past her waist. She was the school beauty, which was why Appa lingered inside the cramped dress shop pretending to look for a blouse that November evening. *Just one drink. Just one dance. Just one. Just one. Just once.*

My doctor reassures me. There's adoption or something— sort of like science fiction—called egg donorship. I'm healthy and could carry a baby. She can recommend someone. I'm remembering summers and winters in Korea; my trans-national search, research, and advocacy; love and fighting for love; arriving and going.

Reuniting in Paris Baguette, Omma embraced me with such ferocity; my body didn't belong to me. Then she examined my hands, matching hers to mine, the curves of our ears and collarbones. She pulled my socks off and recognized the shapes of my toes. She rolled up my sleeves looking for a blue spot, the bruise where my right shoulder scraped. I was born breech in the morning after two nights of labor in my cousin's house.

On the phone, my cousin said she washed me. Omma breast-fed me. Unni said she was there when the car pulled into the gravel driveway. She was just a girl. She couldn't stop my great-aunt from lifting me from the yo and blankets; so she just watched Omma—still weak despite eating seaweed soup—rush out of the backroom as Como Halmoni slid into the passenger's seat. (Her eldest son kept the engine running.) After Como Halmoni's daughter told Unni the orphanage's name in secret, Unni called Omma, and they visited the director who didn't tell them about the orphanage's ties to Eastern Social Welfare Society, which had forwarded me on to Dillon Adoption Agency's office in Oklahoma.

They didn't know that my adoptive mother had tried to conceive for five years, that her husband had served in Vietnam just like Omma's eldest brother, that my adoptive father agreed to a Korean adoption in part because he couldn't imagine loving a Vietnamese child, or that my adoptive parents borrowed money for the agency fees from my adoptive grandmother, whose deceased husband had served in the Korean War. He trained sharpshooters who tracked Koreans in white clothes. The Japanese said Communists always wore white.

How to get rid of the bitter flavor? I'm learning the taste of Omma's hands, the taste of mine making baechu kimchi. I've developed my own recipe based on trial and error and remembering Omma folding seafood and red pepper paste among brined cabbage leaves and wrapping them into parcels.

I know one of Wae Harabeoji's stories. I tell it to my nine-year old choka who reads at a fifth grade level. My younger brother turns down the radio so he can also listen. Still, my choka is too young to understand distances—how these few sentences about his great-grandfather's life took thirteen years of trans-national searching to find, crossed the ocean, and passed through translation to this moment in which we're riding together in his father's truck. How could he understand? He thinks this story is just a story, and in a way, he's right.

Reunion wasn't supposed to be like this. I waited to have a child because I wanted my child to have Korean grandparents, to be safe from the chaos of not knowing our ancestors.

After Omma and I met in the café, we went to her apartment, and she cooked for me. She sang to me. She rubbed my back while I cried. She styled my hair, and she told me I had my father's eyes.

A young woman in her twenties receives between $5,000 and $8,000 from a reproductive medical center for her eggs, and possibly ten times more if she responds to a private ad. She will take powerful drugs that might harm her fertility in the future in order to stimulate her egg production to give "the gift of a child" to an infertile woman with money. In some states, her eggs might be used for medical research without her knowledge.

I didn't know if I wanted a child. I wanted a child. At the root of both truths was an abiding fear—my child turning to me and asking, *where do we come from?* My child's face a kind of mirror of my own, like a ghost trapped in a surface and shimmering. I wasn't ready to release the ghost so soon, but the body has its own answers.

The body has its own logic. Premature ovarian failure is an autoimmune disease. The body attacks itself for no reason. The body can't recognize itself and heal.

My adoptive mother's name resembles the name Omma gave me. If you type 수진 into Google Translate, it appears as Susan.

Omma pestered me about having a child. She sent me home with juice packs of hongsam to improve my health, but they make me sweat because my body already has a lot of heat. She has dreams about her grandchildren. She has ambitions for them and for me.

The potential is overwhelming: an anonymous egg donor with a SAT score of 1500; a birth mother whose healthy newborn can bond easily; the possibility of five, ten, twenty half-siblings unknown to each other.

The day lilies need water. Prairie thistle spikes through the hostas. I'm standing in my kitchen. I'm tired. I want to go home. This loss was never a home, and maybe it wasn't a way either. Maybe it wasn't even a vision. Maybe it was just a drunken conversation at Bada, a bar in Hongdae, with repatriated adoptee friends who were similarly schooled in critical theories.

Maybe home was tentative. Maybe it was the serenity one feels when it's least expected. My choka shows me a dance that he created after listening to his favorite pop song on loop for a whole week. *Everybody have fun tonight. Everybody just have a good time.* He teaches it to me, and I follow. We're in sync, and we're laughing. For a moment, I'm completely in my body, and our bodies are united in a way that can only occur in movement, not in language. Then suddenly he slides and twirls. I stumble. I can't keep up, but that's why we're having fun.

I've booked an appointment for a seminar about IVF treatment. One of the application questions asks if "feelings of loss have been properly addressed." I don't know what loss is anymore. I thought I knew. Through knowing loss, I could re-contour desire. Yet how is it possible to be the entire triad—birth sister/daughter; adopted person; infertile woman whose only hope is adoption or egg donorship—and the space beyond the triangle's conjectures a realm of dreaming?

Who gets to dream? Whose dream shrivels because life has been diverted away? Whose dream ripens? Who is told to dream in the direction of someone else's desire? Whose desire? Your mother gave birth to you through her heart? Her womb is in the shape of a heart? You're her daughter, but you can't have a child. You give life to a dream through taking another woman's child. Your dream takes on a life that no woman's child could ever inhabit. You're that child. You're trying to embody a dream, a flesh and blood dream.

My doctor advises me to schedule a bone density exam. My fatigue might be related to hormonal changes. Something about dryness. We make an off-color joke about "use it or lose it." We agree about staying positive. Who knows? She's being kind.

Sometimes slipping. Sometimes falter.

Sometimes shelter. My choka mispronounces myth. He says "mithe." He asks me about the mithe of Medusa, and I tell him that she was once a beautiful but haughty virgin priestess. The goddess Minerva punished her and transformed her into a monster with the power to turn men into stone. I learned this myth from my adoptive mother who loved Latin, her favorite subject in high school. My choka wants to know what a myth is, and I tell him that it's a story to explain a natural phenomenon. Jupiter throws a thunderbolt, and that's why there's a storm.

These are the last days of summer. Sometimes rain. My doctor tells me to keep in touch if I want to explore egg donorship or to call her if I have more questions about my blood work. "Thank you," I tell her, "I appreciate it." I hang up. All the mothers in my life are somehow in my body, and I'm a woman looking at her backyard. I see Omma's pine mountain in Shillim. I see Susan's redbuds on Cleveland Street.

Does the body listen? Does the body respond?

I notice that my choka has a mole on his left cheek like mine. On Dongsaeng's backyard deck, he sits on my lap while I hold an umbrella to keep us both dry. We test the umbrella to see how it works. I follow his suggestion: Tilt the umbrella to the left and close it slightly. See how it keeps the rain off? *See, Como, see? Hahaha! See!*

---

* This essay was influenced by egg donor testimonies featured in the documentary film *Eggsploitation*, produced by the Center for Bioethics and Culture.

Jacqueline Doyle

Dora

Dora Dreams of Fire

"A house was on fire. My father was standing beside my bed and woke me up. I dressed quickly. Mother wanted to stop and save her jewel-case; but Father said: 'I refuse to let myself and my two children be burnt for the sake of your jewel-case.' We hurried downstairs, and as soon as I was outside I woke up." (7:64)

The jewel box was my mother's. It was not for him to rifle through, pulling out pretty trinkets and holding them up to the light, looking at them this way and that, deciding what was valuable and what was not. He named me "Dora" after his sister's nursemaid, not even her real name, but a name bestowed by her employers. He was protecting my identity in his case history, he claimed. His treasured jewel-case. He took my mother's jewels. He named me, claimed my story.

Dora's First Kiss

"[Herr K.] suddenly clasped the girl to him and pressed a kiss upon her lips. This was surely just the situation to call up a distinct feeling of excitement in a girl of fourteen who had never before been approached. . . . [But] the behaviour of this child of fourteen was already entirely and completely hysterical. . . . Instead of the genital sensation which would

94

certainly have been felt by a healthy girl in such circum-
stances, Dora was overcome by . . . disgust." (7:28, 29)

Herr Zellenka lunged at me, his beard tangled and unkempt, his lips wet, his breath foul with cigarette smoke. The alien, probing tongue was like a worm in my mouth. I squirmed, I pushed him away. I couldn't breathe, could not speak for fear and disgust, wondered, "Does my father know? Is he trading me for Herr Z.'s wife?" For I knew she was his mistress, a fact never in dispute. Who are these men, to make such arrangements? Why has my father arranged to make me lie on this man's couch?

They throng by my bedside. The lecherous Herr Z., who offered me a jewelry box. My syphilitic father, who offered me to Herr Z. and lied to my face. Frau Z., who borrowed my father and offered to lend me her pearls. My mother, offering nothing, running from her burning house without her necklaces, bracelets, rings. Herr Doktor Freud, smoking cigar after cigar, fondling the jewels in his case.

Dora's Jewel Case

" 'Yes, Herr K. had made me a present of an expensive jewel-case a little time before.'

" 'Then a return-present would have been very appropriate. Perhaps you do not know that "jewel-case" [Schmuck-kästchen] is a favourite expression for the same thing that you alluded to not long ago by means of the reticule you were wearing—for the female genitals, I mean.'

" 'I knew you would say that.' " (7:69)

Of course.

Quim, beaver, gash, cunt, pussy, honey pot, snapper, pearl hotel, fuzz box, jewel box, clam. Something to be pried open. Entered. Filled.

Legs tightly together, I lie supine on a divan draped with an oriental carpet and piled high with soft velvet pillows, an ottoman fit for a sultan's seraglio. The air is so thick with cigar smoke that I can hardly breathe. I clutch my small purse. Herr Doktor Freud sits out of sight, just over my head. Toys with fantasies of my incestuous attractions to Father, Herr Z., Frau Z., himself. Strokes his beard. Shifts in his seat, adjusting the family jewels. Sucks on his wet cigar. Talks and talks.

Dora's Purse

"Dora's reticule, which came apart at the top in the usual way, was nothing but a representation of the genitals, and her playing with it, her opening it and putting her finger in it, was an entirely unembarrassed yet unmistakable announcement of what she would like to do with them—namely, to masturbate." (7:77)

I fiddle with my purse. Wonder whether it's time to leave yet. How many weeks it has been.

Dora Dreams of Departure

"[In the dream] I was walking about in a town which I did not know. I saw streets and squares which were strange to me. Then I came into a house where I lived, went to my room, and found a letter from Mother lying there. She wrote saying that as I had left home without my parents' knowledge she had not

wished to write to me to say Father was ill. 'Now he is dead, and if you like you can come.' I then went to the station and asked about a hundred times: 'Where is the station?' I always got the answer: 'Five minutes.' I then saw a thick wood before me which I went into, and there I asked a man whom I met. He said to me: 'Two and a half hours more.' He offered to accompany me. But I refused and went alone. I saw the station in front of me and could not reach it. At the same time, I had the usual feeling of anxiety that one has in dreams when one cannot move forward. Then I was at home. I must have been travelling in the meantime, but I knew nothing about that. I walked into the porter's lodge, and enquired for our flat. The maidservant opened the door to me and replied that Mother and the others were already at the cemetery." (7:94)

Eleven weeks now.

I can see the station. I don't need a man to accompany me there. I can't seem to move forward in the dark thicket and the smoke. My mother's jewel box is lost. I am lost. My father is dead. Herr Doktor Freud is waiting, but I must leave. I will leave a message with the maidservant. Who is the maidservant? It's so hard to move forward, the branches are tangled, I'm short of breath. "Ida, Ida," Herr Doktor Freud says to me, "you are working through the thicket of transference. Let me accompany you to the station. We are almost there." I know he will lead me back through the unfamiliar streets and deserted squares, away from the terminal. I am anxious, I will be lost. "No," I whisper, "I'm leaving now." "Two and a half hours more," he says. "No thank you," I reply, a little louder, but he insists. "Five more minutes." Finally I tell him, my voice returning at last, "I will go alone. I am leaving now."

And I did.

Work Cited

Freud, Sigmund. "Fragment of an Analysis of a Case of Hysteria." *The Standard Edition of the Complete Psychological Works of Sigmund Freud.* Trans. James Strachey, Anna Freud, Alix Strachey, Alan Tyson. Volume 7 (1901-1905). London: Hogarth Press, 1953, 1-122.

Russell Evatt

Pocket Guides

Pocket Guide to Sketching People

Try to figure out what makes a person a person. You will probably not be able to figure it out. None of the people you'll draw will look like the people you wanted to draw. Is it the nose, the casual curve of a nostril that makes someone recognizable? Like I said, you will probably not be able to figure it out. So draw a person and then try to find the person you've drawn, asking on the streets "have you seen this person?" and "does this person look like you or anyone you know?" There will be no takers. Don't dishearten. Draw them anyway, pages and pages of no one, fill up entire notebooks with no one with no way to know for sure if they might be alive somewhere, looking for themselves.

Pocket Guide to Punctuation and Loneliness

All is not complete confusion. Add an apostrophe for ownership. Add an *s* and stop being alone. Remember no set of rules can hope to cover all variations. It's not as easy as anything you've ever said, but variations and peculiar styles can be dealt with. In references to whole centuries, recall the different generations. Roman numerals are used to differentiate related males with the same name. The sentences that follow provide a few broad principles. However, there are many specific situations in which these principles will not apply.

Pocket Guide to Writing a Book Critics will Adore

Compose a book in which each chapter quotes from the previous chapter. In this way the book will talk to itself, about itself. Make sure each chapter is in a vein of argument eerily similar to the preceding line of questioning. This will give the reader an opportunity to observe a highly intelligent conversation between leading experts. You are the leading experts. Your smart friends will call it masturbatory. Your immature friends will laugh at your smart friends. Probably your dead friends will like it the most. Read it to them softly, under your breath, so that no one else can hear.

Pocket Guide to Filling Out the Forms

If you have any questions please refer to the manual, section 1A. If you have any questions about this please refer to the manual, section 1A. We have sustained enormous losses and realized very little to prevent more. If you have any questions about this please refer to the manual, section 1A. If you find that 1A does not suffice, please refer to the manual's instructions, conveniently located in section 1A. Kindly seat yourself. This will take more time than you have.

Pocket Guide to Generating Ideas

Some of your ideas will sell for money you'll never see. Your work will take up billboards and fit nicely between songs on hit radio or between paragraphs in celeb mags. Wrench out a song on piano for parents with kids and kids without parents and parents who are also grandparents. It will be the same song for each. Occasionally you'll run out of things to say so repeat yourself and call it a chorus. If it's catchy everyone will sing along.

Pocket Guide to Watching Reruns from the Nineties

Don't wonder why cameras way back then were so fuzzy. Must've been something in the air. Don't mention you are alone. A decade will pass. No one will know it but you. Wrap God around your fist and have it out with the air. A rigorous applause will radiate from the clouds. After that, speak only with the wind. Friend its gentle touch while counting the birds on the windmill.

Pocket Guide to whether Matt Is/Isn't Smiling

A group of friends will go dancing. One will sing happy birthday to herself. Another will scream "The Star-Spangled Banner" in its entirety. Someone in the city will be laughing at a boy trying to pick up a woman. A joke will tell itself on the sitcom showing on the muted television. *How easy it is to kill the mood in here by defining the mood in here.* The black skirts will all ride up at the same time. Be sure to designate a driver. Someone you don't know. Someone whose belief in the nature of truth will preclude anything on the face resembling a smile.

Pocket Guide to Joining Up without Cause

Be aware every drop has a fall, a steep price to join up. Know that the guard of national supremacy and the furloughed newspapermen with their marriage hats slung low over their eyes can't tell you where to solace. Even money will say it's a fair fight. Be aware the young, who lap up the teachings of illusion and follow along the map of suffering, are drunk on the blood from a grand piano. They don't need to sit up straight and really belt it out. They'll come in handy during the war, those legs. Damn good employees if you ask me. Look out on the beach of conflict; count the little sandcastles of death arguing with the tides.

Wesley Fairman

Emma and the Rain

One thing you should know, the Rain is patient. He can out-last your sunny times, your playing-outside-and-laughing-at-the-absurdity-of-every-living-thing times. He can be silent through your nights which glimmer like crystal broken on the floor, a dropped vase or serving bowl. The Rain can listen without speaking for weeks, hearing your shouts of joy and enduring your guttural, animal night sounds. The Rain accepted years ago that most people would rather he didn't just drop by. The Rain learned eons ago to call before he comes over.

But one shuddering swift night, the Rain fell. He fell for a woman with freckles on her cheeks and nose, not a professional beauty or film femme fatale. She set out to stroll through the gray sky gathering dark, yet soon found herself marching with knees held high to a primal beat, the rap-a-tap of oncoming rain against the soul compelling her to dance. Her so-pale skin glowed as she marched through the kiss-cool quiet, past the finally fading hydrangeas, with her eyes held on the level of the horizon. She marched on for several blocks before finding that she was shuffling along with her feet just above the cracked walkway, its dips and valleys were the Blue Ridge Mountains in miniature. Deeply alive, shock-ingly vital, this woman you would look twice at without knowing her name was suddenly self-aware. Aware of how her hands were hanging just so, with thumbs parallel to thighs; she could practically feel her hair growing wild. Her lips and cheeks tingled with self-consciousness, and she knew, in that moment, she was being watched.

Emma started and turned on her heel, all aboriginal lean-ings vanishing. She could just see the gabled roof of her small yellow house from the corner where she stood. She felt she had walked miles, and yet as she stared, she saw her weather vane spin on its angled axis. The final flowers of summer shed a few pitiful petals among her toes, a satin-soft warning, a silent, sweet reminder that she was exposed.

"Storm," she muttered with a nod. Oppressive clouds gathered and she watched as the stars winked out, the broken shard of crystal swept up and emptied into the dustpan of the night. Eyes on her shoes bruising flowers underfoot, Emma set out for home.

The first drop fell as she approached her white picket gate, a pregnant-heavy drop which landed on her left cheek-bone and ran swiftly toward her mouth, a wet caress. As she closed the gate the violets seemed to call out. "Take me with you," begged some, and they reached out to rub against her wrists and waist. "Run," urged others, and refused to ac-knowledge her further.

The Rain came down and took liberties with her face and neck. He ran down her shoulders, dampening those vestigial wings. He caught in her tangled brown hair and slid behind her ears, dripped off their freckled lobes. She sprinted to her door, but the Rain was faster, slipping down her throat to touch a clavicle. Pooling in the dip made between those bird-like bones and moistening her chest. The Rain saw more of strange, beautiful Emma in that dash to the door than any man could hope to see in weeks.

Emma reached the shelter of her wide front porch as the Rain played a symphony on her old-fashioned tin roof. She slipped into her house and stood inside, back pressed against the door. Clutched in her hands were the violets she had man-aged to save, now slightly wounded as they pressed against her torso. As the Rain used her roof for a tom-tom, Emma buried her face in the violets and sighed alone in the dark.

* * *

A "rainy spell" is what they called it. A week after the Rain met Emma, the old women sat on their porches, watching the water rush toward the storm drains, and talked about the old men who mostly talked about floods which were fading from memory. They gathered together near the slip-slide-silent doors of the grocery store and joked about flood insurance.

Concern was written on the faces of the hustling people passing one another on the streets the next week. Southern people aren't bred to deal with the constant gloom and ever-gray skies that people from Northern regions accept. People meandered slowly through shops, drove slowly and stopped at every yellow light, delaying their return to dripping clothes and wringing-wet hair. Headlights began to fade from constant use; whipping windshield wipers hypnotized children. She cursed when she slipped in the parking lot of the hardware store, exclaimed that the Rain simply must come to an end. Her small packages of foam-backed weatherstripping went skip-scattering across the pavement, and as she bent to retrieve them, wet-warped as they were, the Rain took his time admiring his view. The sky crackled with static electricity, and the clouds formed a roof over Emma's head, making her heavy under the Rain's invisible gaze.

The Rain pressed against her windows as she dressed for work, puddled in front of her door in an effort to feel the rough and smooth of her slightly-too-large feet. The Rain had bubbled up through her basement floor, overwhelming the machinery designed to pump water out and away from the house. He had finally infiltrated one of her windows, had located a hairline slit in the seam and had pushed until he could slip in. Moistening Emma's walls, he watched as she brushed her teeth before bed.

*   *   *

The Rain's Dream

The ocean rushes toward the shore, pounding and pounding rocks against rocks and grinding them into rough gray sand. The ocean feeds my hunger, delivering molecules of water, tiny children, to me constantly. I gather these children together and press them until they are too fat-full to suspend from the sky, and then I release them to bathe Emma and the world.

She will be seeing no one and hearing no one and thinking of no one, and the sand will soften the calluses on her hands and feet. I shower her with my gifts, make music for her against the primordial landscape. I will worship her with my many fingers, protect her with my cloud-cloak cover, and she will love me too. She will dance naked the way so many have, returning my adoration and respecting my might, a rain dancer in a monsoon.

*   *   *

A woman who looks a lot like a girl you knew in high school stepped off a tiny passenger plane; lifted her face to the sun in a moment of relief. She crossed the cracked crumbling pavement, its peaks and valleys a miniature of the Tetons; she hummed a sunny-day song for the first time in weeks. Her bag, when tossed from the hold of the plane, made a satisfying clunk as it collided with the runway, confirming her presence in this unprecedented haven from the Rain.

She presented her passport to the customs officer, admiring her new stamp as she waited for her bag to be returned. She consulted her French-to-English dictionary as she waited for her driver to load her bag into the van. As they sped at a rate only professional drivers are comfortable with, Emma

106

peered out the window. Behind her, watching her progress to her rented chateau, the Rain gathered himself. He pulled from hillside creeks and river valleys, rubbing these foreign molecules together, exciting them. They were warm from the sun and felt good against his mass.

The driver grunted at his rearview mirror, "The Rain," he said, "it comes."

In Spain, the Rain tapped out "Emma please" in dots and dashes on every surface she passed. His pleas gurgled up from overwhelmed storm drains along with a mouse who had died. The tiny rodent bumped against the side of Emma's boot as she crossed the street, causing her to jump with surprise. His gray fur was waterlogged and his tail was wrapped around his body from the force of the current.

Wild-eyed with this mouse, Emma knew that somewhere under the city there was a flooded nest, perhaps the watery grave of one Missus Mouse. She knew that the Rain had invaded that home, too. The Rain was ruining everything.

* * *

The Mouse's Dream

Scurrying dark, and with a full belly. Safe from the constant threat of the sky, from the traps and poisons of humans, the Mouse and his Missus collect scraps of paper, tiny twigs and shed feathers. They weave them cleverly to produce a cozy home. The Mouse and his Missus have no need for travel.

Together they may surface on the street, once their children are tucked away, and watch the Rain pitter-patter against pavement and umbrellas. With water nearby and yet safe from the Rain which could wash away all, the Mouse and his Missus settle down to love one another for the duration of their impossibly short lives.

*   *   *

A woman you would look for in dusty yearbooks sat alone in the processed air reviewing an English-to-Arabic dictionary. Sallow, still dripping from the Rain, she smelled musty, a rug which needs airing. She moved her mouth silently, testing the way the words might feel if she found someone to speak them to. In her mismatched clothes, layers to shed in a new climate, slowly forming puddles on the floor, she looked like someone you might steer your child away from in an alley. Men would put themselves between her and their wives in primal fits of protectiveness.

Stowing her dictionary and preparing to board her flight, Emma glanced toward the Rain, pounding against the plate glass windows. She took her seat on the aisle to ignore his glares, and he pounded against the double panes, beating out a message which came through loud and clear.

*   *   *

Rocking in a chair on her river-wide front porch, there's a woman who is vaguely famous. She has surrendered to the constant humidity and allowed her hair to frizz and matt into a prematurely gray mass. Crow's feet make her look decades older than she is, a result of squinting into the sky. She murmurs as she rocks, the heel of her foot hitting the boards of her porch in an ancient rhythm, and watches, watches the Rain.

Beating against the tin porch roof, the Rain rushes down gutters and wears away the flaking yellow paint. Bubbling up the steps, the Rain reaches out with many fingers to caress her bare toes, washing her feet. Eroding tight-packed dirt around the roots of the trees, it is just a matter of time before the Rain and Emma are truly together.

Elisabeth Frost

GRACE COURT

The Neighborhood

Half-circle, offshoot of no consequence, our horseshoe of
houses isn't a route to anywhere.
    Court, it's called. Judge and jury? King and queen? Or
players—a team.
    The only goal is getting out.

Garfields

Their backyard faces our backyard.
    Their house is bigger than our house, their yard a little
messier. I cut through to get to school sometimes.
    A high gable faces the rear. The white paint is chipping
down to the pine.
    I know the dented trunk of their car, backed into the drive
under a maple. I watch their kid from behind in his lit room,
while Mr. Garfield in pajamas comes out at nine to dump the
trash with a thud.
    Out on Nassau Drive, though, I have to count three in
from the house on the corner to be sure which place is theirs.
The view from their street is strange—the trimmed lawn, the
curtains waiting in the window. Shrubs.
    I know them better than this. It's all a front.

Marxes

When Mr. Marx inspects the hedge in his undershirt, the tiny round flame of his cigar lights his way. It has a drafty, I'm-at-ease stench. He hardly notices me standing like an odd number, hugging the maple, courting the foliage climbing its climb.

He's looking for my mother in a dress like a glass of wine on the nightstand. He evens his side, an eye on the blinds.

My mother says that Mrs. Marx offered up her husband once, on the theory that it would do them all good. But she had her pleasures—why would she want theirs?

Some weekends Mr. Marx clips till his side of the hedge is like pressed asphalt, ours a bushy wilderness.

Deal

If I want to hang out with David and his friends, I have to have a dollar. Since I never have a dollar, I have to pull my pants down.

A quick crumple of jeans toward the knees for Billy Linetti and the rest. Billy gives me a nod, like a receipt, his pretty blond hair brushing his cheeks, and they go back to tilting Cokes to their mouths.

That's it, I'm in. Like a hand stamp at the amusement park—good for the whole afternoon.

Forsytes

When the *The Forsyte Saga* comes on, we move the TV to the porch, and Mom smokes into the dusk. She leans our plastic supper trays between the brick floor and the stucco walls.

Irene's cheating on Soames, even though they're filthy rich. She's in the vestibule in a big fur wrap, her cheeks glowing as he screams.

On the sidewalk kids turn to look for the sound.

Where have you been, Soames wants to know, though he already does—the architect's garret, the creaky iron bed.

All she says, in her blond way, is *Out of this house.*

Finster

He stalked me for weeks, waiting his chance by the oversized elm. Grabbed from behind, I knew it was him. Couldn't have been anybody else.

Then the whispered threats of kidnapping. How he'd burn down my house, burn me at the stake, burn whatever he could lay his hands on.

I kicked for the groin and ran from his doubled-up clutch. Small victory, my hair trailing behind me as I fled. Anyway, he was full of hot air.

These days he's big in the volunteer Fire Department. Saving cats stuck up trees. Still talking stakes and blazes.

Patience

The kids from the block collect where our gravel drive meets the asphalt street. We push the screen door wide. Keds kick the turf the way one dog noses another dog.

A kid opens his mouth—the one in the stiff dungarees.

Inside, we put it to her. Like a riddle. She's chewing gum and playing solitaire on the dining room table. Patience, she calls it.

God dammit! she yells. The dog barks twice. Another

point against them. She hates the town.

Go tell them we're Nudist, she says, and counts out three cards for the pile.

Klebinoffs

The day they move in, Mrs. Klebinoff makes tuna fish sandwiches for all the neighborhood kids and their two, Linda and little Rachel.

Tuna and white bread cut into triangles on a plate. The grown-ups move in and out of rooms, emptying boxes.

I'm in the kitchen when the hard taste of metal makes me gag. I spit out tuna and a small, sharp nail from the brand new house.

Soon Mr. Klebinoff takes up with another woman, Mrs. Klebinoff hooks up with Mr. Kreutzer, and the new Kreutzer family moves down the block—four kids from two marriages in a big new house.

And Rachel, still littlest, with the long, wavy scar down her thigh, is a majorette in the band.

Casey Fuller

Alternate Bios

Alternate Bio 1

Casey Fuller grew up in a trailer park in Olympia, Washington. He was a terrible student in high school and had to take early morning weight training to get enough credit to pass. After stints at rolling burritos, washing cars, and delivering copy paper, Casey Fuller thought the idea of going to college might be pretty okay. So he went to junior college, then The Evergreen State College in Olympia. At Evergreen, Casey found that he enjoyed reading long books and writing obscure papers about the rationalist tradition. But also at Evergreen, Casey Fuller took classes on Shakespeare, myth, the essay, political economy, cognitive science, evolutionary biology, and Robinson Jeffers. It was pretty amazing for Casey Fuller. Eventually he stayed too long and they told him to get out. All of this prepared Casey for a job at the State where he opened envelopes all day and stamped their insides with one word: RECEIVED. This turned out well for Casey Fuller because he could continue to think far thoughts and read Bishop Berkeley. Eventually, Casey Fuller was promoted to the warehouse where he was alone most of the time and took to listening to books on tape. This, too, turned out well because Casey Fuller found there was enough time at the warehouse to go to school while also listening to his tapes. So he went to school for writing and wrote poems between spells of moving cubicle panels and forklifting boxes of forms. Other things happened as they always do, and Casey Fuller decided to quit the State and retire to the People's Republic. Along the way, Casey Fuller got two cats and a wife, a couch, a bed. Things stacked up in a room. Of course, there is always so much to say. Casey Fuller loves so much. He walks up to animals and embraces them freely. He enjoys biking, the wind on his limbs. So much. The smallest thing can shake him forever. There is never enough time, never the right word. *So much*, even those two words, even right now so much is coming right at him.

Alternate Bio 4

Casey Fuller once fed green apples to brown horses. Casey Fuller once saw a real wolf. On Carpenter Road, late one night, low and crossing the second hill, Casey Fuller once saw a cougar. Once, Casey Fuller's docile mostly house-bound kitty, Hailey, hauled a dead rabbit over a seven-foot fence. Once, two stray dogs fought in Casey Fuller's trailer. Once, a Saint Bernard bit Casey Fuller right in the middle of his stomach. One winter a car engine killed two of Casey Fuller's kitties because all they wanted was to stay warm. Casey Fuller once caught tadpoles from a drain ditch and kept them in a coffee can in his room. At night, while he was sleeping, coyotes would run across Casey Fuller's backyard during summer and they were so close he could hear the pat of their paws punctuate their hysterical yelping. On Fourth Avenue, after buying his first computer, Casey Fuller was once stuck in traffic because two gray whales kept swimming under the Fourth and Fifth Avenue bridges. *Animals*—with one word a life can happen. Searching then failing, finding what's there, looking back for one thing then uncovering another, Casey Fuller's work has always been like that: retrieving what's lost, then attaching his name.

Alternate Bio 7

Casey Fuller has two lost uncles. One is named Don, the other Andy. Missed payments, a yard full of cars, the power shut off, a half-hearted garden, Casey Fuller's Uncle Don went the slow way poor people do: fast food, the county cops, a slow eviction. He ended up two towns over living with his ex-wife's mom, only showing up when his dad died. Casey Fuller's other missing uncle was more mysterious. An outdoorsman, a former state trooper, an athlete in college, Casey Fuller once watched this uncle's cut-fastball, clocked at ninety-two miles per hour. He quit being a cop, tried fighting fires, found work at a mill, and decided turning boards over with his hands was better than busting kids for weed. Then he gave his whole heart to fishing. (What Casey Fuller wonders is how we know anything, how we can make any claims, how anybody observing can have any knowledge at all?) Uncle Andy's coworkers said he was hit in the head by a 4x6 and suddenly became cross. He quit the mill, put his few things in storage, and moved into his truck. The last time Casey Fuller saw his Uncle Andy was on a bike trail where he was dressed in fatigues. Casey Fuller and his uncle had a talk then. Does it matter what was said? Does the reader really need to know? Here is what Casey Fuller feels comfortable with: where it happened was so close to Casey Fuller's former place of work it's uncanny. He drove a forklift there, broke down boxes, swept. Vigilant, even wary, completely worried his work would consume him, he hung a heavy bag from a rack to work out frustration. Chin down, elbows in, turning his hands over at the ends of his shots the way his Uncle Andy taught him, Casey Fuller would also practice ducking imaginary punches coming straight for his head.

Alternate Bio 9

Anyone who likes plot will love this story: it's gray, green, brown and starts far off in the sky, but slowly, in the way that long focus gradually begins to shift, colors turn to patches, those patches to trees, and just inside those trees, houses begin, small structures at first, but then much larger homes, ones with substantial design and multiple stories, ones with kept yards near bodies of water where, yes, there she is, the co-star of this story, a girl named Nikki, who is just now nineteen, who is closing the door to her Jeep Wrangler, she is flipping down the visor to mirror-check her hair, to tamp her lips, buckling in, turning the ignition over and starting out down the driveway, past the entire soccer field her dad made for her brother, past her two similarly-housed suitors who have been best friends since the second grade, past the dentists and optometrists who commute from Seattle, out of that opulence, out of the sphere where her dad owns the wood mill three towns over, where Casey Fuller's un-lost uncle still works with his hands, into Casey Fuller's neighborhood, which is nothing more than a semi-circle of doublewides, where she closes her door, jumps out, they embrace, and she and Casey Fuller walk out into the trail behind where he lives, into the woods, where the scene zooms down to a single image, a small circle, a close up of their two held hands.

Alternate Bio 10

Naked, in bed with his girlfriend, sleeping, covered in a quilt his grandma made him, in a complex called—no shit—The Corporate Apartments, where all windows had a view of other windows, in his room, in an apartment he shared with a roommate, Casey Fuller heard a slight rustle, some voices, nothing special, then something louder, some yelling, some dishes breaking, then wrestling, fighting, loud smacks, so he jumped out of bed, opened his door, looked, and saw three men wrestling his roommate to the ground on the living room carpet, pinning her arms behind her back, kneeing her legs down, tightening a wire tie around her wrists, and Casey Fuller, not knowing who they were, not thinking why they were there, not having any clothes on, his scared member completely out for all to see, pulled off the biggest of the three, somehow got him down, had his arm in a tight lock, and seemed to be evening the score until another one of the men pulled out a gun, pointed it casually at Casey Fuller's chest, and with great calm handed Casey Fuller a stack of stapled papers, which said the men were bounty hunters, that they were here for his roommate, that this was legal, completely legal, all of which was on the papers, and all Casey Fuller had to do was read them, which he stood there and did, naked, in that room, as the three men began to haul off his shaking and sobbing roommate, which was Casey Fuller's completely lost half-sister.

Alternate Bio 14

Then Casey Fuller got into a fist fight, in a bar, on Christmas Day. He had just turned 21, his leg was finally healed from being shot, and he just moved back in with his mom one town over. His friend Adam's mom went to Chicago for the holidays. So Casey Fuller and his friend Adam had the place to themselves. The place was huge: three stories, a massive deck, a barn, a stone trail leading out to a rowboat and a pond. They decided to throw a series of 300-person parties the first week Adam's mom was gone. What Casey Fuller remembers is carrying an English wolfhound around while shouting, shooting a real arrow through a fake door, jumping off a banister onto a living room full of drunk, dancing, semi-conscious people. So the second week Casey Fuller and his friend Adam decided to chill. Covert ops to the liquor store. Large bottles of clear vodka. Darts at Denny's. Small tumblers while an under-aged friend drove them around. (This was before Casey Fuller had real work.) On Christmas, everything closed down. Adam looked through the yellow pages and called all the bars. One was open. Casey Fuller and Adam drove there posthaste, without a future for Latin in their foreseeable lives. Another man folded his arms in the doorway. Words were said. He and Casey Fuller decided to flare into mythic images. Ripped shirts, rolled eyes, dumb yelling—what can Casey Fuller tell you about those images you haven't heard before? Running, laughing, limping when he thought he was healed, his hand swelling into a honeyed ham, Casey Fuller's work was to admit it to his friend Adam: today was the day the Son of God was born.

Alternate Bio 15

Casey Fuller was once in a pickup. The pickup was silver, a single cab, a four-cylinder with a white stripe that ran down its sides and met up at the tailgate around one word: MAZDA. He had a baseball bat on his lap. No use wondering where the baseball bat came from (so much is lost forever), here is the part that remains useful: Casey Fuller's friend Adam was riding in the truck bed with a bat. The person who would come to shoot Casey Fuller was driving. Here's what they were doing: out on Hawk's Prairie Road, out on South Bay Road, out on Johnson's Point Road where they would eventually crash, the person who would come to shoot Casey Fuller would pull up to houses with long driveways. Then, in the American grain, with the entire tradition of troublemaking behind them, Casey Fuller and his friend Adam would jump out of the pickup and, with wood bats that may well have gone back to little league, bash mailboxes off their 4x6 posts. Fresh faced and without a need for a razor, seventeen at the time, with a long queue of mailboxes already taken care of, Casey Fuller had an idea. He knew where the governor lived. It wasn't far. If the person who would come to shoot Casey Fuller would drive there, Casey Fuller and his friend Adam could bash the governor's mailbox to a twelve-ounce can of Coke. A background lit with silver, a night so bright it's blinding, who can refute the realm of forms where perfect ideas come from? They went. Someone from the imperfect world saw them. A chase occurred. Who knows who it was, where he was from, whether he was a concerned citizen or an agent from the State? Here is what always happens: a corner is too sharp, a pickup is too fast, the trees are always welcoming. Casey Fuller's work was clear: to embrace those trees. He appeared in those trees that night. And like best friends always, not even midway through the journey of his life, they continue to embrace him like an entire forest.

Alternate Bio 17

Casey Fuller will now tell you what his other lost uncle said to him on the bike trail. It is not much. He hopes you have not been waiting. But now that we're on the subject, Casey Fuller wonders why some instances stay and others gray away, why untold instances often seem so clear, and by saying what happened some part of us somehow frees up and no longer feels frozen. He was there, his uncle, in fatigues. Riding a mountain bike and waving to everybody that passed by. Casey Fuller passed by on his road bike but came back around. Casey Fuller and his lost uncle said hello and . . . laughed. After asking him how things were in the People's Republic, how his wife was, if he had work, Casey Fuller's uncle began to describe a bike he had just seen. A mountain bike made for snow. With double rimmed wheels, an extra-wide frame, a hub that spanned the wheels, disc brakes, and tires wider than a motorcycle's. Then he turned to various people along the trail. How some were good, others bad. He seemed confused but remained specific. Like a former cop, Casey Fuller's lost uncle called some of them "vagrants" and others "campers." He was a camper. He had a truck. So he was a camper. Casey Fuller's lost uncle Andy seemed to know something was off: that he was using a logic others couldn't see, that he talked too long without the other person speaking. So he suddenly said, "Well, I'd better get going now." Casey Fuller said to his uncle it was nice to see him, he was glad he saw him, it was very nice to see him. Still dignified, still with it, still able to recognize what was proper in an awkward situation, Casey Fuller's lost uncle asked—in passing, a last thing, some words to show he knew the score—where Casey Fuller was going. And for a reason he still can't fathom, in words that suddenly became large as soon as he said them, in a flash (knowing that a life can break out and turn in any direction), Casey Fuller realized his job was to tell his lost Uncle Andy the reason he was back, on the bike trail, pedaling through the woods to the city he called home: to meet his friends, to see Shakespeare, to watch Hamlet.

Alternate Bio 21

A cool night, rainy, deep black, a low fog faint but thick around creeks and ponds, so gray and black then, the driver tipsy, stoned, the windrows of haze coming up quickly as the driver presses down on the gas, the person who would come to shoot Casey Fuller sitting beside him, in the back seat, sipping bad beer, in a red and white Chevy Blazer, with a set of subwoofers so loud no one could think, let alone see the mama deer ambling out in front, aimless, innocent, light brown, the driver locking up the bad brakes, uselessly, a side swipe, in her hind quarter, lifting her, spinning her onto the other side of the road, into a field where, rather than asking if everyone was okay, rather than pausing and considering their dumb luck, the driver whips it around, slams it in park, and as near to where the deer disappeared as possible, pulls something silver from the glove compartment, the person who would come to shoot Casey Fuller doing the same from his jacket pocket, and both, laughing loudly, going out to finish the job of the Blazer's busted bumper—and found Casey Fuller, who, looking for a job, followed, into that field fogged with haze, where, to all who might have witnessed it, his work was to appear big-eyed, light brown, aimless, and ready to receive what was coming his way.

Alternate Bio 24

And yet so much still remains: still bright, saturated and ready for the right moment to arrange on the page. So much remains left unsaid. And yet what can ever be done: each brightness fading, each color graying, each room ashing over with what could only be described as clouds. So much, so many directions, never enough time, never the right words. . . . Here is the last thing Casey Fuller will say about his life lived in these poems: remember how Casey Fuller used to drop his mom off and tell her he was going to school, then drive off into the world without a destination at all? One day he felt like going to the ocean. Almost in anticipation, almost as if by looking back it was all part of a plan, he saved his lunch money for three days so he'd have enough gas. It was still cold, an early spring, the camera zoomed out as wide as it would go to take in what he was seeing. The horizon was silver tinged with wisps of blue behind light brown clouds. He was there. All the earth before him was sand. Then, without knowing why, without wondering who was there to see, without regard for what he was wearing, without a strategy, after looking at the waves rolling green on green on green, Casey Fuller did what you hoped he'd do, and walked out into the entire ocean.

Molly Fuller

Hold Your Breath

The Neighborhood Psycho Dreams of Love

All the children on the block follow you like stray cats. I watch you caress their fragile heads, read them stories at the paint-peeling picnic table, toss them smiles. You make them feel so safe.

I want to press the ruffled edges of the hem on your dress to my cheek. I want to caress your fingers, one by one, stuff them in my mouth. Pull one string of hair at a time, count each strand.

I would lock you in my closet, keep your polka-dotted panties in a shoebox under my bed. I saw them once when you were bent over pulling groceries out of your trunk. I offered to help, but you said *I'm fine.*

I watch you smoke on the front stoop. I want to be the unfiltered tobacco on your lips. Your tongue lovingly licking over me, fingers pinching me close for a moment before you flick me away into the dirt.

I want to bury you in my yard under the Japanese maple— your crimson lipstick, the same shade as the fiery red of the leaves in the fall. I would plant flowers in your ribcage each spring to match your bountiful heart. I would rub your left, middle finger, knucklebone all day long like a worry stone to ease my fears. All this is love, I think, rolling down my car window, offering you a light for your cigarette, holding my breath as you lean your face toward the flame.

She Saw Stars

Look, there are two suitcases, one pair of worn out shoes on her feet, one-way bus ticket. A new husband waiting at that last stop. Young Wife leaves in snow, arrives in sunshine. It is too warm for her hand-me-down winter coat. Husband's hands are sleet against her skin.

Watch how after the baby is born, they take it from her arms. They bind her breasts, wrap her tightly with clean white cloth. She cannot catch her breath. She can hardly breathe. She is just eighteen.

Hold your breath as Husband pushes her head under water. The surface goes black, pinpricks of light dance across her eyelids. *Like birthday candles* she thinks *Like constellations at night.*

Count the losses as the baby, the car, Husband, all disappear. He leaves behind the new pink cap and booties, forty dollars in a coffee can. The neighbors don't know. The police say *Wait.* Young Wife sits on the curb, thinks about killing him. The Greyhound back to Ohio, arcing through the night, feels like trying to breathe underwater, like being buried at sea.

Lay your head on her chest. Imagine a baby there and then not there as she strokes your hair, as she whispers in your ear *My love, my one, my only.* She is as distant as the night sky over a still lake, the reflections of stars always out of reach.

Brothers

Their parents leave for work at half past seven; the two boys ride their bikes through the rose garden to the fountain inside the square. Identical hands dip under clear water, pushing through their reflections to grab up fistfuls of change. Pennies are pitched off the bridge onto the highway, the silver saved for something special. After they run out of pennies, the perfect rock is discovered half-buried in the dirt. Prying it loose from the earth, they bloody their fingers.

She is driving the black sedan, knuckles clenched on ten and two. This is her first time manning her husband's car. It takes both boys to carry the rock to the edge. They lift it over the railing, watch it land on her windshield below. Her sharp breath fills her ears as glass splinters into a spider's web. She can't see; she can't feel her feet on the pedals, her hands on the wheel. Her car coasts to the side of the road.

Down the hill they scamper. A noon sun beats on their blond heads as they carry her into the nearby field. They prospect her like a pocket watch, learning how women work. Tall stalks of grass bruise under their weight. Then they put her back together, button up her secretary's blouse, zip her into the long skirt, put her sensible heels on her left foot and then her right. Brushing the dirt away from her still face, they place the quarters over the rouge on her cheeks, shiny mirrors beneath her open eyes.

Match

She pairs cowboy boots with short skirts, wears the tightest tank tops. Wants everything to be out in the open. *Honest* she'll say, and look at you with her sky blue, cornflower blue, blue like the top half of ocean water somewhere tropical blue eyes. They will pull you in like an undertow, knock you over, knock you flat on your back until you're staring up at her, her strong thighs planted on either side of your face so that she can lower herself onto your mouth like an open sunflower.

You'll be left as breathless as the playground merry-go-round. Fix your eyes on a point in the distance, hold tight as she goes spinning by, floating past all those outstretched fin-gertips like a field of dandelion heads gone to seed.

After she breaks the dishes, she sings lullabies, weaves melodies like blankets, like nets, like cocoons. Like being embraced by a hammock in the heat after noon with fresh-squeezed lemonade damp on your lips.

She won't cry yet, standing there again on your doorstep. *A matching pair* she says, a bruise circling each eye.

You've seen this before. You've arranged the getaway car, bought the bus ticket, brought the horse and tied it up to the old oak, tipped your hat and held out your hand like you're asking her to dance.

You should see the other guy she says. Takes the ice wrapped in a flannel shirt. Lays her head in your lap, blue eyes looking up, as you touch the dried salt from her black-eyed-Susan face.

Coats

She is young and blond with a ponytail so shiny we want to touch it. She tells us about her foster son. How he arrived at

126

seventeen, how he brushed his fingers down her cheek that first day, said *You look too young to be a mother.* It is cold enough to see our breath in the meeting room, the heat stalled in the old radiators. We glance at each other, hug ourselves through our winter clothes, think *We aren't like her.* She talks about how she used to raise horses before the boy came. We realize she is not young, that her hair is dyed.

She tells us about the women in the prison where they put her, how she taught those women to read, to write, how she changed their lives, how those women were the gift that God gave her after all. She sings to us about Jesus. Her voice is girlish, innocent; we would have cried if we were alone with that song. We pull our coats tighter to our chests.

She talks about him like he was her real son. Says *I was supposed to protect my baby, I was supposed to care for my boy.* She folds her arms across her breasts when she tells us how she held him tight against her each night while he cried, how she tried to comfort him, tried to be a good mother. *He was so weary* she says *We were so weak.* Sleet strikes the window panes, tapping like hooves against stone. We look down at our hands, reach up to our faces, all of the broken horses brushing our blinders back into place.

Twins

We follow the growing boys like bats, like bees. We wring our hands, we buzz and flap. *They're good boys* says their mother. *Accidents happen* their father says.

They rear themselves in dusky alleys, the crawl space under our porches, along the rusty chain-link fence down by the worn out tracks, like weeds, like spiders, like vines.

We hear the boys ask the twins to prom. Hold our breath and strain to hear the answer. Know the girls have agreed when we see the boys in the driveway, washing their father's white Cadillac, blond heads shining like halos in the sun.

We sit outside with lemonade and iced tea at seven. The boys arrive, like clockwork, ringing the doorbell at half past. We watch them hold out identical corsages of pink blossoms, lead the girls out into the yard, stand them next to the weeping cherry tree. One girl wears mint green, the other dusty rose.

We hear the boys saying *Good evening.* Saying *Fine, thank you.* Their teeth sparkle and flash as Mr. and Mrs. snap their pictures. *The right kind of young men* Mr. calls to us. *Gentlemen* says Mrs., yelling across the lawn. We raise our glasses in a toast. We stay behind our fences.

We nod, we sip, we rock, we watch. We hear they don't find the girls for days. When everything is discovered, recovered, except for the twins' small hands, the boys bare their teeth into vulpine smiles.

Maureen Gibbon

Always Happy and Go Lucky

1.

A couple months after my divorce came through, I was still celebrating. I was in some bar off Hennepin when a guy named Lamar offered to take me to Las Vegas. He also offered to give me seven thousand dollars to spend, since that was the amount he had in a check from his last gig.

"You can have your own ticket," he said. "Open-end return date. You call the shots."

Before I could mull it over, though, he told me too much. "Sexually speaking," he said. "I believe you'd blow a motherfucker's mind."

I told Cary about it the next time I talked to her and she said, "You better come down here. Nothing like that's going to happen to you here."

She and Deak were living in Socorro, New Mexico, not far from the Rio Grande.

"I don't know," I said.

"You've never been out of Minnesota. What, are you afraid?"

"I'm not afraid," I told her. So then I had to fly down there.

After Cary picked me up in Albuquerque and we started the drive south, she told me she just wanted me to be happy.

"You have to make the decision to be happy. Give yourself a chance to think before you get into anything else," she said. "Take it easy. Figure yourself out. Stop drinking."

"I thought you wanted me to be happy," I said.

But I did clean up. Just a beer now and then—no weed, no speed. I wanted to do those things when I was with a man anyway, so there at Cary's, it seemed easy enough to stop.

Cary worked in the school as an aide and she got me on there. What it boiled down to was that every day I tried to teach a girl named Donetta to read, and every day she couldn't. She swallowed lye when she was little, and it burned her throat and eyes, and somehow worked its way up to her brain. Some days as we looked at books, puzzling over *was* and *saw*, Donetta held my hand. I liked the feel of her skin and small fingers. It was like holding a sparrow.

After I got done at the school, I walked through the square in the old part of town and then partway up a long road that led to the mountains behind Magdalena. There was a switchback road all the way up, and I thought someday I would walk it.

Instead of climbing into the mountains, though, I'd go back to the house and pull a lawn chair out into the dirt of the front yard. Sometimes I looked at whatever magazines Cary had lying around, but mostly I watched cars drive by and let the winter sun beat down on me, there beside the yuccas.

2.

Louis has a heart tattoo on his arm with a scroll running through the middle of it. It's a good tattoo. The red's still bright and the blue is good and deep against his dark skin. But the scroll in the center of the heart is blank. In the place where there should be a name, there's no name.

"Who are you saving it for?" I asked the day I met him.

"A woman, or maybe one of my kids. I don't know."

I met Louis on a street not far from Cary's. I saw him walk by in his black jeans. He said "Hi," I said "Hi," and we started walking up School of the Mines Boulevard together. It only took a couple blocks to get him to kiss me.

When I told my sister Cary how I met him, she said "Larue" and made my name about five syllables long.

"Maybe he's my lucky penny," I told her. "You know, finding him in the street like that."

"I hope," she said. "I hope he is."

Cary kept telling me not to rush into things, but she wasn't living my life, so she couldn't know. The first night I spent with Louis, which was the night of the day we met, I knew I wanted to be with him. After we got done having sex for the third time, I went and got a pen from my purse.

"What are you doing?" Louis said through a hank of black hair, face half in a pillow.

"Nothing," I said.

He held still, though, until I finished writing LARUE in fancy letters in the heart on his arm.

"Are you happy now?" he said.

I could say yes to the question, so I did. He pulled me back into bed.

But happy didn't begin to cover it. Each time we made love, Louis whispered to my thighs. I was wet all the time for him and had the feeling of years dropping away, like I was a teenager again. He was so slim-hipped and slight it seemed like I was with a seventeen or eighteen year-old boy, not a man in his thirties. I liked just saying "Louis," which could be *Loo-wiss* or *Lu-eess*. He was half Navajo and wore his hair long, so on top of everything else, I had his beautiful hair to brush.

In a couple of weeks we were moving in together.

"Didn't you learn anything the first time? With you-know-who?" Cary asked when she found out. At least she didn't say my ex-husband's name.

"I learned I will do anything to be happy."

"All right," she said. "All right, already. You know where I am."

"I know," I said. "I love."

"I love too," she said.

3.

I guess it was the confusion of moving and all the fun Louis and I were having christening the "living spaces" of his apartment, including the floors, but I didn't take the pills every day. Sometimes I had to double up and even triple up to get back to the right bubble for that day. I knew it was bad, but I kept telling myself my body wasn't fussy. Or maybe I just thought my luck would hold.

It didn't. When I was late, I said, "I am not going to go through this."

I looked at the pregnancy test box when I said it, not at Louis's face. Then I looked over at the square on the calendar for the seventeenth, the day I should have got my period.

"Maybe you'll fail the test," Louis told me.

"Ha ha," I said. Because I knew what the answer was going to be even before I peed a stream onto the test stick. I felt it, just the way I felt Louis all the way from across the street when I met him.

I was sitting on the toilet, waiting for the five minutes to pass, when Louis walked over to the table and got a pen.

"Goddamn it," I said when I saw what he was doing. I pulled up my pants and went to get the thing away from him, but he twisted toward the refrigerator.

"Larue," he said when he was done writing. "Right there in my heart."

For the second time in that apartment, I lay down on the kitchen floor. I cried, which Louis let me do.

"We were having such a good time," I said.

"Here," Louis said, handing me a tissue. "Blow your nose."

That's when I knew whatever it was had started. There

on the floor I knew that.

4.

It turned out to be a trick. It turned out I had what the doctor called a silent period. No baby, but no blood, either.

"My body is hanging onto its eggs," I told Louis. "I couldn't let one go."

In truth I was trying to figure out why I felt relieved and disappointed at the same time. The relief I understood. The disappointment was harder. There wasn't room in Louis's apartment for a baby unless it slept in a drawer. There definitely wasn't room in my life for a baby. So why did I feel let down? It was my own private mystery, the mystery of me, Larue.

It was not long after me not being able to let an egg go that Louis showed me the picture of his daughter. A blurry, little face, cut out from a bigger picture. So overexposed all I really saw were eyes and a mouth.

"Her heart wasn't right," he said. "She died when she was a baby."

He waited a while and then he said, "Maybe we didn't take enough good care of her."

I didn't say anything. There wasn't anything to say. I held Louis's hand, though, and we sat a long time, looking out at the street, at the cars passing, the roofs of his neighbors.

"Dawn was her name," Louis said. "Now you know."

"I think I knew before," I said.

All the years he spent drinking, it would have been hard not to start a family. You get careless or you think it's going to make everything better between the two of you. That's where Cary and I came from. I almost did the same thing.

"I could have had a baby," I said to Louis. I played for a while with the pepper shaker.

"But you didn't."

133

"I didn't."

No babies for me. Not with all the drinking and the weed and whatever else I did.

"I stopped that baby before she even got started," I said.

We sat thinking there at the table, none of our children around us. Free to come and go as we pleased.

V.

Later, I said, "What about your heart? Why didn't you put the baby's name in your tattoo?"

"I held her when she died, and after she died, I brought her all the way to Rapid City to her mother's people, wrapped in a star quilt," he said. "Her name already is in my heart."

Louis told me he felt her there with him sometimes. At first he was scared, but he had come to know her presence, had come to know it was her.

"I always think I can hear her baby shoes," he said. "They had bells on them. You probably think that's crazy."

But I didn't, and that night I dreamed about her and my own kid, the one I didn't have.

In the dream she and Dawn swam together in a river, and then slept beneath the water like fish. The two of them nestled down in the water weeds, and their bodies waved gently back and forth in the current.

When I woke up from that dream it was still night. I listened to Louis snore for a long time.

VI.

This is what our rental house looks like:

Adobe, on Central Street, not far from Cary's place. Blue

curb out in front. A walkway up to the front room, which is really a closed-in porch with a cement floor. Louis and I can sleep there when it gets hot. The kitchen has a lumpy vinyl floor with sunbursts on it. There's an attic you have to climb up into like a bat. The adobe walls are painted white, and the living room has a fireplace with one red tile missing. When Louis saw that missing tile, he said he could replace it.

"No," I said. "I like the gap. And I like the lumpy floor and the wavy walls."

"You like everything," Louis said.

"And there's a problem with that?"

"It's not all going to be a honeymoon, you know."

Still, the first night we were there, just being in the house felt like a party to me. Cary and Deak helped us move, and Cary hugged Louis when she and Deak were saying goodbye. Deak shook Louis's hand and cuffed him on the arm in a guy way.

"Let us know if you need anything," he told Louis.

After Deak and Cary left, Louis told me, "You and your sister were beaming like headlights."

I was giddy with the day, but I thought it was the funniest thing I ever heard.

"Do you know what?" I ask Louis now.

"What?"

We're in bed, making out, and I'm the one on top, holding Louis's arms up above his head as I kiss him. He thinks I'm going to say something sexy, but I don't.

"There's an old cookie in the nightstand," I tell him.

"What?"

"The nightstand we got at the garage sale. There's a cookie in the drawer."

I slide off of him, scoot over to the edge of the bed, and reach down into the bottom drawer of the nightstand.

"See?" I say, holding up the pink and brown cookie. "The brown means chocolate and the pink means strawberry. The colors let you know what flavor you're going to taste."

"Throw it out," Louis says. "Who knows where that's been. Come here."

I make like I'm putting the cookie in the trash, but I don't. I put it on the floor behind the trash. Later I can sneak it back into the drawer where it has not been hurting anything.

When Louis goes to lick open my thighs, I touch his hair so he stops with his mouth just above me.

"What?" he says.

I want to tell him more about my philosophy of the cookie, about how you start to taste things with your eyes before they even get to your tongue. But I just look down at his face, which I think is the kindest face I've ever seen. And I don't tell him what I thought I was going to tell him.

"Nothing," I say. "Just sweet on you."

Sarah Goldstein

from *Fables*

1.

Many old wives' tales persist in town, such as: *take an orphan child hunting, you will return with threefold the bounty.* Although law forbids observing such advice, a hard winter is coming. Some adults decide to take a few of these unfortunate children into the woods. The hunt yields nothing. After several days the adults become frustrated, and the already grief-stricken children know something is wrong. Sunlight fails through the tree canopy, and the children see ever more owls and bats. They sneak away from the hunting party and wander the forest. Nightjars and swifts circle, alight on their arms, pinch them. Swallows dive and take tufts of their hair. Exhausted, the children crawl into the undergrowth. They feel safe and sleep, but wake without memory of themselves. When they cry it is the sounds of the whippoorwills. The nightingales become their mothers, and pheasants usher them to winter quarters. Meanwhile, the adults have returned to town to face the others. Everyone grimaces, hearing only what they decide to understand.

2.

They call him hatchet-head, spoon-nose, moon-face. His friends are a worn-out bicycle and the family dog, who is graying and slow. They barely endure his talking at home and his mother frequently buries small talismans in the backyard after his father has gone to sleep. One night she nods off in the yard, waking to find her son holding a bouquet of fiddle-heads, puffballs, and sumac. She feels very hot, as though the sun is out. But it is only that the moon has risen to a bright-ness she no longer anticipates and she hears the river recede into its rocky bed. Her son's face is nodding and difficult to see, yellow in a blurring glow.

3.

Not so long ago the crops were terrible, and the farmer came home each night worried and wondering how to keep going. Usually there were chickens and rabbits for his wife to cook, but not anymore: now they are almost out of everything. The wife opens her window and lays out a few crumbs of bread on the sill as she has every day for the past several years. The sparrows come, heads cocked. In return for the crumbs they have cleaned her bushes of centipedes, crickets, and biting spiders. They hear her whisper, see the trail laid out for them. That night the farmer returns to a better meal than usual, crunches down the stringy, bone-ridden bits in the stew. Strange, but satisfying, he tells her, before going to bed. She stays up a bit longer by the dying cinders, fingers tapping the rhythms of birdsong. Her insides are fluttering with the beats of tiny organs; there's something stuck in her throat and her eyes are wide and barely blinking.

4.

After enduring many years of abuse, the children decide to do away with their father. With some effort they manage to turn him out of the house like a sack of flour. Before dawn comes they must heave him to the field and bury him, although one girl suggests a burned corpse is harder to identify. They enlist some spiteful friends to help, but only after bribes of candy and their father's remaining stash of cigarettes and liquor. By daylight everyone's chest is indented with cowardice and sorrow. At school that day some of them kill a toad and leave it on the teacher's chair. When no one confesses all are made to sit, palms up, to receive the lashing. Laughter cuts through the otherwise silent classroom in between the cracking of rulers.

5.

You and I have an agreement, don't we? We shall cross the country by foot and sleep in the barns and cabins of unsuspecting city folk who are away until the weekend. Or we will find shelter in garages, through unlocked cellar doors, maybe curl up together in blankets on beds of leaves, pine needles, under hemlocks. Each day we will move just beyond sight of the highways, we will forge new trails at the edge of farmers' fields, we will steal apples from the orchards and cream from the vats in the milking sheds. These parts of the economy sputter onward, but the cities are dying. Better to make this our new life, embrace it, than rot in spirit and body in the embers of the crumbling urban commerce. To see the rabbit slung across your shoulder as you return from the hunt is all the retirement plan I will ever require.

Jeffrey Greene

Domestic Narratives

1. A Little Something for Everyone

While this city has a little something for everyone, the Trinity Parish has dumped its soup kitchen. The problem is that it was ruining the neighborhood, too many unwanteds begging morning, noon, and night—such sacrifice cannot go on forever. What was that last soup like when the gang broke up, tattered, unshaven, climbing steps from the cellar to wander into November rain? Each soup finished, the bread gone, chairs pulled out, pushed back in again, that tired note, dumb grin, resignation as in family arguments when there's nowhere left to begin.

2. Gone to Pieces

When I was young, mothers went to pieces. That's all over. Now it's whole neighborhoods. Still, I remember my mother or my mother's friends going to pieces. It was a way of getting kids to stop doing kid things, like mooning oncoming traffic. Today, my wife went to pieces holding a knocked-out wren in the gentle cup of her two hands. It was so small she could have drowned it near her face. I'm such a fool, she said, tears to her chin, eyes shut tight. I had to wonder if it was only the bird. But damn it if it didn't wake up just then.

3. Family Math

Someone must write a history of glitches, genetic glitches like burnt-out stars still glittering, the truth having to travel so many light years to reach us. My father, the math whiz, and my aunt, his little sister, as children slept in the same bed as the Jewish doctor, the neighborhood friend. Their mother was in the hospital long before anti-hallucinogenic medicine. Meanwhile, the family math was simple—everyone who stayed in Europe still glitters like a burnt-out star.

4. Passing Through Gotham

Batman is in full costume, black pointed ears, black cape, black boots, only he totes a Colt .45 from the Old West and goes around the room like a mixed metaphor, shooting his good stepfather first and then the visitors who are drinking kir and speaking science in two languages. Batman's mother shouts when he runs across the couch, muzzle grazing the temples of forbearing guests. For this and for slapping his mother's forearm, Batman is removed to his cave. She holds him firmly by the shoulders, her voice caressing him with small waves of reason. He can feel the full force of her need, signs of reconciliation, but he's stuck in that ancient place between capitulation and pride, never raising his head above the safe space of his mother's breasts.

5. Family Tradition

For fifteen years my cremated grandmother was forgotten at the funeral home. This was, after all, the family tradition—when you die you're on your own. Then for some reason, my mother rescued her, though she'd never loved her. My grand-mother sat on the mantle like a tin of cookies. The joke was did you want one. Another fifteen years passed, my mother retired. My brother and I were middle-aged men caught in the stupor of how fast life had gone. We all took the tin to the ocean, the one place where my grandmother had been happy when the century was young. But to spite her daughter and grandsons, the tin didn't sink, but kept rocking in the small waves, first toward gray islands, then toward freedom.

6. The Pilgrimage

I make my lunch-hour pilgrimage down to the Department of Motor Vehicles to report the stolen plates from my stolen car in which some ghosts are cruising around. They wear my new sunglasses and thumb through my books of literary crit-icism left on the back seat or quote Emily Dickinson out loud—I felt a funeral in my brain. What else do they have to do but discover how Dickinson fits the continuity of the Pu-ritan tradition? And because ghosts never stray far, they travel the same streets in the town that I live in. Past the schools I went to, children at recess, the houses that I knew that still look the same. One ghost reads—I like a look of agony be-cause I know it's true.

7. Living on Air

My father, who has no money, calls to say that the stock mar-ket is on its fifth leg in the meta-pattern of fives that will bring back the great crash or worse. I listen in earnest, but I never learned the language my father spoke to his father. Now, the charts come in the mail—the dollar, gold, and stock indexes superimposed with blue ballpoint, in patterns of five. I have no doubt he'll be right, world economies hanging over the abyss my father sees. They'll plunge off the page into the Depression of his childhood, the ghost generations of the Czarist past, living with the scent of someone else's earth, making their fortunes on air.

8. Sermonizing at 2 a.m.

Black tracks and blue marsh all the way to New Haven, road work of the ungodly hour when I head home in the underworld of talk radio: Is he sick or just another loser, the baseball great cut from the team, his own worst enemy? Of course, none of us are angels, though some long-time listener first-time caller says his father broke his back working, brought five kids into the world, and never hit his good wife. Still he drank enough wine to keep Niagara flowing for five days. The guy worshipped his father, and maybe we are responsible for our weaknesses, but at 2 a.m. as one darkened town borders another, I wonder how much wine that is, five days over Niagara.

9. Report Card for the Unknown Child

The best school in town sends a report card for the child you never had. It's not that you didn't try—sperm spun down in clinics, you wife charting the mild climate of her body. A few times it worked for a while. Now it's early dark. November. The child is on her way home from a school project with a friend, a neighbor. From where you stand, she appears in the rush of leaves and steady porch light, almost out of breath.

143

10. Love and Solitude

If you don't believe in ESP, then why is it that when you make love, the telephone rings or your little dog begins to hear a ghost in the hallway, creeping around? Something in this town begrudges you ecstasy. When its unregenerate rival has brushed her hair and goes quietly down the stairs, your little dog can get some sleep. The phone gives its last feverish ring. Then ecstasy comes on its own terms, offered up like an odor against the odds. After all, you have been loved, and now a steady snow falls between the window and a wall.

Sonia Greenfield

In Parts

It's called harvesting, which is the same thing as reaping, which now sounds close to raping. Reaping what was sown by a delivery truck on a slick, moonless night, because I'm really trying to look at this harvesting as giving instead of taking away. So maybe the surgeons lift grain from the field of his open body, maybe they lift away wet bags of husked rice or green bundles of sorghum, and maybe he'll feed not only other bodies in need but everyone they reach out to touch. Just a week ago golden tassels of corn bent to brush against our necks when we wound through a corn maze shaped like the state of Washington. I kept losing him around every bend but it was so easy then to simply follow his voice. How do I not think about the land *after* the harvest? We've seen it on our many road trips: muddied, brown, mown down.

Over beers two months ago at the dining room table, him still in his lamb-stained chef's coat, I complained about our baby feeding every two hours, and it was two in the morning, and my husband was just getting home. I was almost angry about almost everything, and my mouth kept giving up the ghost of weariness, and I said how I wished he had a normal job, and I said that our son was making me crazy even as I admitted there was nothing else like the way his small mouth pulled a new kind of desire from me with ropes of milk he used to drag me around. I said, *if you're never going to be around to help, I might as well just do it all myself.* I didn't mean that. I still wanted him around. All the same, if I had been able to choose between him and our son, the unfolding of these events would likely be no different, even if I woke in the morning to find our son asleep across my husband's lamb-stained chest. This fixture above the dining room table gives off a terrible light. I've never liked it.

Heart. Drop the metaphor and consider the muscles. Consider the efficiency. Right atrium, right ventricle. Left atrium, left ventricle. Blood goes in, blood flows out. Actually, no: Don't consider blood. Don't consider the variations of red. Consider, instead, the word *heartened*: like another wife, the one who might finally put on a little make-up, who might trace the pink welt running down her husband's chest where his living skin closed over our terrible story. Who might put her ear there to hear what is now his *lub-dub*. Lulled. Lullaby. The sound maker for our baby plays recordings of the heart. It hangs at the side of his crib and casts a pink glow on his cheek. We find it comforting. I guess the other wife can have that metaphor, too. I'll take *pump*, which is still metaphor, though scrubbed clean of meaning and strictly mechanical.

Not long after graduation and before his first sous chef position, he tried to take me out for sweetbreads, but I didn't know what they were. He said they were awful, but I thought he was joking the way he pronounced the word. I assumed it was some kind of bread pudding or tea cakes. The restaurant was one of those cavernous green spaces, spot-lit with candles, awash in a slur of murmuring punctuated with bursts of sudden laughter. And he said, *no, goofus, not "awful." It's "offal," like "off all," meaning the off-cuts from the carcass.* I didn't know why anyone would want to eat the "off-cuts," and I said as much. I said I would just take the chocolate torte thank you very much, and he said he was disappointed with my lack of adventure. When his sweetbreads came, he said the capers really complimented the pancreas, but I refused to taste it. I refused to be goaded. *You go ahead,* I said. I could hear his knife cut the crisped skin, and of the preparation he said, *look, it's oozing meat juice.* I said, *don't be gross.*

Two nights ago, skin still gluey from sex, with the bedding pushed off the bottom end of the mattress, my dead husband confessed to infidelity with a stripper of all things. What a thing to dream about. What a way to conjure him. My sleeping mind, at least, still had a sense of humor. In this dream we talked of what some call *open marriage* and I felt liberated to exploit my anger. In my revenge dream I found another man to sleep with in the same bed, the same sticky skin, but he was him again. Same dirty blond hair, same pale eyes. *In my dream my husband walked in on me sleeping with my husband.* Tell me how I'm expected to move on when I couldn't even cheat on a cheater. Of course he wasn't upset. I think he gloated. My desire exists with nothing to cling to. I'm going to take it and all those damp cotton sheets to the cleaners and forget to pick them up.

In my ignorance of anatomy, I somehow thought it was the whole eye. That his actual eyes are in someone, seeing. I saw myself traveling with our son through some blond European town trying to trace his father's lineage, and we'd pass a woman on the street with mild blue eyes, and I would stop and grab her sleeve. I'd ask, *"Kenne ich dich?"* and she would pull away and nervously say, *"Ich glaube nicht."* And our son, who has his father's eyes, would lead me to a hotel lobby bar to buy his long-widowed mother a *Doppelbock.* But now I know the cornea is just a lens, not, as they say, the mirror to the soul. Just something that lets the blinded see, say, a field of cornflowers on their lanky stems, also known as bachelor's buttons, made to wave goodbye by the matter-of-fact breeze, or see the back of someone familiar and beloved hurrying away.

Before we were married, before he completed culinary

school, well before the birth of our child, we were visiting friends in New York, downtown just a blur of headlamps, horns, and dirty snow. I ate only salty nuts and olives run through with plastic swords. I said a dirty martini had to be sordid and briny as I drank four and blathered for an hour in a dark Tribeca bar. On the way back uptown the cab tilted and the buildings bent, so we headed for the subway, but I could barely make it off the 6 Train. He had to strong-arm me through the closing doors while I swayed completely shit-faced, almost swallowed by the tunnel, nearly spirited away to Harlem. I slept with one foot on the floor, and the next morning he tipped my head back in his lap and washed my burning eyes with saline, the tears running down his calves. I had never seen him drunk, and I said I hoped my liver was as good as his, which, I'm told, was a good one after all.

Some useful statistics: bicyclist fatalities still account for two percent of all traffic fatalities. For example—and I'm counting on the cold coinage of numbers here—you and your new Cannondale bought at REI, tempted by a rare, balmy October. Do you know how much I hate that one flickering streetlight on Eastlake? Did you know that when a motorist and bicyclist are on parallel paths, the most frequent of crashes involve the motorist turning or merging into the path of a bicyclist? Your new NiteRider headlight gave off a useless glow. And not all white panel trucks are the same. I heard the driver tried to help. That he was just out making his usual deliveries. You with your bike-short tan-lines in the wrong place at the wrong time. You: trying to churn your way home, just another night to tick off, your journey rote, everything in its proper place.

Carol Guess

Revival of Rosemaling

The Ruined Garden

Everyone lost someone in the avalanche that year. Nights, we held dances in the ruined garden. Wolves wove the trail but stopped short of the fireline. The mountain refused to name what it knew. When a dog, child, or mitten went missing we wore miner's headlamps, bright sieves for thick dark. Everyone waltzed, but not everyone tangoed. Hard-packed snow tumbled, gathering speed, eating ice farmers, sentries, and skis. We shouted questions, but our questions stirred rocks. We had to learn not to talk—to move mutely, we of the valley—and to bury the bodies when spring thawed ice walls. Our dead came down perfect, red in their cheeks, palms flexed as if resisting the pyre.

Marietta

No one knew about the cabin. People thought I lived in town in a wooden house with a bright red door. No one had ever seen the house because the house wasn't real. I lived in a cabin on the outskirts of town. I had to haul my garbage to the dump. When someone got hurt, the ambulance came from somewhere else. No one could see the cabin from the road, although I could see the road and the bay. No one could see what I was doing or who I was with. All winter, snow kept the shape of snow, sirens muffled, Amtrak derailed. Llamas stumbled into the field and slept standing up, manes brittle with frost. Once a hawk flew into the window. Once you dressed me up as a boy. Once you came home in a stranger's coat and shook strange snow onto the concrete floor.

Crown Hill

Stairs spiraled up to an attic filled with salt. We slept thin as tripwire, taut among pillows. One night strangers stared down through the skylight. Glass divided stage from audience. What we wanted was applause. We showed them everything, and when it rained they never went home again. Our hands signed the story of what it meant to be warm.

Field

We fled the city at night. I was distracted by your body. My suitcase chipped at the bone in my thigh. Thieves stole doorways and sold them to trees, scrubby oaks that grew up on the street. Beyond the factory we slept in a field littered with swan's-down, beer husks, and bees. We fed a fire to blister coyotes. We strung death along on thinness alone.

Museum

The house that lived beside us is gone, replaced by concrete for a three-car garage. At the estate sale, dealers priced Norwegian dolls. We saved a squirrel from a tangle of chard. Maybe *charm* got confused with *harm* by someone like me or maybe by me. We chipped ice from bootprints to brew into tea. What did we know of strangeness? What might've saved us lived somewhere else. We hung aces from trees axed for newfangled holidays. We knit shadows from snow, leading wolves to false prey.

Jessica Rae Hahn

The Keeper of Records

To Start in the Dark

It was when man stole the moon from its sapphire cradle to make coins that things turned sour. The skyward silver dollar was no longer around to guide and deliver. Hands outstretched to find our way, we began feeling without seeing— the scent of a newly minted coin to lead us.

But my people never held such things. Even as all the town girls brought aprons full of the shiny coins in trade of daisies, heavy cream to bake the best man-bait, and silver embellished mirrors to search out their futures, I went without. Back then, the woods women still visited the river for soothsayers, prayed to all things airy to bring a good life—a woodsman with soft hands and an empty leg to store extra food. We blushed our cheeks with a fierce pinch. Our futures, no longer decreed by that empty sky, were ours for the taking.

Without such a guide, we wandered, found things out. What grandpa really did in that shed, the paint chipping down the sides, the granddaughter with nightmares of green-faced witches. This is how the story goes, we say. This is what we require, what we want, and what we absolutely desire.

He Reminds Me

It is night again and dark. But I've found who I was sent look-

152

ing for and now feel another coiled urge. Without food tonight, my grandfather dies, and along with him, the tiny, writhing child that lives within me, the one who calls out when I attempt to calm the fire.

Grandfather coughs a little and sleeps a little and reminds me that there is no use in fear, or anxiety. But, I think to myself, if I don't need those things, what do I have left? All we amount to is energy, he tells me. And all I can think is to sleep. To feel the soft cotton sheets on my skin. To disappear. "We are here to be seen and heard," my grandfather says to me. "Why else would we be given such senses?"

I can't tell what to make of it. He's strong, even this close to the end. The animals can smell death. Those who are warm-blooded draw near in support. Cows in the pasture raise their heads from a gnawing mash of grass to let him know they are still there, thinking of him.

The Keeper of Records

The Keeper of Records stows away in a stream of woods walkers who fill the land with pull-apart shelters, and who dare dying animals to reclaim their territory. At night I dip my long hair in wax to make candles for my lover. It is said that The Keeper works through fault lines of meerschaum, but already, secretly, worms have created kingdoms connecting it all. Does anything work so greedily to devour forgotten earth?

So, they say, glean the teeth. Keep the mouth if it fits you, if it tells the correct dream. This is how I remember: two boats in the crook of shore with thousands of paddles dragging them under. Twilight sliced the even sun. He buried me in the sand, grain by grain, taking his time to fill the fragile curve of my nose, my eyes. I lost his scent. And there I stayed. Buried, awaiting my new guide.

Marie Harris

Dear Scorpio:
Letters to My Mother-Self

1.

Look, Mom!
   You didn't tilt your head to squint up at the topmost branches of the oak tree. You didn't turn to see them plummeting off the granite cliff into icy quarry water. You didn't watch as they propelled sleds over precipices. But you always *kept* watch.

2.

Your Gethsemanes: the waiting rooms: those outer chambers with their molded plastic chairs and shelves of glossy, anodyne *women's* magazines. The offices of principals. Bedsides. You did keep watch. (*Don't cry. Don't worry. Just sleep. Don't die.*) Until the middle of that night when they woke into the long night-of-no-mother.

3.

Face it. You had to put the oxygen mask on yourself before assisting minors. Your plane was in free fall. Ordinary household objects, stripped of their innocent uses, had become lethal projectiles. Your understanding of the basic physics of

154

family was coming apart like rivets popping one by one off the skin of a wing. You had to think quickly, make split-second decisions. But you could always reconsider once equilibrium was restored.

4.

If you'd kept them you'd have taken them to Disneyland. If you'd kept them you'd have gone to every soccer game. No basketball tournament would have gone uncheered. If you'd kept them you'd have run interference like a tight end down the streets of pre-dawn paper routes and the dangerous halls of public schools. If you'd kept them nothing bad would ever have happened to them. Ever. (You're lying. You wouldn't have taken them to Disneyland.)

5.

So your childhood was idyllic. As was theirs when you think about it. All you did was blow your Fifties bubble into their Sixties bathtub. Bikes & sleds & basketballs & baseball gloves & books & puzzles & swim fins. Plus the puppies & dogs, kittens & cats, goats, chickens, ducks, geese. And talk about friends! The best! OK. So *you* didn't have to change towns and schools and friends and parents as often as they did. But at least you knew how important it was to leave them to their own devices. That's got to count for something, right? Ask them why don't you?

6.

Maybe it's the Purgatory-to-Heaven guarantee that keeps you kneeling in this perpetual Gethsemane—sweaty bait for deer flies and mosquitoes, bending into the green beans, trying to thin impossibly tiny carrot shoots, picking disgusting bugs off a variety of squash leaves, hand weeding—offering up your long-suffering for the souls who almost made it, the ones crowding around the back gate with their weepy eyes on the prize of everlasting life. But you don't believe in any of it. Even, for that matter, the possibility of eggplant.

7.

Remember how, later, they used to say that you, oldest of ten, must have known everything there was to know about raising children? You, who considered yourself an only child with nine siblings. You tomboy, secret reader, rider of the purplest sage, sailor on the bounding main, girl detective. What did anyone think you could possibly have brought to the changing table? And your mother. Her parting words, as she carried a wedding-morning breakfast to your childhood bed on a tray set with her antique yellow and pale blue china: *Never say no to your husband.* Remember how beautiful you looked wearing her elegant dress? Remember your exquisite ambivalence?

8.

You knew a few things. Little brothers sick together (tonsils chickenpox mumps measles); little brothers hurt together (stitches bandages); little brothers wounded together (parents fighting parents disappearing); little brothers stick together.

9.

So what do you think you can still make of your stubborn regret? That bargain basement hair shirt. Do you really want to wear it for another season? They've forgiven you your trespasses long since. Isn't it time you stopped *crying again?*

10.

And shouldn't we consider love? You know, that common plant with its companion herb. At once a venom and its antidote. A scourge and its cure. A sore distress and its comfort.

11.

You and I would do well to read those tabloid horoscopes once in a while, standing in line at the supermarket, to remind us that we are (*perceptive & intuitive strong willed with a highly developed sense of sensuality, possessive, jealous, manipulative & controlling, intensely loyal, charming, often misunderstood*) who we were then, who we are now. I love you.

Jim Harrison

Hospital

I was chest-high in the wheat field with wind blowing in shimmering circles. A girl on horseback came by on a trail and the horse smelled sweet with the wheat. How blessed horses smell in this bitter world.

I could see the hospital in the distance and imagined the surgeons in the basement sharpening their knives. Tomorrow they will cut me from neck bone to tailbone to correct mysterious imperfections that keep me from walking. I want to walk like other kids in the fields with my noble dog.

After surgery I didn't get well and they sent me to Mayo in Minnesota, an immense Pentagon of health machinery. In an ambulance-plane I ate a bad sandwich in keeping with the tradition of bad food that would last until my secretary brought take-out from a nearby restaurant.

Each night I sang along with a bedsore cantata from the endless halls, the thousand electronic gizmos beeping, and also people entering my room for "tests." I was endlessly sacrificed at the medical gizmo altar. There was no red wine and no cigarettes—only the sick who tore at the heart.

A beautiful girl Payton couldn't walk. I'd shudder whenever I passed her room.

On very long sleepless nights I'd gaze at the well-lit statue of Saint Francis across the courtyard. I'm not Catholic but he bore me up with birds on his shoulders. One night the planet Venus dropped unwelcome on his neck. Francis with Venus is not right. I don't think he knew a woman. I saw the same thing in Narbonne, France, one night with a million blackbirds flocking above the canal for the trip south across the Mediterranean. Venus was blurred on the peak of the cathedral.

My spine aches from top to bottom. Also my shingles burn, a special punishment. Francis heard my crying over Payton. He doesn't care about her beauty I suppose. There were no beauty contests among his birds.

I heard Mozart's last trio late last night, a spine-tickler, like the night I heard Thelonius Monk in Grand Central. There are so many emotions on earth, especially trapped here where moment by moment I surge with emotions. I'm told this place is admired throughout the world, though my brain waves tell me different. The nurses were kind and friendly while the doctors tended toward smug and arrogant. Hundreds of doctors looking for something wrong are suspicious.

The old bugaboo of depression slid in. I wanted to sleep on the floor but was frozen in an electric bed. I began to have delusions and at one point I was in Paris at my favorite food store buying cheeses with my grandson. Another night I was wailing and the attendant shook me awake. "I'm dying," I said. "No you're not, you're just wailing." I ate an apple and went back to staring at Saint Francis and his birds. Without birds I'm dead. They are my drug that lifts me up to flight. Thousands of kinds of birds I've studied, even in the rain when they seem more blessed on the branches.

What *is* wailing? A death-drawn crooning. It hurts to hear noises from the pediatric ward—the innocent crying out. I am thoroughly guilty in a long life.

159

I wanted to be a cello. I hear cellos when I'm trout fishing. The green banks with wild roses capture the cellos and thousands of birds, many sweet-sounding warblers and colorful western tanagers. Will I fish again with this badly ruptured spine? The scar looks like the bite of an ancient creature.

There is a place in us to weep for others. I found it at night with daytime eyes, whirling the memories so fresh you could smell the pain within is dark and raw. This great sprawl of sick people craving the outside, to walk in a forest beside a lake, the air full of birds in the greenery. Saint Francis dozing against a tree, a yellow warbler perched on his shoulder. There is no way out of this prison we have built so clumsily. Hellish in its ugliness, most of us want to stay. I can't die when I want to go back to Narbonne and my secret room where I write so much. They cut me open in a long strip and luckily sewed me back up. In hospitals we are mostly artful sewage systems.

I need my secret place in the Upper Peninsula near Lake Superior, my dark thicket covered by winter. It is night in there but I can watch passing animals, a deer, bear, even possums which I love for their humility. The thicket is flooded with birds, a few inches from my good eye. Francis would love this thicket. Maybe I'll take him there someday. And best of all a stump in a gully that I can crawl into and sit up. My place of grace on earth, my only church. The gods live there.

How to get out of this hospital? I planned three departures but a doctor won't sign my release. I am desperate for home and my lovely wife. They want to keep me here though departure is supposedly voluntary. Finally a friend in California sent a jet and saved me. We loaded up my daughter, my secretary and her daughter and were soaring back to Montana.

160

A green glade of soft marsh grass near a pool in a creek. There are a dozen white birches and I curl in the grass. The last day I saw a drop of blood on a tile. Be careful, our blood falls easily.

Pamela Hart

Zuihitsu of a Spartan Woman

Cities & Signs & War

If all cities are Venice and all Venice is memory, then where
will you be deployed. Will you see Venice in Kabul. Their
architectures spreading across arid plain and narrow canal.
You can walk and walk and not see anything real and when
you do see a thing maybe you'll know that thing as a sign of
another thing. At least according to Calvino. There you go.
Your M-4 across your shoulder. Marco Polo tells Khan, "Your
gaze scans the streets as if they were written pages: the city
says everything you must think." You are reading an unruly
discourse. It may have nothing or everything to do with the
city of your deployment. Your face burns as it hunts. The
signs are signs of other things. What do I as your mother
know of this. Nothing.

War Stories

Stories of war begin mid-sentence is one way to start. This
isn't a story of war. This is the mother on the idea of the son
at war. And how does the mother feel. The mother doesn't
like that word. The mother likes the word *think*. Will the
mother blame herself could be a story. Can he kill is another.
Will ideas versus feelings get in the way. Is this the story of
mothers of soldiers. The mothers' lives are windy. The air is
elastic. The story is a story on the idea of war and the son
who might kill or be killed. She could change this.

Your Soldier

At Mount Vernon they manage lines. Here's one snaking through the house, library and dining room, the low-ceilinged bedrooms, kitchen and pantry, along the back stairway to the outside, where it is March and warm above the Potomac. I am looking back now. I am writing backwards to figure out forwards. Gesturing behind to describe what's approaching. This May morning the early fog helicopters over the pond, the meadow. I hear it rise and dissipate. This March afternoon I stand with my son in a line that moves in an orderly fashion. We chitchat. He is a young man. The breeze is in the line too. It follows us into the house, listens as the guide explains the colors in the dining room. It is and is not the same breeze that annoyed Mr. Washington in March is something I consider while looking at unruly May greens chattering in the trees. I'm not good with plot. While I fiddle with the shape of these lines, my son one morning gets in line and there are other soldiers with him.

Playing War

Your first gun is a dinosaur. Then the wooden rubber band gun crafted from pine. Later, you study the problem of land mines in Afghanistan. Princess Diana hates them too. In a photograph plastic soldiers crouch behind switchbacks of sand and twigs. Several lie sideways in the dirt. Their small pedestals like helpless turtles. Miniature paper flags askew near the enemy's berm. Elsewhere, the mustard-yellow cowboy, his hat hanging off the back of his head as the pistol is fired. The green chief, decked out in headdress and chaps, rifle in one hand and bow in the other. Plastic cowboys and Indians placed on a wall, in a tree branch. I take several home.

On the Soldier's Twenty-fifth Birthday

The son waits in line for mortar class. A good career move he says. The mother reads Clausewitz. "Danger in war belongs to its friction," he writes. "The light of reason . . . is not refracted in the same manner as in speculative contemplation." Her day proceeds. The moon being nearly full, she watches it puddle on the driveway as she walks the dog. An owl somewhere in the woods calls out. The soldier son will set coordinates, call for mortar strikes. Danger may be far off or nearby. "The true difficulty begins with the fray itself," says Sun-Tzu. The soldier son was small and perfect at birth. He required rocking and walking. Did she raise him up to be a warrior. The Spartan women have their doubts.

Contour Drawing

When you make a contour drawing you do not look at the paper. Only at what you draw. You put your pencil on the sheet and do not lift it. Your hand and pencil mimic the form, mark an imaginary line before you. You are looking. The thing you look at pierces your eyes. You are so close. What if I make a contour drawing of the son's head. Hair shaved to the skull. Its shape honed. Against the backdrop of wall or sky. Or the infant head. Or head on a pillow. Head wearing the striped baseball cap. The head of the soldier is the head of the boy. You see this as your pencil makes its way into the story of the son's shaved head.

The Map is Not the Territory

The city isn't to be confused with the words that describe it, says Calvino. My mother's letters. Blue ink on onionskin paper. Palimpsest of her hand. Ghost image of her voice. A frottage of syntax revealed under script. Her younger self a house I construct of twigs and handmade paper, suspending it over my desk. Which isn't my map. Someone else can describe the city's story. Marco Polo had his version. What to do with report cards and notebooks. CDs on a shelf, sneakers on the floor. What file folder for you.

Code Talk

Along the Chattahoochee we walk. Men fish in its muddy shoals. Also cormorants. Pelicans. I'm proud. It's the marching. The uniform. The order. Heat oozes. Fish break the cinnamon surface. I notice your eyelashes. How dark. You were a blond baby. Now you are a dark soldier. You have an Adam's apple I see. Your skin is clear. I hear my father saying your skin is clear. I talk to him for a very long time in the parking lot of the Red Barn restaurant. It's our last lunch. I don't know this then. See how the mind is torn from topic to topic. We don't visit Carson McCullers' house. She married a soldier from Fort Benning. Its stucco houses, the red-tiled roofs. You liked to paint. You were not an artist. There's no rushing mountain stream to this story.

M16/M4

Firing your weapon is like a long discussion on some big philosophical question over coffee in a café. I study Wikipedia. The M4 is replacing the M16. The soldier's friend posts an eleven-second video. Guns are fired. Clouds sweep over a line of men. Sunrays slice the billows in hyperbolic algorithms. Cardboard for practice. A piece of paper shivers near a boot. The bullets are real. The paper isn't the target. "A machine beloved for its fatal qualities," writes Rimbaud.

Rules of Engagement

She should read Thucydides, slog through the Peloponnesian Wars. To understand, "knees pressed in the dust. Trojan spears smashed and Greek spears smashed." Go backward to look at forward. "Now," writes Aeschylus, "things are where they are. And will end where they're destined to end." That's not how she sees it. Reading and comprehension will rearrange destiny. But Ajax rages and murders before killing himself in a field. His trauma god-made or war-made. Twice the pain, says Sophocles after a decade of war, is twice the sorrow. Athena and her web-weaving, "working into the weft the endless bloody struggles." The mother surrounds her body with a great shield of books. Dickinson and Woolf. Why not go where "loveliness reigned and stillness. . . ." So the mind wanders and leavings accumulate on her eyes. Kaleidoscopic colors explode in the dark.

Land Navigation

Lately the mother believes in the concept of the map. She remembers some maps. The map on the cover of *Swallows and Amazons*. The stack on a seat of the family wagon as it rumbled cross-country. She's not good with maps. She holds an unfolded grid of blue and red lines in front of her. To imagine what's ahead. For instance, the map of Afghanistan. How the topography moves is hard to pin down. She's not good with details. Night vision goggles could be useful. Measure the coordinates. Point A, when the son first mentions the Army, to Point B. Which is what and where. Slow the racing sentences. Study gradient points. The associative mind is restless. Language is messy.

Holly Iglesias

Nothing to Declare

Near the end, there were gold purses and cinch belts and giant sunglasses, men in guayaberas, women with two-carat studs, platinum shrimp forks and rock-crystal ashtrays. I had children then and was free of disease. An undocumented woman ironed in the garage all day long, the same shirts over and over, and a man shocked the pool every other week. They will tell you I left of my own accord, but observe what happens when I smell Paco Rabanne Pour Homme.

* * *

No words precede the reef, none follow. Only sea fans, brain coral, a bank of clouds miles above the surface. The glint of sun, of barracuda and baitfish in flight. The Gulf Stream sweeps by, squeezing between Florida and Cuba, the true Cuba, the solid one, not the wet seduction of dreams. Ahead, the drop, the sea floor sinking, the mask pressing its mark into skin.

* * *

Another afternoon downpour and nothing to do but wait. It will pass, as it passes in Caracas, Havana, San Juan, in all the damp summer places of the hemisphere. Half water, half sugar, Cubans stay inside, they say, so they don't melt. In the battle between Amnesia and Nostalgia, Nostalgia always wins, memories of home solid as sugar or gunmetal, Amnesia a mere vapor wafting through the transom unannounced.

*　　*　　*

Bomb, echoic, derives from the Greek for a deep, hollow sound, for when a man eyes the armhole of a sleeveless cotton blouse, gauging what is visible against the sweet ache of all that is potential, assessing with the same easy pleasure his finger takes when circling the headlight of a Lamborghini, and when the tanned arm, the pale breast but inches from the armhole is that of his daughter, thirteen, something detonates, thundering within the body's chambers, seismic at first, then settling into a rumble, its half-life beyond measure.

*　　*　　*

You depend so on the machete to keep the strangler figs at bay. Forgive me—the plums gone, my letters in the icebox now—I can't sleep, the machete under the bed so cold.

*　　*　　*

The spoons of people dead before your birth, sterling like this one, the bowl demure, somewhere between demitasse and teaspoon, my great aunt's initials at the bottom, one flourish more ornate than the next. The patina soft, like that of the cream and sugar set my mother bought during the war, which you have, or I suppose you do. I gave it to you when you married, when it looked as though we had made it, as though the knives and lies were behind us. Before the new regime and the hiding of gifts.

*　　*　　*

Cloudbank flecked peach, ochre, orchid, day dancing with night, the old world with the new. Strains of a distant bolero, the seduction more breeze than gust, a hat with a veil, say, or a lipstick called New Bruise. Body, ocean, melody, all of it fades to a shade neither gray nor blue.

Siel Ju

The Locust of Desire

boy with black arm socks at Insomnia – Los Angeles

You're not the usual guy I date, but maybe it's practical to date men your friends find slightly repulsive.

blue polo shirt guy at Urth Caffé – West Hollywood

You were with a girl who I think was your girlfriend, but you looked unhappy. I overheard you say something about the locus (locust?) of desire. The most important moments are the most mundane ones enacted at the right places, then narrated with insolence.

caffeinated dogwalker at Coral Tree Café – Brentwood

We were there before the lunch rush. You gently tied the leash to the parking meter, gave each dog an approval pat before going in. The intimate relationship between strangers.

gray suit sans tie at Bread & Porridge – Santa Monica

You looked a little breathless, like you'd been running, standing by the eye-level shelf with its eight glasses, lined up, lip down. Above, a bronze ceiling fan spun athletically. Cheap brown leather couches crowded into a blank space punctuated by a few large, leafy floor plants. They matched each other, but nothing else. In the corner, a stand of condiments and five wooden pepper mills watched us inhale, exhale in harmony. You were the perfect complement to the setting.

boy eating herring at Warszawa – Santa Monica

You watched my surreptitious shedding of socks, laughed back when I looked up and noticed you were watching. Later, your friend came over and asked to buy me a drink. Societal norms seem an overwrought mass of laughable formalities, don't they?

boy in oversized art books section at library – Downtown

By the time you walked in, everyone else already looked like they'd come to terms with their loneliness.

guy with green bookbag in Fairmont Hotel – Santa Monica

You were walking with someone who looked like your father,

and I think you thought I was looking at him. I'd like to think of myself as the kind of girl who has affairs with older men, that I give them a fair shot to turn me on. But it's impossible to get past the receding hairline, the slightly protruding belly, the striped golf shirt, the sunburned and overeager smile. I was in the narrow bar with my laptop open, playing business girl getting a few clicks of work done before the big industry conference tomorrow. Maybe you're too young to join me for a drink, but I hope you'll relish the anonymity of the city. Strangers, whether desirable or frightening, will disappear forever by the 11 a.m. checkout time.

guy with black hat at Stephen Cohen – Los Angeles

When we spoke, I had a hangover pain under my left eye. Everyone else had been to therapists with the same training as mine. When I opened my mouth, they looked at me actively and punctuated the ends of my sentences with an individualized assent that sounded unlike the usual uh-huh. Today, the physical pain isn't as acute. The people we know are completely random. And I suppose there's a beauty in it, but most of the time it just seems like a fucking mess.

boy reading *Monkeybicycle* at Dutton's – Brentwood

I could see you were reading a poem, tracing your finger below each line to focus an attention that wanted out. I remember liking the idea of poetry, but now it's difficult for me to figure out what, if anything, I enjoy. Meaning: everything seems enjoyable in a stuffing-envelopes sort of way. Stuffing a lot of envelopes and watching a stack grow becomes mildly satisfying. Write and black letters fill up a page, except there's that question of substance. I suppose you could get nitpicky about stuffing envelopes, too—folding letters in perfectly creased thirds, moistening the lip of the envelope without wobbles, putting the stamp an exact eighth of an inch from both the top and right edges. With poetry I can be attentive—pay attention to handwriting, grammar, syntax, all of that—but in the end I may as well have filled the pages with *S*'s. Or *O*'s. Or just diagonal slashes.

Elizabeth Kerlikowske

Self-Portrait with Tutu

Forever Tutu

Saying "tutu" is the best part of tutus which are made from Brillo pads, the flesh of little girls, and wishes. Tutus stand alone in corners waiting to smother some hips or hang upside down like bats that only come alive in footlights. I thought they had to be earned but come to find out, they can be bought. Pink as fingernails, as Candy's baby mice, they can support a french fry dropped before the recital. You can lose a bracelet in their froth. And a tutu, even on a whale like Maryanne, frosted her with grace like a figurine on a wedding cake. Tutus turn a pencil box of girls into a flock of gyroscopes careening across a pock-marked stage.

Time Steps

Shuffle ball change. Shuffle ball change. Shuffle ball change. Stomp. Switch feet. Shuffle ball change. Shuffle ball change. Shuffle ball change. Stomp.

Shuffle hop step fa-lap step. Shuffle hop step fa-lap step. Shuffle hop step fa-lap step. Shuffle hop step fa-lap step. Next.

I stopped. The rest tapped on.

Shuffle hop shuffle step fa-lap step. Shuffle hop shuffle step fa-lap step. Shuffle hop shuffle step fa-lap step. Stomp. Stomp.

My ears knew the words, but my feet could not keep up.

Studio Rats

Barbara is eating Roseanne's lunch, I concluded, more due to Roseanne's inability to digest dairy and chew carrots with braces than because Barbara's mother is "incompetent." In other words, it's toe shoe economics, TipToe. According to the *Dancing Chronicles of 2010*, stealing and eating a lunch like Rosanne's takes an average of fifty eight seconds compared with eight seconds for Susie's and three seconds for Maryanne's, because she's a heifer and keeps her lunch within reach. Eating Roseanne's stolen lunch takes seventy-four seconds if Roseanne's mother packs oranges, but seven seconds if Susie's mom packs Twinkies. Roseanne's neatly Saran-wrapped sandwich of high quality meats and wrap-up cheese is twice as tasty as Susie's, which is stale bread with organic peanut butter. Peanut butter can add a full minute. I'm not at the studio long enough to need a lunch. I envy the brown bags. Candy gets salmon loaf on Friday with bones in it. I beg her to invite me over after dance class to that heaven of smells: banana bread, salmon, armpits, cigarette smoke, oily hair.

Fitting Room

Alyce Hogan Dance Studio was an old two-story house that had been gutted for space. A few lilacs and lilies of the valley were covered with soot. Once a year, the little studio upstairs became a measurement and fitting room for the spring recital. Alyce's mother, pushing ninety, commanded the phalanx of mothers who sewed away a percentage of their daughters' lessons. Even with shawls, Alyce could not conceal the great hump on her back, and her mother's hump was twice as large, as if she were pregnant with another back. We shivered in our underwear under the bare light bulb. The older girls smoked and tried to guess our cup letters, if we had cups. Experienced talons ran the measuring tape around our parts. Alyce's mother called the numbers out in Polish. In a week, the costumes would be ready for fitting. More touching and exposure, as the trolls twisted their necks to look up in my face. "Is that good? Is this what you want? How does it feel?"

The Max Factor

I trudged downstairs at 6 p.m. My costume dragged behind me almost on a hanger. My face was plain. My hair was straight. I was clearly a conscript. The real dancing girls chattered and skittered like chipmunks hot on the trail of a bird feeder, their ringlets all slinkied on their heads. Each dressing room had a list of names of those who needed a costume change. In the center of the basement the make-up bay was lined with huge mirrors, and the stage mothers perched there with tubes and sticks and puffs and sprays and ashtrays. They drank from matching coffee cups with lipstick prints, lipstick prints on the filters of their cigarettes as they waited for their Shirley Temples. I brought a book and made myself scarce. My costume was sky blue; therefore, I was easy to overlook. Maybe I was a cloud in the WPA mural in the lobby. Maybe I was peeling paint in the tunnel that led to the backstage. But as the younger dancers disappeared for their debuts, my plain face became obvious as the moon, and one of the mothers pitied me. She shellacked my hair into a bun. She caulked my pores with foundation, drew on eyebrows and the shame of peacock blue eye shadow. My eyes were aqua silver dollars; the stubborn rouge skidded across my cheeks. Haphazard Tangee lipstick completed the mask. She forced me to look in the mirror and admire myself. I hid my book under a sofa cushion; I didn't want it to see me.

Dress Rehearsal

A kind of glamour heated up under the lights along with the temper of Miss Alyce. The pit band passed a paper bag. The emcee smoked, and the smoke was wounded magic in the follow spots. He blew rings and waited in the wings as Miss Alyce's heels cracked across the stage. She bellowed instructions to the lighting guys. We were the first act and already she was swearing. "Put the goddamn gel in and keep it steady. Jesus Christ." She turned to us, "Sorry, kids," and put her cigarette out in her hand. We squatted in our starting position. I could see her skull through her dyed red hair. The first notes of our song, "If I was a frog, I'd hop to town"—but Miss Alyce stomped her foot and marched to the center of the stage. "Could you tune the goddamn horn since the piano is too much to ask for? Jesus Christ." We stayed squatting. I was in the center, as I would be my entire dancing career due to my great height. Overhead, a light exploded. And then a trickle of water ran downstage from the left. And then one from the right. A ripple of whimpering and giggling. Miss Alyce turned to us and said, "What is this now? Pee? Oh, Jesus Christ."

Frankie and Johnny

To the fathers, *Frankie and Johnny* was the highlight of every recital, and as the closing number of the first act, it kept many a father in his seat who otherwise would have wandered down to the Cottage Inn for a quick one and a smoke. "Frankie and Johnny were lovers" and so were Barbara and Alyce Hogan's son. They smoked outside the studio; they smoked on stage for verisimilitude, though no one knew that word. "He was her man, and he done her wrong." Frankie's breasts were cuddled up under her chin; her red sequined dress left plenty of room for her thighs to breathe. Her scarlet heels were railroad spikes. "Oh Lordy how they could love." Johnny wore a yellow zoot suit and fedora, watch fob for emphasis, and a skinny mustache. He swung Frankie between his legs; he tossed her in the smoky air. He twisted her around his waist like a belt. No wonder she killed him, I thought, but the dads were spellbound, gaping toddlers at their first monkey house. And even when Frankie shot Johnny, she was never hotter. The curtain dropped on her shoulders. She planted her heel on Johnny's chest, she and the gun and Johnny still smokin'.

The Price

From the plush worn seats in the house of St. Cecilia, the audience couldn't see the acne scabs on Susie's face or her tiara's grippers digging into her scalp, just her blue pancake tutu a-swish in the solo spotlight. They couldn't see her mousey mother at the keyboard in the practice room playing the same tunes for years to pay for lessons. When Maryanne contorted herself in harem pants and walked up blocks on her hands, they couldn't see her mother, all jowls and bald spots, hunched under a lamp with spreadsheets, calling other parents about their overdue bills. Barbara tapped in scarlet toe shoes, and from far away, the parents couldn't tell she was pregnant. When stuck-up Rosanne slithered across the stage performing what Grand Rapids thought was modern jazz, splits and fish flops, they didn't know her mother had her own key to the studio where she went each night to mop the floor.

Robert King

Looking at Houses

One of my grandmother's favorite evening activities was "looking at houses," my grandfather driving the family slowly through south Denver neighborhoods while she studied the picture windows of the 1940s, one display after another, little stage-sets of furniture, a lamp spreading its cozy varnish over the arrangements made of the family's life. A child, I dreaded our one-car procession dragging past the lighted rectangles of strangers.

Later, driving by the tawny stretch of prairie around Kimball—called Antelopeville when she was born there in western Nebraska—and remembering she moved to eastern Colorado, almost the same blank escape of earth, I imagined the relief of moving into Denver's deep congregations of trees sheltering the cool and almost holy neighborhoods. A multitude of the saved had been brought inside the city and safely nestled down and she inspected them, one after another.

*   *   *

Traveling in North Dakota, I once turned off at an historic-marker sign to read the bronze plaque beside a small hump of hill. Eric Watne and his wife found a dugout abandoned by early wagoneers, moved in and stayed, living in a mound of earth. He stayed when his sister's family moved in while building in the northeast pasture and then moved out, stayed when a daughter was born, stayed even when his wife died, sleeping each night almost at her level in the thick familiar

181

vault. The finest root hairs of bluestem grass rot in one day and night, and I felt what green energy must have shuddered around both of them. Finally, with a second wife and child, he emerged up into the light.

I thought of the dugout in eastern Colorado where grandfather first went to school, for we have had little choice. In a land of stones, we live inside stone; in a forest, we live in wood. Here, where I have spent most of my life, there is only what is underfoot.

During the Second World War, turning horror into play as children easily do, I dug the small grave of a foxhole into the backyard and crouched down while friends pretending at enemies hurled dirt clods skyward to arch and fall against my occupied position. Other days, I climbed into the earth alone, thrilled simply at my invisibility from the world, at the silky walls against my fingers, at the cool, rich scent of underground. Last year, as a volunteer working beside archaeology students, I smelled it again in the successive layers of a sixteenth century pit house a little farther from the Missouri now, in a forest which had been grassland. On our knees, a posture of continual worship, we skimmed our trowels back and forth, slicing off a centimeter at a time to find the floor where the family lived, collecting shards of pottery and bits of flint. One afternoon a girl, working the screens with her bare hands, cried out and I climbed up with the first-aid kit. She'd cut herself on the flaked edge of someone's broken attempt at a spear point and was bleeding vividly, five hundred years later.

Later, the Watne dugout became a blacksmith shop for the crews running the railroad brightly through, the clang and chime of work, but the line was abandoned, the rails cloudy now, rust spreading out around the spikes. I took a photograph of the plaque, edgy with that irony, and then another, on impulse, of the huge white house standing a quarter mile down the road, surrounded by the enormous rolls of hay the new machines can swirl, spirals of stem and seed rusting in the air as the roots of hot grass beneath us continue to sprout and fiercely die. From the car, the memorial hill looked like an enormous ancient grave, or a tunnel that had collapsed upon those who had been escaping for a hundred years.

*   *   *

I once admitted to a friend that when I took a neighborhood stroll at night I found myself studying lighted second-story windows although I didn't know why. He did the same thing but he knew. Some night, he promised, abashed with self-awareness, there was going to be a naked woman in the window.

He didn't actually need to see more naked women, he shrugged, so he supposed the motive lay more in the thrill of observing, undetected, a moment in life, the way art allowed us to contemplate the gesture of a woman Renoir curved in a bathing dish, perhaps, her skin a matter of light's impressions. But whatever his motive, or mine, everyone is safe: all that can be known of a second-story room from the street is the color of a ceiling, the choice of a light fixture, the top two feet of wallpaper.

It even occurred to me that a woman dropping her clothing like a veil of water sliding down smooth stone and coming to the window to look down from the glare of her room would only be a faceless form of darkness to me if I should happen to look up.

*   *   *

These nights, I often walk around a nearby neighborhood where families have turned their backs on the streets, down which only the private few may glide, and stand at the end of their large lawns without sidewalks, there being no reason

183

for anyone to walk from house to house. Only occasionally do I see in—a bookcase against a wall or the splotch of a painting in an entryway, sometimes an empty armchair watching a television, the splinters of light exploding from the screen every few seconds so the room itself flickers unsteadily with dark and bright.

Then I walk back to my own neighborhood where we have grown wary, guarding ourselves with detectors that sense the movement of a passerby and suddenly flood light outward to the street. When I walk past, even though I am finished with looking into houses where I can no longer see, I trigger light after light, driveways suddenly ablaze against the burglar, the assassin, the spy, houses totally intent on keeping their secrets.

I come to my own home, this time made from brick and tree because I have settled inside the town and have forgotten the look of the surrounding landscape and its deep spaces for the night. Behind me the modern houses wait minutes for an answer to their challenge, alert to unimaginable danger, and then, perhaps reluctantly, turn themselves off, summoning the next eternal darkness.

Jenn Koiter

True/False

1.

Candy Jones was five-nine. Candy Jones was five-ten. Candy Jones was six feet tall. Six-foot-four. Six-foot-seven in three-inch heels. Candy Jones was famous. Everyone knew Candy Jones, especially servicemen. Candy Jones—tall, tall, famous Candy Jones—could wear a dark wig and not be recognized by anyone. Anyone could be Candy Jones. I could be Candy Jones, and I look nothing like Candy Jones. Candy Jones looks nothing like Candy Jones. I have a friend, a professor friend. Her colleagues treat her with more respect since she started wearing three-inch heels. I never wear three-inch heels. I am five-foot-nine. I am six feet tall when I wear three-inch heels.

2.

Harry Conover invented the Cover Girl. Candy Jones was a Cover Girl. Candy Jones's marketing campaign was genius. Candy-striped dresses and candy-box purses and red and white cards that told Manhattan "Candy Jones Was Here." All that candy-striped shit didn't do a damn thing. Candy Jones was a beauty expert. Candy Jones wrote books. Candy Jones appeared often on the radio. I hate the sound of voices on the radio. Candy Jones joined Long John Nebel's radio show. Then she ran the show alone. I can't not listen. Then she was replaced by Larry King. The voices insist.

3.

When Candy Jones was a child, her mother locked her in a dark closet over and over. Candy Jones was thrilled when her mother came to live with her in Manhattan. Harry Conover was Candy Jones's first husband. He was bisexual. He was gay. Harry Conover would only come on to Candy Jones if he was drunk. Candy Jones didn't know any better because she never dated much. Candy Jones dated Orson Welles. Orson Welles really just liked playing cards with Candy Jones's darling mother.

4.

As a child, Candy Jones had imaginary friends. Intelligent children often have imaginary friends. I had no imaginary friends, and my Barbies had complicated sex lives. There was always a good Barbie and a bad Barbie. Neither of their names were Barbie. There was always a good Ken and a bad Ken. Always a bad Ken. The bad Ken is necessary.

5.

One of Candy Jones's imaginary friends was named Arlene. Arlene was not imaginary. Arlene disappeared. Arlene stayed.

The hypnotist found Arlene and brought her back. Arlene despised Candy Jones, weak, girly Candy Jones. Arlene learned to kill with a hat pin dipped in poison lipstick. Arlene learned to kill with her bare hands.

6.

Candy Jones was never a spy. Candy Jones just carried messages to California. Candy Jones just carried messages to Asia. The messages were vitally important to national security. None of the messages mattered. Candy Jones was captured and tortured by Native Americans. Candy Jones was captured and tortured by Chinese men. No, Chinese women. No, white men in white coats. They sent her to Asia wearing a dark wig. They ran too much electric current through her thumb. They held a lighted candle to her genitals. They programmed her to kill herself in the Bahamas. What mattered was that they could.

7.

The whole thing was a hoax, concocted by Long John Nebel for their radio show. Candy Jones, who always knew her audience, went along. The whole thing was a hoax, invented by the government to make the Soviets think that they could do everything Candy Jones claimed. Candy Jones made the whole thing up and laughed all the way to her grave. The whole thing was one all-encompassing fuck you. Fuck you, Miss Atlantic City. Fuck you, Model of the Year. Fuck you, beauty tips and interviews. Fuck you, girdles and garters and high-heeled shoes. Fuck you, lipstick and pancake makeup. Fuck you, Harry Conover. Fuck you, respectable employment. Fuck you, manners and mores. Fuck you, Mother. Fuck you, Orson Welles.

Elizabeth Langemak

You

But All of the Foxes are Dancing

You say, *I'm so glad it's summer,* and I agree. You say, I *hope we never grow tired of each other,* and I think this is an odd thing to say in the context of summer. I say, *you think that I am the crazy one, but really you are the one prone to fits of non sequitur,* but you argue you make the most sense. You say you were thinking of summer as a long, hot hallway, empty but for two people with nothing but themselves to please the other, and I counter that, really, this is not a thought about summer, but a thought about life, or maybe marriage. We have just left our car in the hot parking lot where, on NPR, a woman was interviewing the director who had made a cartoon about talking foxes. She wanted to argue about logic. *But all of the foxes are dancing,* she said once, twice, and I said it a third time and then a fourth, which you thought sounded crazy but what I wanted then was what you were about to do, which was to lift the sentence from its moment like a lid from a jar and then not to look inside but to open the next jar, and the next, and to go on down the line without eating anything.

Making Ourselves into the Morning

Once I saw you upset about the state of poetry. *Oh crap,* I thought, *not you too,* but there you were. Personifying the morning was a mistake, you were saying, as if that were news. Everyone, everyone knows, is always making themselves into the morning. Almost every day I catch myself unbolting the locks in the same way I might open a book about myself, taking the train downtown in the third person, passing autonomy out the window to breezes and mailboxes as if it were something they wanted. I tried to tell you quickly. I said something about moderation, or selflessness, about how sometimes mistakes are what we do anyway, how making ourselves into the morning is—like the morning itself—unavoidable, even with the best of intentions. I couldn't tell if you'd heard me, and even though it was evening and the black surface of the window gave up nothing, you kept staring as if the sun had just come up, its rays glancing off the microwave and that breath inhaling the tickled fabric through the frame.

An Apology

Even young I knew: imagination was mainly for seeing how things would not be. I practiced on my dog. I imagined him hit by a car, frozen, fallen into a permanent sleep. When he developed a cancerous limp instead, I understood that nothing I could think of would be as I thought. I moved on to bigger things, worked on technique: twenty thoughts on college roommates, thirty guesses about where I might live, how I might meet my husband. Each came to me unexpected, as I could not have foreseen them. I wouldn't have wanted to know and so I thought harder. I imagined my work, my friends, the ways I thought I could love people. It was good not to glimpse these: they were not blurry or dim but totally out of my range, they did not shock or startle but each as it happened let itself in, a stranger with a key to the room where I waited. For pleasure, I tried small things: the color of my first car, how good I would be at racquetball, if dinner would taste like the picture made it smell. None were as I thought. After a while surprise no longer surprised me; I knew I could not even say what I felt, when I practiced beforehand. When I met you, I looked for each word I wanted to speak and when it was not there I was not amazed, because by then I knew imagination was a machine for not knowing. All of this is to say that last night when you said I was not thinking of you when I thought of us, I said, *I think of you always,* but I see now how I have actually imagined everything else. Sometimes I think of what we might be instead. I know I am not quite what I thought, that I cannot say well what I most want to say. You are not what I expected either. Forgive me for imagining you otherwise.

Steeplechase

Watching your back, I think of watching it when you are fifty, seventy-five, broad as it ever was, shoulders riding its span like neck-and-neck jockeys caught in a contest on relentless horses, all your angles pushing forward over fences never straddled nor knocked over by your muscle tight and tied to your core of bone and bang. Yours is a race pitching clods of roots-and-all soil over the heads of the crowd. A race that steams flanks under your weight.

Gian Lombardo

Equations

Three times know-you-like-a-book divided by the summation of each utterance of you-should-have-known-better.

* * *

What passes for love raised to the power of what passes for intellect.

* * *

Giggling over the integral of moaning (from pain to ecstasy) less the diffusion of an itch.

* * *

The square root of one game, the two of clubs, three wise men, five o'clock shadow and eight legs.

* * *

Finding the certainty of a single existence divided by two times the shock of discovering metempsychosis is true multiplied by itself times the ratio of the circumference of a soul to its diameter.

* * *

Splitting the difference between meaning what you say and saying what you mean.

*   *   *

The aggregate of not taking it lying down and standing up for one's self.

*   *   *

A smile, its width relaxed until its remainder, when contained by a moment of doubt, matches the factor of a laugh.

Christina Manweller

Shucking

I. Beauty vs. Pressure

It's said Frank Lloyd Wright's Guggenheim design was based on the nautilus, which, if you visit the building, is pretty darn self-evident. In 1943 Wright was tasked by Solomon Guggenheim to create a "temple of the spirit" to house his collection of modern art. Walk into that space, stop under the massive spider-web-inspired skylight six stories up, feel how the staircase that's rising over and around you, reaching toward the skylight, encases you womb-like (albeit a 90-foot-high womb)—just stand, let awe settle over and into you. Light on light. Remember: breathe.

The half-nautilus shell here on my desk makes me think of the museum and its spiraling interior. It's a miracle of design more amazing in its diminutive glory than Wright's replica. The shell's insides glow with a pearlescent radiance and the exterior's silver sheen reminds me of a spaceship. It's a compact, perfect womb-shell.

A cephalopod like the octopus, the nautilus reaches its ninety or so arms out of a shell that grows in a logarithmic spiral. Named the *spira mirabilis*, or miraculous spiral, by 17th century mathematician Jacob Bernoulli, its shell is often used to illustrate the golden mean, also known as the divine proportion, considered especially pleasing to the human mind and closely related to the Fibonacci sequence. The golden mean shows up all over the place. Picking up a pinecone on my walk this morning, I turned it over to find the scales spiraling in and out and around in symmetrical perfection. The golden mean. I've been captivated by a similar design in a giant sunflower's helical seed pattern. It's true that this is a pleasing form. Even human DNA molecules fit the golden mean, though the unseen is often less miraculous to us than the seen. The nautilus shell's beauty always makes me pause.

Endowed with a high level of intelligence and a complex nervous system, the nautilus is an undersea wonder unerringly adapted to its environment. The chambered shell enables buoyancy at various depths and supports the body through extreme pressure changes. Still, beyond a certain depth, say 2,600 feet (imagine the darkness down there! the quiet!), its shell implodes. Yes, scientists have tested this on the poor collapsing creatures. The ability to adapt to such incredible pressure differences is unusual. I mourn my own inability to do so while fingering the shell, appreciating its form and luminescence, how it's a neat little cathedral where the part of my mind not colonized by pressures and fear might worship.

2. Silence vs. Primal Noise

Rainer Maria Rilke fantasized that the skull's occipital sutures could be played by placing a needle in the groove in the same manner a phonographic recording is played. The seams that so captivated him resemble the impressions of recorded sound waves.

When he was a boy, his science class had built a crude phonograph from items at hand: cardboard, paper, wax and a bristle. The enthralled children heard their own voices coming back at them for the first time. Rilke was enraptured by the tracings in wax.

Alone with a skull (brain-womb) at night in the candlelight, sutures standing out in relief, Rilke thought of the soundprints he and his schoolmates had made all those years before. Later he said that even as a boy he was more interested in sound's signature left behind in the wax than the sound itself.

In a 1919 publication he supposed that were the skull played, it would emit a primal sound, *Ur-geräusch*. He imagined that the skull's once-living inhabitant's emotions might be revealed in this way, having been sealed into the bone. (What, I wonder, would pleasure's raw tracing look like? Or anger's?)

He was excited by the idea that playing the coronal suture would bridge what he called "the abyss" separating the senses. What had been experienced through sight or touch could now be heard. The unseen, become the seen.

Friedrich Kittler writes of Rilke in *Gramophone, Film, Typewriter,* "Before him, nobody had ever suggested to decode a trace that nobody had encoded and that encoded nothing."

Speaking of primal noise: physicists and astronomers say they're studying remnants of sound laid down 380,000 years post-big-bang (by today's estimate, that would be 380,000 years after 13.8 billion years before now). Once upon a time, our universe was chock full of sound; it seems it's still discernible as an imprint in the cosmic microwave background. Apparently, at the moment sound turned off—sound doesn't exist in today's space vacuum—during an event called Recombination, the tracings were preserved and are still detectible.

According to Hindus, *Om* is the sound vibrated into being as the universe was created: the first sound, sacred, primeval, representing God's name. It is Rilke's *Urgeräusch* and the scientists' billions and billions years'-old sound imprint; maybe it's what the skull would sing were it played record-player fashion.

"If only we could find the Silence which is the source of sound!" Quaker mystic Thomas Kelly wrote. If only. Hard as I may listen, the universal *Om*, the *Urgeräusch*, first word, God's name, will continue to elude me, submerged beneath the yelling of kids from next door, my backyard wind chimes, street traffic—and if all that is silenced, it will be masked by my own biological noises: nervous system, blood circulation. Even in an anechoic chamber, the body's sounds are audible.

I think of Rilke's skull, of how he wanted to play it, of how morbid that is, but also compelling.

3. The Transitory vs. The Not-So-Transitory

Artist Albrecht Dürer spent his life investigating beauty, defining symmetry. A contemporary of Leonardo da Vinci, the Nuremberger studied mathematics and applied that knowledge to art, creating precise and detailed paintings, drawings, prints and engravings. The compass and the rule were his favored tools along with the brush and engraver's burin. He traveled to Italy several times to meet artists and well-known mathematicians (though not, apparently, da Vinci). A theorist and a writer, he published treatises on math, especially geometry, on perspective and proportion, even one on how to form letters, with painstaking instructions for each character, *a* to *z*.

I saw a Dürer exhibit at the Kunsthistorisches Museum in Vienna in 1994. The famous hare painting (*Feldhase*) and the delicate nature-study watercolor known as *The Great Piece of Turf* (*Das große Rasenstück*) please me, but his dark works with their apocalyptic themes (these include a series of fifteen woodcuts published in 1498 based on the *Book of Revelation*) are heavy and unintelligible to my mind. The human skull turns up again and again. In *Knight, Death and the Devil* (*Ritter, Tod und Teufel*) from 1513, the year Dürer's mother died an agonizing death, a skull lies in the path about to be trampled by horses ridden by a knight and Satan. One of his most famous engravings, *Melencolia I*, teems with mathematical allusions and tools, including a compass, a geometric solid, a magic square said to pertain to the Fibonacci sequence. The engraving is also chock full of death symbolism (including a skull drawn on a polyhedron, an hourglass, a bell, a pair of scales). In 1521, he painted St. Jerome at his desk, hand resting on a skull, a finger laid on a long fracture as if to trace it.

Dürer treasured certain physical objects, as I do—witness my shells and pinecones, rocks and dried flowers. Forms that please. Traveling to the Netherlands in 1520 and 1521 he collected items for his Wunderkammer and sent them home, including:

    a spear
    a buffalo horn
    coral

    shields (fish-scale and wood)
    cloth
    a turtle shell

    ivory
    fins
    bird wings
    a coconut

His accumulations are more extravagant than my shells and pinecones, than the cobblestone I lifted from the streets of Prague and the rocks I've lugged home from California, New Mexico, Nova Scotia; still, I love my little collection, the items that will outlive me. But my own Wunderkammer, stocked with memories and mis-memories (memories of memories, some of which others dispute me on), obsessions, transitory thoughts and images, impressions, etc., exists in my mind and will perish when I do. It's a cabinet filled with personality-makings, the bits that, while not soul, are perhaps brushed with intimations of the deeper self, of the part of me that I hope lives on when this husk gives up the ghost.

Dürer's ghost? Solving mathematical problems no doubt.

Debra Marquart

Whisker Meditations

1.

When I told my fiancé's mother about my persistent, recurring whisker—lower right, underside of my chin—she smiled sideways, said, "Be glad it's only one."

2.

I was parked in the lot outside Bed, Bath & Beyond with my then-husband. I was applying lipstick in the mirror the first time I spotted it—my whisker enjoying a stretch of unchecked growth.

It was hot in the car. We were laughing. My husband tried to pull it out with his fingertips. When that failed, he offered to tweeze it with his teeth. What an act of extreme devotion. It makes me wonder why I ever let him go.

3.

It begins, a smooth bump on the skin that you must worry for days with your fingertips. Then, a small nub, slight friction in the follicle, nothing visible. Hours pass, days. You forget. Then one day you catch it in silhouette or sunlight—a long tendril like a pliable scrap of piano wire sprung from your chin.

4.

My friend Jenny tells me about one night after she and Colin made love. Lying there, sweaty, happy, Colin spotted a long brown hair on Jenny's chest—his hair, he thought. When he tried to pick it off, the skin lifted, the follicle resisted. It was connected. "Get it off me," Jenny screamed. "Get it off!"

5.

This sliver of iron ore spun from the lava core of the earth, one thin chin wire rising through Cambrian, Devonian, up through continental shelves, bedrock, shale, topsoil. This tendril—manganese, copper, platinum—must have pierced my heel, threaded my first step, wound around tendons, up shin, thigh, groin, traveled through heart, breast, throat to arrive here on my chin in my fortieth year.

6.

Sometimes in meetings at work, I catch myself stroking my sad whisker when contemplating problems. I better understand now the gestures of my bearded colleagues who, over the years, have cradled their chins, stroked with the grain, against the grain, or, when really perplexed, vigorously scratched a stubbled cheek.

7.

In the bathroom of a four-star hotel—marble shower, terrazzo floors—I turn on the lighted magnifying mirror hanging near the vanity. Never mind crow's feet, enlarged pores, the natural exigencies of age.

But, oh, in the magnifying glass, under that terrifying light—constellations of age spots, catastrophe of eyebrows, oh, whisker. All the while my fiancé is knocking on the frosted glass door. *What are you doing in there?*

8.

And now my whisker has attracted an evil twin, albino white, emerging from the doorway of the neighboring pore. How long, how long, will it be before the rest of the family arrives—the older brother, the in-laws and parents, not to mention the car full of California cousins.

9.

To pluck it, you must stand by the window, blinds open in full light with a tweezers and a hand mirror. Try to tuck yourself behind the billow of the curtain. No need for you to star in a YouTube video entitled, "My Crazy Old Neighbor Lady Plucks Her Whisker Again."

10.

You'll never get it on the first try or the second. You have to poke around. Then one day, the tweezer's edge will land, small suction as the follicle releases. When it happens to me, I hold the whisker up in the light, say, *Got it! You bastard!*

A small moment of satisfaction followed by silence, vacuous air, as I contemplate the many hours and days, the many weeks it will take for this grave act to be undone.

Kathleen McGookey

Nine Letters

Dear Death, can't you see we're busy riding bikes in the sun? Later we'll cut out paper hearts and sprinkle them with glitter. I have had enough of you. I'd rather learn facts about penguins: what they eat, how much they weigh, how they stay warm in the Antarctic. Some are called Emperor. Some, Rockhopper. First-graders with gap-toothed smiles hold out the class guinea pig for me to pet. Let's pretend you forget all about us.

*   *   *

Death, yesterday my neighbor's boxer, glossy and muscular, charged me again, kicking up dead leaves. This time, it snarled and jammed its open mouth against my calf. I had picked up my daughter and was walking away. It didn't draw blood. So far, you have been more considerate. You don't pick fights. As for theories, I like luck. But each morning, when I hear the white-throated sparrow making its threats at dawn, I know you're not far behind.

*   *   *

Pull up your red pickup to school, Death, it's time for Mrs. Keizer's class party. If you haven't brought Valentines for everyone, you may not pass them out. But you're welcome to braid a friendship bracelet and balance an Oreo on your forehead. Cupcakes go next to the juice boxes. Even with the windows open, the room gets hot. And you should compliment the other moms about their children. No fair watching the moon grow distinct in February's bare sky. Surely you've noticed some child's dead-on free throws or skill with sharp objects? It's okay if you don't exactly fit in. No one wants to believe you are here.

*   *   *

Death, if Maggie lives four thousand yards from school, and Clarissa three miles, which girl stands a chance of outrunning you? How many students can finish their worksheets before their desks burst into flame? The class is tired of math. But they are quick and practical, and set up a bucket brigade for those in need. In a moment of panic, they douse each other with water. It'll be a while before they can write anything in their soggy notebooks again. Why don't you tell about the time you watched a goddess, years and years ago, transform a swan with frozen wings into a rabbit, handily saving its life. I'm guessing your perspective on that miracle is not often heard.

*   *   *

Death, now where's the skinny stray that's already killed a finch and a robin? She's littered feathers like petals in the yard. For three days, she followed us to the bus stop, but she vanished when I prepared a box. Did you know I planned to drive that cozy box to the shelter? Did you know I told my kids, *There's a chance this cat will find a home?* I know truth is precarious. And here you've sent a curtain of rain for the cat to hide behind. In winter, I imagined, she would starve and freeze. In summer, she watches with you. . . .

*   *   *

I said give me the stray cat, Death, not these confused wren fledglings, trapped in my open garage, calling, while their parents answer from the pines. Is this frantic symphony pleasing to your ears? My son says, *Close one big door*, and then two fly out the windows. At least he knows what to do. When I bring the door up again, the last one crashes between the fridge and wall. I don't call my husband to identify it. Are you comfortable in your armchair, Death? The baby bird weighs nothing in my palm. When I lay it beneath the pines, I don't feel anything.

*   *   *

Death, I prefer you in the abstract. Where someone else might prepare a place for you and your sleight of hand. Get a job at the casino, why don't you? The parking lot's always full. Even in summer. Even when sunrise washes the pavement in ordinary light and no one rejoices. The staff in impeccable uniforms, the machines flashing in the haze remind you of some other place. Get busy with your deck of cards. So you'll have an excuse when I ask to send a message to my friend, the one you took last week, the one with the china doll face.

*   *   *

P.S., Death, Lucy just handed me a crumpled page—crayoned numbers orbiting Venus and Mars. The first grade finished their unit on space and started infinity. Our frail neighbor died today, the one who used to watch her swim. Are you chilly up there in your ratty robe and slippers? Lucy would offer you crackers and juice, then lead you to the monkey bars. You'd have fun. But I don't want you to feel at home here.

*   *   *

Take this scrap of my words, Death, and fold it into your pocket, snug over your hip. The three white feathers from my pillow smell like my lemon perfume. Don't worry that your pocket has a hole. This time of year, swallows dive for feathers to line their nests. After it cartwheels over the daffodils, the scrap will land in the gravel. A sparrow will snatch it up. Now what will you remember me by?

Monica Nawrocki

Vancouver Conversations

1.

I am walking down Robson, as I do every day. Up ahead, in front of Shopper's Drug Mart, the guy with the really blue eyes who doesn't talk very well is shaking his paper cup of coins and muttering his line at people. He used to be further down the block, but since he took over this spot—from the guy with the wheelchair who was always asleep—I have discerned that he is saying, "Have a good day." So now I know how to respond when I come to drop off prescriptions and pick up my partner's never-ending parade of transplant drugs. By the time I draw even with the blue-eyed man, he is attempting a conversation with the owner of the neighborhood Art car—a Volkswagen bug completely covered in kitsch. There is only a suggestion of baby blue floating behind the glued-on items that cover every square inch. The owner stands beside it, trying to make out what Ol' Blue Eyes is saying as he points to a little flag of Newfoundland on a rear panel, his face ecstatic.

"Newfoundland, yes," says Mr. Art Car.

Blue Eyes thumps himself on the chest so hard, he stumbles backward a step.

"You're from Newfoundland?" asks Art.

Blue nods blissfully and caresses the flag.

"You're from Newfoundland," says Art.

I can feel them smiling at each other as I pull open the pharmacy door.

2.

Hyper-vigilance is the one thing I always have with me in the waiting room of C6 at Vancouver General Hospital. No patience or peace. Just hyper-vigilance bordering on hyperventilation.

And sometimes coffee.

Today, I concentrate on my breathing. I elongate each breath to a normal length so I won't go into the doctor's office light-headed and crabby, like last time. My partner sits beside me, breathing normally.

A man occupies the chair on the other side of me. He has quite a bit of hair—must be post-transplant by four or five months. A woman walks in, breathless, with bags and a jacket and an umbrella and some hair. She greets the man beside me.

"Hey! How are you? Are you well? You look fantastic."

"Thanks, I'm feeling pretty good. How are you?"

I tune them out semi-successfully and go back to my breathing. The doctor has never been less than thirty minutes late and we are only ten minutes past our appointment time. Lots of breathing still to come.

The words "Hickman line" draw me back to the hair people. I glance at my bald partner to see if she is listening. Her Hickman line has been in a few months already but I'm still a little freaked out by the tube that lies below her skin, running from her jugular vein to her chest, then protruding through the skin and dividing into three color-coded caps: red is always for drawing blood, blue is for medications going in, and white can be used for either. It's prudent to have an extra access valve to your jugular, I always say.

She wears a soft cotton ribbon around her neck, attached to the bulldog clip that holds the three caps so the weight doesn't pull on the line. Also, the caps are cold and scratchy against her skin so we bought soft infant socks to hold her "junk."

When they first put the line in I could only glance at the exit site without feeling sick. Now, I change the dressing regularly and flush the lines with heparin and saline.

Hair guy: "My line came out easy. Why, how was yours?"

Breathless lady: "It was horrible. When they yanked it out, flesh had grown onto it and it ripped me up and then I got an infection."

I gulp for air as the woman continues.

"Should we walk a little?" I ask my partner.

"No. She might come for us."

"Are you kidding? It's only 2:15. How about some water?"

"Okay, thanks." She doesn't move.

"Why don't we both go?"

She turns and looks at me. "What's wrong with you?"

I'm no good at this. I want to be subtle, but it's a bit late to learn now, isn't it? "Whatever you do, don't listen to those two over there. Let's move to the other side of the room, okay?"

She peers past me to the couple.

"Ya, okay," she says, and picks up her backpack.

3.

"Fact: he's a bit too old for me. Fact: he actually looks quite good with his silver hair. Fact: the guys my age I've dated have all been losers."

I'm in the women's washroom at Sears, sitting on the toilet trying not to pee so that I don't miss a word of this riveting monologue. There is another woman with the Fact Lady but her contributions thus far have been limited to those two-syllable responses that can mean anything, including, *I think you might be a little crazy.*

"Fact: when we went to the bar, he was really fun and considerate and I had a great time with him."

"Hmm-mm."

"Fact: if I ditch him just because he's older than me, I may really regret it."

"You might, ya . . ."

"Fact: these bathrooms have not been redecorated since about 1955."

And they're gone.

That night, as I hold my beloved in her twitching, groaning, morphine sleep, I imagine the glorious luxury of life as a series of irrefutable facts that line neatly up, one after the other.

Maybe I could tie them together, throw them out the window, and escape.

Pamela Painter

Art Tells Us . . .

What I See

Those sinewy lines are real. I'm standing on the edge of a friend's blue tile swimming pool, and just this instant I realize that those lines I saw and was amused by in a David Hockney painting are the real thing. I turn to call to my wife but she is deep in conversation with Max, who is generously mixing her one of his slushy margaritas. His wife is sunbathing, against all reason, her eyes closed. I turn back to those yellow wavy lines in my friend's pool. I'm seeing them for the first time. Hockney has made me see something I discounted in his painting as an artist's license to paint anything. Even silly lines. These lines must be ridges reflecting the Cape summer sun—lines most apparent in Hockney's painting *Peter Getting out of Nick's Pool*. Sinewy lines made up of thin reeds of red and orange, and before this moment totally unbelievable.

At the MFA exhibit, I marveled at the nerve of Hockney to paint those lines, when his rendering of Peter's naked back as he perhaps contemplates getting out of the pool is so marvelously real. His hands flat on the hot concrete surrounding the pool. His wide shoulders hunched around his neck, his head turned to the right, his mouth hidden by his raised right shoulder. Strong shoulders taper to a waist, then the slight flare of hips made for holding on to when what I thought of as imaginary lines approach his bare buttocks. His cleft is a rich sienna or raw umber slash with one wavery, solid watery line in particular moving through his slightly parted legs—a

211

line that surely ends somewhere. Peter is looking off to the right—he doesn't seem to be getting out of the pool. Perhaps he is looking for Nick. Perhaps he is waiting for an invitation. Perhaps the tension in his arms is the real invitation.

Hockney has made me see. I look around my friend's pool to see what else I see. I see hummingbirds with invisible wings, crimson trumpet vines eclipsing whatever structure lies beneath its canopy, becoming the more solid of the two. I see my wife deep in conversation with my best friend, Max—her gaze locked on his, their drinks held in silent salutation, an invisible filament between them as tangible, as breakable now, as glass.

A View: *Office at Night*

They don't seem to be working, though up to a few minutes ago she was filing papers in a tall filing cabinet. Beside the cabinet, her boss sits reading a page at his desk, holding it beneath a green banker's light. Her plump right arm bends to encompass a generous bosom, and her right hand rests on the edge of the open drawer. Seconds ago she turned toward the man at the desk. Her face is vulnerable, intent. She is waiting. Partly hidden by the desk, a piece of paper lies on the floor between her and the man at the desk. We are led to believe that Edward Hopper is in a train, passing by on the El. The most voluptuous curve in all of Hopper's paintings, almost to a surreal degree, belongs to this secretary in the night-blue dress in *Office at Night*, an oil on canvas, 1940. What word, in 1940, would have been used to describe those two rounded globes beneath the stretch of the blue dress's skirt?

If it weren't for that piece of paper on the floor, we might believe the curator's prim description of this painting: "The secretary's exaggerated sexualized persona contrasts with the buttoned-up indifference of her boss; the frisson of their intimate overtime is undermined by a sense that the scene's erotic expectations are not likely to be met."

Wrong! The man is not indifferent. He is intent on the paper he is reading—but too intent, and he is not sitting head-on at his desk. He is turned—slightly—toward the secretary, his left elbow firmly on the desk, and his right elbow nearer her is uncomfortably balanced on the desk's edge. His mouth is slightly open as if to speak. His left ear is red. It is. It is red.

And what of their day. Her desk faces his in this small cramped office. They have no privacy because the wall to the hallway beyond does not reach the ceiling. He must have looked up from his papers, glanced up from his desk to say to her as she faced him behind her black typewriter, that tonight they must stay late. Did the secretary call her mother, or the two roommates she met while attending Katherine Gibbs, to say her boss asked her to stay late? By this time, on other evenings, she would have finished dinner, perhaps been mending her stockings, or watching the newsreel preceding the cinema's double feature.

Tonight she is working late. Yes, her dress has a chaste white collar, but the deep V of the neckline will surely fall open when she stoops to retrieve the paper that was dropped. She is looking at the paper. Was it she who dropped it? Though another object lies solidly on the chair behind her? Or did her boss drop the paper—and she is acknowledging this before she follows through on stooping over, perhaps bending at the knees over her spiffy black pumps, to retrieve the page. It resembles the papers on his desk. But note that another paper, curved slightly, its edge rising, has been nudged toward the desk's edge. The topmost paper shows a refusal to lie flat in the slight breeze from the window. This evening breeze is blowing the blind into the office, has curved the pull-cord with its sweet, soft ring. Other papers, but not all, are held in place by the 1940's black telephone, so heavy that in a B movie it could do service as the murder weapon.

Perhaps this story began at an earlier time. It might already be a situation, a situation that just this morning made the young woman choose to wear this particular blue dress. A dress equal to a request to stay late in the office at night. Somehow we are all in the middle of their drama. It isn't over yet. We are mesmerized by the piece of paper on the floor. She will bend before him. Someone will turn off the lights. Certainly they will leave before midnight. Perhaps it won't turn out well; maybe nothing good can come of this. But for now the blue dress cannot be ignored. Hopper's brush painting her, painting her dress blue, made sure of that.

Artist as Guest in the Hamptons

First of all, his wife informed him, we can't possibly have the Horstels to dinner with the Jimm Smythhs because the long dining room wall—the only space large enough for the 6' by 15' paintings they each gave us—is occupied, so to speak. Hanging there is that sixty-pound oil and gouache titled *Whale and Water* that Xu Xui announced was her "house-gift" in the thank you note she sent express mail a month after her three-week stay. Remember, since she used real glass, *Whale and Water* was too heavy when we tried to lug it down to the basement.

He remembered all too well. Besides, he was still feeling the after-effects of last fall's hernia from carrying the Lindstrom bronze porpoise from the potting shed to the patio when Sven Lindsrom mentioned he was coming to visit them in the Hamptons to reinvigorate his artistic vision. And no doubt acquire another muse, his wife said. So in addition to having the Horstels and Smythhs separately to dinner we'll have to wait till our roaming son Charlie is home from his RISDI internship to unseat the Xu Xui and haul either the

Horstel or Smythh up from the basement, depending on the guest list, to the "place of honor" in the dining room. There the artist was always circumspectly seated across from his or her work, which occasionally had a stultifying effect on conversation, but could also lead to some interesting anecdotes, like the story Tioni used to tell about his painted wooden leg's adventures in Italy before he died. Lord knows where in the garage Tioni's *Afternoon of the Fun* is buried.

Meanwhile, his wife said, about tomorrow's dinner party: the small, lush Klayton watercolor—let's see, that was his house gift four years ago—should probably be moved from the guest bathroom to the entrance way, though it does match the new marble tiles perfectly, and goodness, we can't forget to bring his wife's multicolored, jelly-bean platter down from the attic, though we still aren't sure Janine didn't mean it as a joke. And we must call the art restorer to see if he's replaced the matting on the Binner, since they're good friends of the Horstels, and we must also ask if he was able to disinfect the canvas so there is no hint of Nero's recurring bladder problem; it proved so ruinous to the Mendoza triptych that we can only dine out with them, and of course pick up the check, year after year after year.

And by the way, his wife said, the Hampton Art Museum called to remind us that we still haven't retrieved the Missy Massey painting that we'd donated to their auction last year. We told her we were donating it, so heaven forbid she asks what it went for. The director suggested that requiring the opening bid begin at $200 might have been a bit high. Surely, her husband said wistfully, someone might be at this year's art auction who really loves Peoria, as in *I "heart" Peoria,* since the Finleys have stopped speaking to us ever since Finn found his *I "heart" Frogs* behind the ficus in the library. Or was it in the closet?

What is this anyway, his wife said, why can't our artist friends arrive with two exquisite ripe cheeses? Or, he said, a vintage Bordeaux or a good bottle of champagne—house gifts, they agreed, that would disappear at evening's end into the Hamptons' own starry night.

Irena Praitis

Bread

Römhild Labor Camp, Germany, 1945

1.

I look up and see my brother walking, back toward me, his broad shoulders squared against the backdrop of green leaves in late summer glory. He's here in prison, here with me in the camp. Now I know I will survive. He slams his arm to strike a man beneath him, cursing for the man to hurry up and eat, kicking him, spilling the man's soup. The frantic man scrapes and licks at the grass. My brother turns, and I see my mistake. This is not my brother, though it could be. The prison stripes make us all look alike. This stranger's build is so like my brother's it makes my throat ache. He sees me looking and walks my way. I bend my head to eat, slurping the gray soup and gnawing the bread. With my head down I see the shoes he wears: shoes, not clogs, not rags, shoes. "Why were you staring?" he roars at me. "You're new and you will learn!" His truncheon feels as if it will plow through my body to the ground. He pounds it twice on my shoulder blades. The bones crack. My skin burns and throbs in pain. I've dropped my food without knowing it. He grabs the last of my bread. I look at him. He's a Russian, like me, a prisoner, like me. "What is with you!" I shriek out before I can stop myself. "You're not an animal. You're one of us!" He drives his knee into my chin. My teeth clamp hard against each other as I fall on my back. "You want to know what I am," he snarls, "I'm not one of you. I'm alive. This stick means that

217

I'll stay that way." "Fascist slave," I spit. He steps on my hand, grinding his shoe across the bones. "Life is my master and I'll make deals with any vile thing earth spews up to serve it. My wife was pregnant when they forced me to the front. My friends died, but I survived. Captured, they shipped me here. I'll see my firstborn. Damn it all. I'll see my child despite this fucked up world. This club I beat you with means food, shoes, a blanket. That will make the difference when the cold comes. You? You're already a dead man. You couldn't even hold your first day's bread or keep your head down." "I've a family, too," I seethe. "When I see them again, I'll meet their eyes without the shame of what I've done haunting me." He laughs. "You're new. You'll see. If you live long enough." He walks away. The whistle blows. Kapos push and shove us into line to march us to the mine. My stomach seizes. My jaws ache. With my spit rising sickly sweet in the back of my throat, I descend the rough wooden stairs to the basalt pit.

2.

I turn just in time to see the boy catch the potato. I snatch his wrist and bite his fingers as hard as I can. He screams and beats my temple with his free hand but I don't let go. I taste the rusty saltiness of his blood as he loosens his grip and I gnaw through the potato, shoving all of it into my mouth. The boy curls around his hand, cradling it as we're jostled forward, shoved along by prisoners near the SS guards who strike with rifle butts. I don't look at him long, but I can see he's young. Eleven? Twelve? Skinny as his skeleton, like all of us. Russian. Like me. He starts to lag. I lose sight of him, his blood still smeared on my chin. I look up to see my would-be brother smirk at me. He doesn't hold a truncheon now. He's just another prisoner, forced to march with no food. Not quick enough this time to steal the mealy hard potato, caked in dirt. I swallow.

I clench my teeth and throat not to gag. I refuse to know if the wailing I hear comes from the boy I bit or some other lost soul about to lose his sorry life for not keeping up. The rifle's quick report ends it all.

3.

They herd us near the walls of the farmhouse. I don't know why. We've marched in rain so it can't be shelter that they're shoving us toward. I hear a shout, thrashing, pushing, I know there's food and I claw against the shoulders slamming into me. The word "cabbage" floats above us as I hear wood splintering and water sloshing. The flailing's intense. I'm clawing now for food, and food or not, if I don't fight I know I'll be trampled. The guards curse, slamming a pathway through us with their guns, striking shoulders to the ground. They push to the center and grab three men by their necks, beating them about the head until they kneel. A space opens. I see a broken barrel, a large cloverleaf of wet where pickling leaks out of the sides, a cabbage, leaves open like the petals of a flower, lies in the mud, one large gouge in its top from someone biting it. The three kneeling men hold hands to their heads. I recognize him once again—the man who would be my brother. A guard behind the kneeling men, shoots one through the skull, then the second, and then my brother's mimic. He falls, head to the side, jaw blown away, looking at me as light fades from his eyes. Who will see his child? I think. Who survives? I made it. Not you. I survive. Not you.

4.

He licked all the butter off the bread, then chewed it bit by bit, my son. He liked to eat that way. He begged for prune

219

jam before he slept. My wife's scolding never changed him. He was strong and stubborn. Like me. They say he never had a chance, our house was approached first. Others had a warning. They saw what was happening and ran for the woods. But Marya didn't see it coming. They shot her there against the southern wall, my child standing there, too, holding her hand, too stunned to cry. Then each head crushed with a rifle butt, just in case. My neighbor saw it from the woods, my wife's frantic calling let him know something was wrong. He hid in the woods for days until the troops moved through, taking all the livestock, all the food, everything with them. He buried them for me, quick, but deep enough to keep the dogs and foxes away. "At least you know they're here," he said. As I stood looking over them, looking at the place he pointed to, their laughter I couldn't hear, their laughter I wouldn't hear kept swirling around inside of me. Why did I survive? For what? I shouldn't have survived. I fall onto their dirt, my arms spread wide to hold them, the soil grainy in my mouth, on my teeth as I try to kiss them, try to will them to me, me to them. But I know I will not die here. I will not die here. The selfishness that kept me living all this time will not release me now. I'm doomed to live without them. Cursed.

5.

She says, "I cannot leave the butter out"—she runs her finger all across the top to scoop it in her mouth then eats her bread dry. "We hid the cow in the woods for two years. At least we won't starve now." The child looks at me, and I see your eyes, my would-be brother, watching me through her, so steady, relentless. It wasn't far to travel and I needed to walk a ways. I thought, "Why not? I should go. I should tell her what happened to her father." "Part of me died when he left," she continues. "I believed even then he would not be coming back."

220

Your child doesn't flinch at your widow's words, my friend, but stares at me, the imposter, the one who makes her mother weep. "He loved you more than anything," I say, "No one loves like that these days. He did all he could to make it back." As your wife bends her head, and clenches her teeth against the pain, your daughter looks at me, fierce and un-afraid. She is your child, my friend, do you see? Do you see your child? Look through me. Do you see?

Alizabeth Rasmussen

Commuting

1.

All day long, he walks up the hill, down, and back again, each day dressed in the same jeans, t-shirt, and black leather jacket, carrying the same oversized umbrella that, even in the rain, he uses as a walking stick.

He seems destination-less but not direction-less, in no hurry, on no schedule, yet quite deliberate wherever he happens to be.

2.

A lifetime ago in a small Midwest town, my six-block walk to school felt like miles. Around the corner, through the park, looking both ways before crossing the street. I wore a Catholic-school uniform, carried a backpack too heavy and a cautiousness too weighty for a first grader.

3.

Today, I follow a couple on a royal blue Vespa past markets, bookstores and bars. I admire the passenger's mint green helmet, her impeccable posture, the way her flowy pants wave in the breeze.

I know this couple's story. They love each other and the

Vespa. But of course they also have a car . . . they don't love the Vespa in the Seattle rain.

4.

Eventually, the school bus will come by to collect the single, small passenger who waits in front of my downtown office building. Last year's backpack had a cartoon shark on it. This year's is black with red trim, much more grown-up.

For a moment today I thought the boy was on his own, but then I saw his grandmother rounding the corner at the end of the block, following far behind, watching out for him from a distance.

5.

I love the Vespa. And more than that, I love the story I've given its owners.

6.

At my building, doormen greet me when I come and go, there's small talk of weather and weekend well-wishing; the woman at the fire station down the block keeps a bag of treats at her desk just for my dog.

7.

The man steps into the crosswalk. He holds a black helmet so shiny it catches the early morning sun, diverting my attention

223

to the distorted reflection it captures. He studies the couple on the Vespa. They are oblivious to his scrutiny, the slight tilt and barely noticeable shake of his head.

In the story I give this biker, he is serious about his motorcycle, has zero respect for the Vespa, even less patience for the love story I imagine.

8.

On that first-grade walk through the snow in the early morning mist, I saw a man on the other side of the park—standing, watching, waiting. For me?

I walked to school afraid, looking over my shoulder. From the afternoon paper I learned the truth. He was a reporter and photographer, doing his job, taking pictures in the park on another slow news day.

9.

If the grandmother looks at me at all these mornings, it's with a combination of suspicion and derision, what seems a mask of protection separating her from the world. As for the boy, I used to see a flicker of a smile on his face, sometimes. He looks away now, avoids my gaze.

I linger at the stoplight before crossing the street, waiting to see if, like last year, he will wave to her through the window of the bus as they both head off into whatever the day holds.

10.

In college I waited for buses, walked miles through big-city streets, and learned the vast difference between well-founded, appropriate fear and unfounded kid-fear.

I said *no* when the man in the truck pulled over, told me he thought he was having a heart attack, wanted me to drive him to the hospital. I admit, there was a moment of hesitation.

11.

I've seen the man with the full-length umbrella almost every day for the past five years on these streets that are a playground for my son. Suspicion has given way to a quiet acceptance born of familiarity. Now, I drive by and wish him well.

12.

I wonder how my son sees the world, beyond what he shows me. Have I done a good enough job teaching him to-not-talk-to-not-trust-not-take-things-from-strangers? What if I have and, in the process, taught him to fear angels?

13.

In the story I write, strangers are known as "perfect" not because they are so entirely unknown to us, but because of the precision with which their stories intersect with our own.
In the story I write, it is safe to let people show us who we are.

William Reichard

In Smith's Mill

Burn (1)

We inhabit the houses we live in, and they, as much, inhabit us. I have a photograph of a large, gray door. It came from the house I grew up in, though I can't say to which threshold it belonged, or how it came to rest, finally, against the old picnic table in the back yard. I don't know what happened to it. Weathered by years of winters and summers, warped, rotted, my mother probably burned it in the large wire fire pit she built in the middle of the half-acre where we used to grow all the potatoes we'd need for a winter. Eventually, everything ended up there. She had no taste for the past. Nostalgia had too cloying a scent. When she finally left that house, after nearly fifty years, she ended up in the place she now owns— her little old lady house—which could fit, entirely, into the first floor of our old home. And as for that, it burned down a few years ago. Bad wiring or arson. No one could say. The new owners built a sprawling ranch style over the pit where our old house sank. Fire takes everything, everyone, in the end. It's an efficient way to erase the past, empty our lives, make way for the new things we'll one day long to be rid of.

Burn (2)

My grandfather was a pyromaniac. He saw fire as a way to cleanse the world of all the junk that filled it. He grew up poor in Northern Italy, lived in a house inhabited only by what was necessary. When something broke and couldn't be fixed, you burned it. A small mound of ashes takes up so much less room than a boxful of broken bowls or an abandoned car. Grandfather lived with us when I was a child, and though we were poor, we still managed to collect things. That was a different age, filled with disposable materials. In the country there is no curbside garbage service, so as things broke, as trash cans filled, it all ended up in a pile back behind the house. Maybe it was more than a pile. Maybe it was a hill, or even a mountain in our flat terrain. Grandfather couldn't stand it. It seemed perfectly normal to me—having been around for at least as long as I had. His solution was simple: burn it. Let the trash mountain crumble in upon itself, turn to ash, then scatter the ash in the garden. But there was so much of it. He underestimated how far the flames would leap. It turned into not a bonfire, but a conflagration. It nearly burned the house down and my family had to fight the flames for hours. My grandfather didn't understand why my mother was so angry with him, but several weeks later she loaded him into the car and drove him home to Nebraska. I never saw him again. My mother has acquired her own love of fire and every day consigns more of our past to the flames. My family has taken to the cremation of our dead. As for me, I've never liked to get too close to fire. I'm afraid to light a match.

Sitting in The Living Room with My Sister, Who Is Dying (Jeanette 1)

So familiar, the wet, drowning cough, the breath's rasp, like heavy sandpaper on wood. We've been here before. Another sister, another city, twenty-five years ago. Now the first sister has been dead almost as long as she was alive. Her voice still lives inside my ear. And so Jeanette, with her own note of un-willing passing. She reclines on the couch and we watch television. It doesn't matter what's on, only that something is there to fill the void between our two worlds. Twice a month, she makes an eight-hour bus trip from Sioux Falls to Saint Paul to take an experimental drug that could save her life. She says she'd risk anything for that, even the side effect of possible hair loss, or the growth of hair all over her body. It's a new drug, an inexact science. We joke about were-wolves and electrolysis, but we know she's serious. Any cost for life. At fifty-five she's ancient in the cystic fibrosis com-munity. Linda died at thirty. The doctors then considered her old. I feed Jeanette rich foods to fatten her up, homemade ice cream, protein bars, anything to add some weight. On a windy day like today, when autumn is carrying summer away, I fear she could rise on a draft and fly all the way to the next world. How far is that? So I tether her with heavy blankets and heavy food. She wants, she says, to have her own apart-ment one day, away from her daughter and grandchildren, their noisy lives. I pray she lives that long, to the day when all that she can see will be her own.

The Crows (Jeanette 2)

The hollow field, stripped of corn and stalks, is carpeted by dozens of them. When a car passes, they all take flight at once, a black cloud against October's sharp blue sky. I'm told they have two languages. One, the familiar social call, the caw-caw announcing: I am here. The other is quieter. A low chirping spoken only in the family nest, nothing meant for outsiders.

I ride the elevators with my sister, who is dying and needs new lungs. The hospital is enormous, a hollow concrete box that towers dozens of stories into the sky, digs dozens of stories below. We travel from floor to floor, lab to lab, doctor to doctor. Everyone measures something but no one makes any promises. In this, they are all very precise.

When a crow dies, others will gather in a tree above the dead. No language here, only silent observation, a voiceless wake. When it's time, each bird will know to fly off alone.

We hadn't spoken for months when I heard my friend had died. I knew it was inevitable, but tried to pretend that silence was equal to salvation, a miracle cure for the cancer that consumed her. Now I hear her voice in my head. She is laughing. We always spoke quietly, privately, with a trust not meant for others' ears.

My sister doesn't say anything after the last appointment, just finds me reading in the waiting room and says, "Let's go home." The list, it seems, is not for her. The line for a new set of lungs is long, and her body is starved for oxygen. We don't speak on the drive back.

A murder of crows. Such a menacing name for these intelligent birds. Studies show they possess long-term memory, are as intelligent as a typical three-year-old. When I was a boy, a neighbor kept one as a pet. It loved shiny things, would fly down to snatch up a foil gum wrapper or a lost ring, anything that glinted in the sun, caught the light in a way that made it radiant.

We sit, silent, in the living room as the television rambles and the cats seek out the last of the late afternoon sun. Silence is the secret language in our family, the long gaps between what we can and cannot say. She dozes under a heavy quilt as I stare out the picture window, then get up slowly and walk away.

Richard Robbins

Betrayals

1. Memoir

My life isn't that important, but I remember that afternoon
seeing you run away and only get so far. You cried on the
lawn next to your lawn. The high hedge grew mountainous
between them. You'd wrapped your things in a bandana and
tied them to the end of a stick. Behind you, the shrub bent
with its load of pomegranates. On the ground, one of the
globes had torn open, spilling its red tears. I left my Chinese
elm and crossed the street to sit down with you. The man who
owned that lawn, the man we hardly ever saw, flew a biplane
along the coast of North Africa. He smuggled guns for
Tunisian rebels. He had ripped off the ears of temporary cap-
tors. He had left scorpions in the limp gloves of spies. We
wondered if his curtains would suddenly open and we'd see
him again at his picture window, like that time he sat there
all month, his arm in plaster, his forehead stitched, smoking
cigarette after cigarette and grinning as he exhaled, grinning
as the smoke snaked back into his nose.

We lay on our backs, the grass itching our necks. Now
there was the sky deep blue with autumn, and now there was
the problem of how to go back home. In your bandana was a
pair of socks, a change of underwear, the missal you received
for your First Communion, a Werewolf comic book, a Mars
bar, a pencil with a broken tip, a travel comb, a Stardust Hotel
ash tray you used to keep coins in before you ran away, one
three-cent postcard stamp, a piece of chalk taken from Mrs.
McGovern's classroom, a Charles Atlas ad snipped from the

230

back of another comic book, a length of yarn, a skate key. Now there was the problem of how to go back home. All your things spread out like items at a sad picnic. Under them, a paisley pattern rippled across the uneven altitudes of grass.

You broke the Mars bar in half and shared it. There were lines on your cheeks where tears had cut trails through the dust. You gathered your bundle together. You broke the stick in half and threw it under the hedge. You made me swear I never saw you cry. We crossed our hearts. The green of that street scratched us. The blue of that street made us shiver. A stranger might have watched through the drapes. I crossed my heart. My life doesn't add up to much, but that was the moment I betrayed you, even though it took all these years until now to see it through.

2. Starch

When it rains, he thinks of the cleaners, the shop smothering with steam presses, the breathable air leaching starch. What a pleasure to walk out the front door to an offshore breeze salty and cold. Any direction made sense, uptown or toward the beach. Any place waves broke within earshot and swallows patched their mud nests above him.

That day the crazy lance corporal puked his guts on the counter, slammed down his laundry, shot himself in the head. That day. No one on the sidewalk saw through the fogged-up window. No one in the back—blind-stitching trouser cuffs, bundling fluff-dry in blue crinkly wrap—heard a thing until the second round of screams from the high-school girl at the till. She dragged her way to the back, small red planets on her sleeve. She'd been screaming since it happened. He'd been sewing red chevrons on a pair of dress blues.

What happened next made no sense at all, how she exited to the alley, leaned over the hood of a car like she was praying, looked up between the backs of buildings at one cloud like she was praying, until the policeman with a small notebook asked her to come inside and sit down, and she said *No, let's talk out here,* and he said *No,* standing at the door, waves of heat pushing their way around him into the alley's fetid air. *No,* he told her, *you need to do right now what I say.*

3. Marks

When I was a kid, two Japanese monks dressed in long robes appeared on a TV variety show. One held a samurai sword, the other an armful of different-sized fruit. One monk lay down on his back and balanced a watermelon on his stomach. The other raised the sword high over his head and brought it down in a flash until the two halves of watermelon fell to the floor. The monk on his back was clearly untouched by the blade.

The two men switched roles. One monk placed the curve of a banana on the curve of his head. The other swung a wide, horizontal arc so that, after the blade penetrated the fruit, one third fell to the right shoulder of the monk, one third fell to the left, and the middle third balanced on the flat, upturned side of the sword. Not a strand of hair had moved. The monks dealt in their turn with an orange, a kiwi, and finally two blueberries poised in the cleft of one man's chin.

After I moved out of the house, my first roommate hated that I would slice an onion without a cutting board under it. I asked her to show me any marks I had made on the countertop, but she never could find them. Many years later, a man I loved claimed all I needed to do was to run my hands over his stomach before he could feel tiny slices being made of his liver. He sometimes woke up choking in the middle of the night after dreaming I had kissed him, turning his tongue to filets.

As Lao-Tzu might say, the vegetable cuts as deep as the knife. The potato skin lets the blade in, but it reaches around the knife too, almost as if a grief lived in the steel, some hard sharp thing only a milky juice could soothe. You or I might watch this and not know anything is happening. We'd look for marks but find nothing.

4. A Map of the World

Maybe we have come finally that far, where the afternoon of lazy reading in the heat no longer matters, only planting perennials near the billion-year-old gneiss, only buying grain without stone, grain without its hound's tooth of blood. We could try to move back to the last city. From the bridge, we could see the backs of trout then, rippling green as green water, nosing toward the sea. The horse met us at the back fence, taking off the tops of our roses. We fed it apples any way. Our child lay new to us on new grass.

Maybe this street has already tricked its neighbors, routed them elsewhere toward oblivion of pine or static. Somehow we have come finally far enough to know we're hearing this intersection for the first time, without echo. The car driving by carries teenagers talking, talking, each on the way to some ultimate damage. Chickadees tick in the elm.

Or maybe the map, the first dreamscape, made a place for us here. After the woman had the house built, after homes surrounded the farmstead, after covenants against Jews and Indians, after oak, maple, and plum set their roots, after the next woman died ironing in the basement, after one across the street lost her daughter, after the man down the block his arm, after the trolley disappeared right in front of them, after a tornado three streets away, after the rage one summer burning the near part of town, after flooding creek bed and river, after music came down from the sky one warm, humid night,

233

the insects humming.

After a long winter, neighbors sit on their front steps. Others are doing the same thing on the other side of the world.

The world gave us wind, the breath between human beings. It gave us the road shoulder anywhere on earth, a place between the blue lines of a map. What do we say to the others when their rice reaches our plate. What do they say to us, wearing shorts and shirts we recognize. What do they say to us, waving their greeting, the day we march, a slow green wall, into their veins.

Jim Ruland

At the Orpheu Café

Séance

Oh, it looks cheerful enough now: blue wallpaper blooming with fat bright birds and red flowers. Opposite, a bench with a headboard and enough crushed green velvet to fashion cloaks for a dozen nymphs of the forest. Baristas invite you to be comfortable as they place dainty cups of strong Portuguese coffee and sweating glasses of lemonade with mint and cinnamon on your table. But after hours, when the café is closed to regular customers, the lights are dimmed, the candelabras lit, and the séance commences. James Joyce and Fernando Pessoa shuffle in through the back entrance, each mistaking the other for Charlie Chaplin, and talk for hours about nothing but poontang, poontang, poontang.

Pharmacy

The bar is a nurse's station where the prescription is always booze. The diners wander about a sloping green lawn like inmates at an asylum. Someone shouts, "Nurse, I'm worse!" while we go off the rails on medicinal gin, awful in any dosage. Let's play thousand-yard stare. I'll be Wilfred Owen. You be Siegfried Sassoon. On a table draped with a cloth of deepest burgundy we draw up plans for the coming skirmish. We're going to need Cuban cigars and Italian espresso. Definitely champagne. Possibly lube. A busker performs feats of beggarly magic. Bullshit with fire and burning tobacco that's hard to ignore. Sunlight swims across the satellite dishes. Vendors prepare the fish snacks and chocolate sausages. The bill is presented in a plastic pill bottle, like a message washed up on the shore. We take cover under canopies like sailboats keeled over on their sides. Balloons blow over the churches, giving away our position. We dash to the sea and wait for friendly fire to chop us down.

Missed Connection

The Estonian barista needs a hug. Cold rain smears the windows all year round in this place where summer is a euphemism for being aroused by advertisements for tanning oil. The sun here is indifferent. Only the flatness is exceptional. Tumbleweeds, wind chimes, and kites have been outlawed, and all the wind does is blow. He is the only one in the airport who hears the cold electronic ambiance. A soundtrack to the terminal drama of ceaseless coming and going. It is meant to soothe the harried travelers but it pools in his ears like sludge. The barista has a Baltic brain and a Mediterranean soul. He can grind your beans in one hundred and fifty three languages, but can only say, "I love you" in one.

F. Daniel Rzicznek

from *Leafmold*

Like a bug, I was born in August, well outside the panoramic winter. Under the influence of mercenaries, I woke with the rain between my teeth and the citadel looming on the mother-of-pearl cloudiness. It's best to go all the way out where the houses end, lift a handful of dust and lose it, little by little, until you're halfway back to all of it. The lords reveal themselves as green, quietly rustling stands of grass. Guided by long-horned beetles, by cuckoo wasps, I practice compassionate aggression in this unwindowed greenhouse, like a heart searing inside a postulant—nearly scientific the way it caverns, daubers, sixes me; sixed, caverned, daubered like a wasp nest smoking to match the dusk. The green, quietly. The mother-of-pearl, the teeth, and the citadel. There were waves like hair beneath the boat—the sea-hair, the sought-for romance materializing above the invaders' halberds, and then the planks crashing forward, the disco of all those feet hitting the glop, souls spilling through the eye of the surgeon's enslaved needle. (Empty suits and empty ties crashing forward.) Death to the Crusades! *In death, I draw the line.*

*   *   *

Fluked tail after fluked tail breaking the sea's onyx surface when longships rolled in great herds and the careless stars were busy predicting napalm and microchips. No more will I turn away from it—a thing is a thing is a thing. *Always*: time and space plucking kisses at last in the roughest of forms, a word—one that strikes endless paths in every direction at once. Achilles, in his tent, hears owl music and he wails like

237

a widower. The difference, topographically, between Mexico and Texas is not so strenuous—the Gulf insists it all is one. Nothing blazes a trail into memory like an object. Exposed roots submerged in snow, miles of rock and debris beneath our unsteady feet—the dog and I hear a weathervane screech in the night and we dash indoors. Anyhow above over and beyond: air becomes our last limb eventually. Crossing out a line, you feel the universe's temper buckle—and brightly-plumed birds pour from the seam.

*   *   *

I write with green ink to fool the crows—they think the words *grass* and *turn away*. I become a shadow again. Snow falling against thought, or really just the thought of snow falling against itself—laughter in the next room. To take, to buy, to burn, to meddle, to withdraw, to rehearse, to pour out—to sneeze and almost immediately sneeze a second time. Don't eat a whole roll of mints at once, don't push a boulder off a cliff onto poor Piggy's head, don't dye your hair in the middle of the day, don't turn a reward into a punishment, don't forget to say "God bless you" and don't forget to mean it. Three dreams in a night: a woman I know and her nonexistent identical twin attack me with a pressure washer, cackling—it's quite humiliating; at the edge of an invented park in Dearborn, Michigan, I argue with an old man over the body of a dead mallard; the dog has grown wings and is flying with a pack of geese, a silver ring through his nose—I follow him home by it.

*   *   *

As if the world was coming to me from ten angles at once only to collapse after passing. A hundred years from now they'll say we lived in a simpler time. Cold as the grave but clear tonight—ochre devils hiding in the grass and cursing in French. A well made of wood or a well made of stones? A well made of wood and stones? I spent an hour over bad Thai noodles and gravy with green-bottled beer wondering how to make you happy while also making myself happy. Sharp-shinned hawk, here is my heart for you to carry above the mountains. Here is my pride, my wakefulness, my lust, my generosity. Too muddy—the brain muddy and magenta spikes of whiplash muddying the corner of meadow still visible, the brain rewinding forward into nowhere. Samson running rabbits through fog in his sleep—scrape of nails against your leg and lazy whimperings. I wake and the world bottoms out—the wake is you, beloved—morning bulldozing itself back into poppies and rainwater, a (what is it, what do I conjure?) nothing—be nothing now, be nothing, be still. Yes: always two things at once.

*　*　*

Burial at sea! Burial at sea! A shadow rages below—voluminous disasters notwithstanding, here's an apple, here's a pear, here's black mud in your November ear. The fire surgeon came too late—my alter ego's doppelganger now reconstituted. No sense of season: self-flagellation, hot candle wax down a shirtsleeve, a hammer in the hand of a dormant seraph. Crazy before your time with rocks blinking awake beneath holy floorboards: in my sleep I climb large stones backwards—hooking my feet over the tops and pulling myself up upside-down. And I see two green, high-backed chairs in an anteroom of sorrow. Upward across the mountain by car: two deer cautiously chewing in the wood-shade. A thing asks me a question about the desert—where does the face of God hide there—in what tunnel of rock did the sunlight first descend—in what strange hall did I touch the last oak of a dead forest? I refuse to describe it because it has yet to happen—something crashes in the next room followed by young pigs squealing.

*   *   *

Death slaps a paw on your shoulder and you laugh—that skeletal lion in a black robe is just as unreal as you happen to be. Months later, the pen begins to move again—painful, cautious, but continuous, like someone walking into a hospital. Time to put my mask back to my face and sleep in the woods—the smell of the open sea unlocking the microscopic door at the base of my skull. I haven't set foot in this room for what feels like a heaven-sized eternity (cloud-rot, tarnished gowns, and a mouthful of nettles). Fate flashes by— a thing that happens with no one present. A notion from an older world—a chance that takes itself and takes itself and takes itself. I could never sleep in the woods. See where the fabric fails—never torn, merely unwoven? The raft of smoke threatens always to reappear—old animals flying against the Amazon wind at noonday. A politician walks out of the hospital with her lips sewn together—again and again and again and again and again.

*   *   *

I'm in paradise with my mother watching swans fly the marsh—windmills on the loose, white blades locking over mud the color of dark tea. Paradise is the epicenter of confusion. I am in paradise with my father maintaining a delusional calm. Paradise is the desert of inheritance. I'm in paradise with my mother, muttering apologies to her. Paradise is the transaction of agreeing on a radio station. I'm in paradise in the car with Amanda, the windows down, the windows up. Paradise is choosing not to answer the phone, and also choosing not to hear it. *Not to own a phone.* I'm in paradise with Amanda now that we're married and swimming it and not

240

talking on the phone so much. Paradise is the fragrance of day-old sweat. I'm in paradise with my late self. Paradise is being late for work—being diligently late for work. I'm in paradise with my childhood undergoing the miles from here to there. Paradise is a fitful night by the river's edge. I'm in paradise with nothing in particular—exactly, in fact, in-between things and not thinking much. *Not thinking much.*

Lucas Southworth

A Dainty Network of Bones

Bluebeard was a killer. Pursuing young women kept him rapt with pleasure. To marry them, to place the cold keys in their palms. An obsession is always an obsession, and Bluebeard gave them one. Then he waited, his hands tightening to little fists. For a while, he hoped his wives could withstand. He whispered: You must resist so I can resist. But soon each wife would fit that smallest key into that smallest keyhole. And Bluebeard would lick his lips to stop the tingle.

Deep in his crumbling castle, the dragon slept alongside his treasure. Mostly, people were too afraid to approach him, and the dragon wanted this. He knew the edge of the world should remain a lonely place. That humans must not tiptoe to it or topple over. Sometimes knights tried sneaking into the dragon's decrepit corridors. Wrapped in dirty and dull armor, they moved slowly. They carried swords so heavy they could barely lift them. On by one, the dragon killed these knights, keeping safe his gold coins, his goblets, his fair-haired maidens.

The ogres were killers too, as were their cousins, the trolls and giants. To them, killing was living, as natural as river water cascading over rocks, or earthworms surfacing to drown in the rain. These ogres, these trolls, these giants, were protectors. They guarded places that were supposed to remain empty: the stinking bog, the cragged gorge, the sky. Something had to keep the humans from crossing where they didn't belong. Something had to shield the world from too much beauty. So the ogres, the trolls and giants, destroyed what they could. They kept the scales balanced. They held things in line. Rarely did they consider the future. If they did, they imagined the impossible: a time when all the world reeked with the bad breath of cannibals.

On her birthday, the witch moved into a house of gingerbread and candy. Lounging in a new armchair, she smiled, dusted her hands. But soon she discovered she couldn't eat the food that surrounded her. Good things like sugar and candy had no taste; they churned in her mouth like concrete. She'd built this house, never intending it to be a trap. Now it lured children, fattened them up. Guilt is always guilt, but comfort and survival are more necessary. Before long the witch had little trouble slitting the children from end to end, scraping fat from the inside of their skins. There were so many of them, the witch reasoned. So many uncared for. So many unwanted. Each year she needed only two to stay warm and alive. Who could deny her these basic pleasures?

Since a pup, the wolf had always lived a life of hunger. Pain had always needled his stomach; his limbs had always shook. But when he spotted his prey—the rabbit, the squirrel, the little child—he didn't pounce. He folded up his claws and teeth, and began to play. Laughing, he juggled the squirrels and mice. Grinning, he strung rabbits by the ears and tickled their bellies with the tip of his tongue. When children came along, the wolf spoke to them. He promised them beautiful flowers and enticed them from the path. For a while, these entertainments helped the wolf forget his hunger. They helped him forget the difference between instinct and lies, games and death.

Sometimes humans could be killers; sometimes they even killed each other. There was one who kept severed heads in

243

his refrigerator. In his closet, skulls and bones. In the freezer, a human heart. To the killer, this heart stood for love, and love for loneliness, and loneliness for sex. At night, the smell was awful. It was intoxicating. Lying in bed, the killer remembered all the bodies. The ones he'd entered, the ones he'd split in half. He recalled how, in fits of rage, he'd once tried eating them. The flesh had tasted terrible, but the killer had swallowed anyway, hoping it might be the thing to finally fill him. In the freezer, it didn't take long for the heart to turn gray, chip with ice. The killer never touched it. He never freed it from the cold.

Like all killers, Bluebeard's house was his body, and the twists of the hallways the twists of his mind. He enjoyed removing eyeballs with a spoon, unwrapping flesh from the fingers until a dainty network of bones lay cradled in his palm. Bluebeard loved his prey; he'd married it, brought it here, chained it up. Once disassembled, each wife became a skeleton, a collection of pieces and parts. Their shrieks, free from their bodies, wandered the dark corridors for hours until they collapsed, exhausted on the dirty stones. And at night, their dead voices rose up again, curling. Be proud you are not like me, Bluebeard told them. And soon they understood. Still, he would not open the door. He would not allow them to lose themselves among the weeds.

Like all killers, the wolf knew the forest well. He knew the safe places and didn't hunt there. He'd found that deceit was best: costumes, a slight change of inflection, a thatch of ferns, a concealing shadow. To be a hunter is always to hunt. To kill is always to use one's teeth and claws. And the wolf's sad knowledge was that more prey would always come skipping down the path. Like all hunters, his pleasure had never been in the killing and eating. The wolf knew that once he'd killed, once he'd eaten, the hunger would only return. So his pleasure remained in the moment he spied the children in red; the moment he devised a plan. They were the perfect prey, these children. They were never in a hurry; they were always willing to trust, to be led away. And to comfort them, the wolf ran a paw along their cheeks. To forget his hunger, he attempted to coax them into his mouth.

Wherever the ogres and trolls and giants walked, fire spurted from the ground. Howls came from their stomachs. Birds stayed hidden in trees. Protecting the mud and air was a quiet curse. Humans were adept at filling space. They carried beauty with them; they created it anew. Soon they would build bridges and plod across. Soon they would dare to sprout wings. Soon they would harden the ground with sand. So the ogres and trolls and giants killed quickly: a rock to the skull, a slash of the axe, a snap of the neck. Separated from the safety of their cities, the humans were small and weak. They begged for mercy. Each day, after the killing was finished, the ogres and trolls and giants scattered back to the ugly dark, leaving the bodies behind, bleeding in the sun.

At the end of the world, the scorched bodies of knights lay about the floor. In the corners, piles of bones, cleaned by rats and mice, climbed the walls. It was cold, and the dragon shivered. He spouted a bit of fire to warm the room. Outside, the wind hurtled itself against the faces of the cliffs. He knew these knights had been determined once. Once, they'd been a part of their own valiant stories. They'd heard tales of those who'd managed to kill the dragon. They'd believed them; they'd tried to write one themselves. Ambitions are always ambitions, and they will always stretch too far. As long as there is a dragon, humans will always seek to kill him. They will always fail.

After months of eating candy, the children had gained enough fat for the witch to fry their fingers a thousand times. They had gained enough fat for the witch to heat her house the entire winter. On the morning the witch planned to kill and clean these children, she sharpened her dagger. Catching her reflection in the kitchen mirror, she recognized the nasty blade, the cruel and wretched face. The witch knew she was a killer. She understood that in the end, killers are killed too. They are outsmarted, outmuscled. They are taken in by their victims. So when the children pushed her and she stumbled into the burning heat, the witch wasn't surprised. In the oven, her skin bubbled and blistered. Around her, gumdrops sizzled; sugar browned and charred; gingerbread walls, once so sturdy, folded in on themselves. The witch didn't cry or complain. She knew that living was a pleasure. She knew how easily it would end.

And then there's the human killer, the killer of humans. Nothing is valiant about the end of his story. Yet we tell it: a victim abducted, drugged, tied up, somehow managing to slip away. Free from the apartment, the victim ran barefoot across the street. Blood flowed down his face; blood flowed down the insides of his thighs. He didn't notice the bruises until the police stopped him. He didn't notice he couldn't speak until they started asking him questions. Under the streetlamp, the victim stood dumb, marveling at the loveliness of his own hands. He finally led the police to the bodies of those who had not escaped, and they found the decaying parts cooling in the fridge and swimming in vats of acid and oil. Years passed before the human killer was murdered in prison. But as he died, he remembered the gray heart in his freezer and how he'd once considered opening his own chest, shoving the dead thing inside.

Things are often simple. Sometimes, they are not. These are the killers that haunted my youth. They are the reason I am afraid of heights. The reason I stay away from places I don't belong. Why I refuse to open my eyes in the dark. To kill is always to kill, but to be a killer is something else. So if you're thinking of it, come with me down the path. We'll bring a full basket, a full bottle of wine. We'll stroll toward edge of the world. Together, we'll bring our bodies so we can feel pain. Together, we'll bring our lives so we can lose them.

Julie Stotz-Ghosh

Haiku Sequence for Snow

1.

Frances counts syllables in the first poem of her new series: "Haiku Sequence for Snow." *All afternoon, low gray clouds.* Seven. Living in Michigan, you know snow is coming when the clouds get low and gray, light gray, like cement (not the angry, dark gray of thunder clouds, the kind that seem to roll in, the kind that tower and intimidate). Snow clouds cover the sky like a blanket, but she can't write "cover the sky like a blanket." She can't write that snow clouds and short December days make her sad; she has to show it. *Wind chases snow down the street.* Seven. She is snow; wind is sadness. *Wind makes sport of snow.* Five. She doesn't think you'll understand.

She's tired of games. She wants to write: *I'm lonely in my house because even the furnace sounds like wind whipping snow off the roof,* but she can't write, "like wind whipping snow." She wants to write: *Icicles look sinister like pointed animal teeth along the gutters of my neighbors' houses*, but she can't write, "like pointed animal teeth." She wants to write: *My brother is unfairly mad at me because I forgot to pay him for the honey he gave me straight from the hives of his bees, the honey he had to boil especially for me so that I could give it as holiday presents to my neighbors who live inside ice-covered homes,* but she can't write, "hives of his bees," or "holiday presents," or "ice-covered homes," and don't even bother counting the syllables.

248

She feels ice-covered. She wants you to know that it's a metaphor for loss. She's afraid you won't understand. She wants to write, *I lost a baby*. Five. But she can't write "baby" or "lost."

2.

When she was young enough to curl into small spaces, Frances liked to fall asleep like a cat against her mother in the blue light of late-night news shows. In the blue light of the ultrasound room, Frances watches images that look like snow-covered mountains—outer space satellite transmissions of white river beds. The technician maps out hills and valleys, measures distances. Everything is winter. Outside, December breaks its promise. Snow melts—drips and slides off buildings and cars. Icicles fall wickedly in chunks from eaves.

When it's time to leave, Frances can't remember where she parked her car. People walk in circles around her, talking loudly.

Laura Tansley

The Wake She Leaves like a Whirlpool

Something must have happened between then and now, here and there, because Imogen has been ignoring my smiles. It becomes clear I've done something wrong when she pulls my hand from the small of her back like a plug from a sink. I washed your hair earlier, I think; washed it clean of the gel and wax you use that leaves a damp film on my pillows, and there are only so many times I can turn them over.

She plays with the snags of skin around her nails while we wait for our table. I drink Campari to pass the time and bang my knees on the glass front of the bar when I try to cross my legs. Perhaps tomorrow I'll prove this with dark, blue bruises.

I ask her to delete the short film of me she has on her phone. "It's unflattering," I say with a smirk, hoping to prick the tension. "I don't like where it centers."

Imogen runs a hand through her hair, pulling away loose threads. She stretches strands over the flame of a candle till they fizzle like a fuse and snap.

*   *   *

Victorian lamps and the film of cloud that lies over the city keep me warm, but in the shadow of the arches of the viaduct I notice the goosebumps on the parts of my skin that are exposed, hairs raised in anxiety since she walked out during dessert. Maybe by the time I get home, by the time I boil the kettle and fill the teapot, by the time she has decided to come home, I will know how to soak this all up, wring it all out.

*   *   *

There was a time when she gnawed my fingers, chewing an ache like growing pains into my bones. She liked to bite her way into the center of attention, to carve an impression with her teeth. At parties she'd reach across conversations to leave little purple punctuations in my skin.

*   *   *

CrownGate shopping center is full of the hulks of black and empty buses. She slept in one once, broke in and made a bed across a row of seats because coming home hard and angry wasn't enough, she wanted me haunted. So I stand on tiptoes, peer through the curved glass that makes a mockery of my face, looking for signs of her.

*   *   *

Imogen doesn't have periods; she's got an implant which stops them. It makes my pallor all the more noticeable when I get my own, when it feels as if my skin is being stretched. But my time of the month has become exhausting because of the weight of her. A pale film of desire and frustration settles over her round face. She is rampant, and crosses her fingers when they're inside me.

*   *   *

As I cross the Severn Bridge I think I can see Imogen coming out of the hedged entrance of Cripplegate Park, but it's not her. This woman isn't walking slowly, holding her weight on each hip for long enough to think she might pause, for long enough to think she might sit down there-and-then like a child having a tantrum. The possibility of her, the rumor of her, is like the sweat that runs down a cold bottle of something, of beer, of water, of wine. And when she's not here there's not much else to say except that hopefully she'll be back soon.

* * *

The street lamps cause a shimmer on the cling-film that covers my wrist and hand and I think again about how I'm going to get money out of my bag, sign my name if I need to, or go to the bathroom. My arm stays bent upwards, poised in the air, while the rest of me slides across the back seat of the black cab as it moves through the center of town. Warmth comes in waves like cross words from the puckered skin. I should tell Imogen, tell her what happened. How the lid of the kettle, if you pour it like that, at the wrong angle, will fall open. How a blister can appear in an instant, needs no friction sometimes, but boils up from underneath. I take my phone out of my pocket but only check the time.

* * *

I'll call her eventually. She won't speak but I know she'll cross herself. Not for me, but for the benefit of whoever is around. Two fingers touching the skin of her forehead, her chest, the left shoulder, and then the right. She'll hang up and say, "needs her Imogen," to whoever she's with, but there'll be time to finish her drink first. It will play out like a film; a chase down a hospital corridor, a reunion, a kiss. Her at the center of it all.

Bob Thurber

ABCDEFG

(A)

I met her at a CYO dance I wasn't supposed to be at because I was neither a dancer nor a Catholic. Her name was Donna. She wasn't pretty and she wasn't rich but her daddy owned a business and her family lived in a big house with a wrap-around porch, which made them rich in my book.

After one slow dance, before I even knew her name, she let me French kiss her between the air conditioner and the Coke machine. She had a wide mouth overcrowded with perfectly straight teeth and a tongue like an angry snake.

(B)

Eighteen months later, I suggested we climb a mountain, a small mountain. I studied some maps, found a low peak. A short, zigzagging, two-mile hike. She had scaled a few mountains prior, and I had camped on a couple of steep hillsides with the Scouts, but this was our first mountain together. We planned to kiss at the summit. She didn't know about the ring. To be safe we had each invited a pair of friends to climb along and witness our affections, and to help carry sandwiches, water and wine, and add to the general spirit and to the joy. Plus, I wanted pictures taken of me proposing on one knee. In a clearing marked "Last Trash Can" we broke for lunch. Cold air swallowed us up. People and warnings started float-

253

ing down. Hikers hurried past us, shouting downhill. The weather had shifted. There was wind and ice and snow above the tree line. Ruddy-faced climbers with backpacks and knitted caps turned back. We had nothing. We were six kids in denim jackets. We were children.

(C)

At the altar, while reciting my vows, which I had written a week earlier and thoroughly memorized—a sort of long rambling prose poem expressing loyalty, devotion, joy, happiness, really sappy stuff, most of it penned while I was stoned—about halfway through, my throat tightened up and my voice broke into this shrill falsetto one might expect from a prepubescent choir boy. My knees and elbows began to shake; one leg felt ready to buckle; I thought I was going down faster than you can say "Take this ring."

My bride detected my malfunction in a heartbeat. Under the pretense of adjusting her veil, she poked her elbow into my ribcage. The jab made me flinch, straighten, and gulp for breath.

Turns out a little air was all I needed.

Two or three slow breaths later, still shaky but less woozy, I prepared to continue from where I'd left off. Problem was my mind had gone blank. Though I knew my lines by heart, and could have recited them from the beginning, mentally I'd lost my place. For a long moment the church was as quiet as a funeral. The priest wavered his eyebrows. The pretty bride shuffled her feet.

At a traditional Catholic ceremony the veil remains down until the very end, so I couldn't see Donna's face, but fearing another jab I coughed to clear my throat then skipped over everything I had written, summing up in a croaky but level voice that I'd love Donna all the days of my life.

No one but the priest had reviewed my notes, so no one else in attendance was the wiser. The thing is, I left out a substantial portion of what I had intended to say that morning, much of it gushy and sentimental, though all of it heartfelt. Considering how things ended up—the marriage imploded after eighteen months—that's just as well. More than a dozen people were videotaping, making a permanent record, and I'd really hate for Donna—or anyone for that matter—to know what a lovesick fool I was back then.

(D)

Our first weekend back from the honeymoon we went to a Chinese restaurant on Mineral Spring Avenue in Pawtucket. We sat in a padded booth, waiting for menus, staring at eachother across the Formica tabletop with our placemats showing the signs of the Chinese zodiac.

I didn't know anything about the Chinese zodiac but within minutes I discovered my new wife had been born in the year of the tiger while I had been born in the year of the snake.

When I pointed that out to her, she didn't seem impressed. An Asian girl brought us menus. They were like a giant children's book: six pages of block type surrounded by drawings of red dragons attacking Chinese sailing ships.

"Are we going to get a bunch of side dishes to split or eat separate meals?"

"I don't know what I want," I said.

I remember her lighting a cigarette in that hollow-cheek fashion that she always used to light her cigarettes, every one. She was six weeks pregnant, already hurting the baby's lungs, heart and brain, but we didn't know that yet.

Streaming smoke at me, she said, "Why the look?" and I kept staring, straining my muscles to balance the corners of my face, thinking, God damn, this crude smile is going to collapse and give me away, tip my hand, reveal my honest feelings. And that was the first time I admitted to myself that we weren't going to make it, no matter what I said. So I recorded that moment like a history lesson, taking special note of the brief life we had shared.

(E)

I was having trouble finding a place I could afford. Every night I slept on the couch. She still did my laundry and made my meals. I still helped with the baby. Day after day we talked about how things would be after. These discussions were uncommonly civil and frank. I began to look forward to them.

I think we were chatting about how often I would visit and how much I would pay, when out of nowhere she slapped me.

I could take a slap in those days. It didn't faze me. I didn't do more than blink.

After a long silence she raised her arm like she was winding up for a second shot, then slowly brought her hand to her mouth. Tears streamed down her cheeks.

"Hurt your hand?" I said.

She nodded, trembling all over.

"Let me see."

"It's all right," she said.

"Let me have a look."

She shook her head no, then extended the hand, limp, listless.

I held it, rubbed my thumb across her knuckles, then turned it over and looked at her palm.

It was flushed red but it looked all right.

"It hurts," she said

"Can you move your fingers?"

She moved one after another until she'd moved them all. Her eyes looked raw.

"You know I'll never forgive you," she said. "You know that, right?"

(F)

My first night in that cramped, attic room I didn't sleep. Not a wink. I simply lay on my back, still as a corpse, sunk deep into the bowed, rank-smelling mattress. I thought about a great number of things, including my wife, while listening to the sounds of mice scurrying through the walls. Of course, I didn't know they were mice. I mistook the scratchy noise for the tapping of summer rain upon the roof.

The room I'd rented was a windowless space adjacent to a filthy kitchen shared by eight other roomers, all men, all of us running away from something. Each night mice traveled past my room and squeezed though holes and cracks to raid our kitchen. Previous roomers had plugged many of these entrances with cardboard and scraps of wood, but they hadn't gotten all of them, and each night the mice came and went pretty much as they pleased.

Every morning we would assess the damage—the half-gnawed boxes of corn flakes, oatmeal, pasta. We'd follow the path of mouse droppings back to some new entry point. Then seal that hole as best we could.

There was more to it, of course. The agonizing day-to-day, the petty arguments and drunken fights. Sometimes a death due to a heart attack, or an overdose. But essentially that is how we lived, tracing trails of mouse shit, discovering holes then blocking them, setting traps, spreading poison, working collectively, until someone moved out or got themselves evicted, or returned to his wife, leaving the rest of us to carry on, battling things we couldn't see.

(G)

One Saturday, shortly after all the papers had been filed and we were just waiting for the court to make it official, she called and said, "What are you doing?"

I said, "Laundry. Why?"

She said, "Feel like chatting?"

And the way she overextended her syllables made me suspect she had been drinking.

"Where's the baby," I said.

"At my mom's, why?"

"How is she," I said.

"My mother?"

"No. My daughter".

After a long silence, she said, "We're all absolutely fine, thank you for asking."

And that came out bitter and cold, like she wasn't quite drunk enough.

So I explained how things worked with a shared laundry room in a house with eight other tenants.

"Oh, poor you," she said.

I said, "Is there something special you wanted?"

And she said, "Yeah. I wanted you to know that somehow someway I'm going to make you fall in love with me again."

"What would be the point of that," I said.

"Just to make you hurt," she said.

(H)

On the Fourth of July I stopped by the house to hand over money and drop off a box of sparklers for my daughter. She was far too young to hold one herself but I thought she'd enjoy watching the fizzle and spark.

Naturally, Donna wanted to talk again, even though there was nothing left to talk about. And wouldn't be, not for a good long while. I had signed a lease, put down a security deposit, advanced two months rent.

She nursed the baby to sleep, showing more breast than she needed to. Then she set the kid on the La-Z-Boy and boxed her in with a couch pillow. We split a beer and smoked a thin joint. I wondered where she had found money to buy marijuana.

The smoke tasted cool, sweet, thick. Really potent shit. We got goofy high and I suggested we go outside and burn the sparklers.

She said, "Sure, but I want to show you something first." Then she led me by the hand into the bedroom. She crossed her arms around my neck and said, "Miss me?"

I didn't know what to answer so I kissed her very hard on the mouth. But after five minutes I got sick of kissing her. I pushed her onto the bed and rolled her over. She pretended she was dead. I lifted her skirt and she propped up on her elbows. "Careful, that's silk," she said.

Her underwear was printed with rows of pink hearts. I pulled the fabric to one side. "Let me do it," she said.

It had been months since we'd touched with any degree of kindness. I couldn't remember the last time we'd made love in daylight. I heard the baby squeak from the other room. The kid was waking up, so I put my hand on the back of D's neck and pushed her face into the pillows.

She raised her ass a little higher.

259

"Be nice," she said.

Those words were the last in a long series of serious misinterpretations between us.

Alison Townsend

Coyote Crossings

I saw the animal on my way home from the dog park. It was crossing the ice on the Rutland-Dunn Road Marsh. At first, I didn't understand what I was seeing. The long, bushy, black tail, the pointed ears, and narrow, pointed face all looked dog-like, resembling the two collies panting in the back seat. *Was it a German shepherd?* I wondered. *Or maybe a small Alaskan husky? What was a dog doing out there, alone on the ice?* I could feel my mind twist and turn in its traces, as it does when we attempt to register exactly what lies before us. *Who would let their dog run loose that way?* Then I noticed the tail again. It was carried down, not up and waving or straight out behind, like a dog or wolf. I noted the animal's rich rust-colored coat and the smooth efficiency of its loping gait. It was a coyote. A coyote, in the middle of the day, though they are diurnal, active primarily at dawn or dusk. *What was it doing out there?* Worried, I slowed the car, straining to see more clearly. The ice looked thin. Farmers shoot coyotes around here. It was on Department of Natural Resources land and there isn't a single hunting restriction on coyotes in Wisconsin. Then, as if it knew all these things, the coyote covered the rest of the white expanse in a few quick steps and was gone, disappearing like smoke into the woods.

One day early last fall, as I set out for the long walk that has, with mid-life and injuries, replaced running for me, I encountered a dead coyote. I was less than a quarter mile out when I saw something large, brown, and motionless at the side of our road. *Dog,* I thought, my mind conducting the same riffle

261

it did with the coyote at the marsh. Looking closer, I took in the lean torso, the slender, fox-like muzzle, the long legs and lanky build. It was a coyote. A perfect, beautiful, dead coyote, with the thick, cinnamon brown-colored plush of its winter coat just coming in. The tire tracks leading to its body through tall grass suggested that someone had swerved, hitting it deliberately, as I have heard some in this state do for "sport." Although I have seen coyotes many times, it was the closest I have ever been to a one. And it was dead. I stood beside the body for a long time, memorizing its shape, color, and dimensions, one hand over my heart, saying a prayer for its spirit. The walk ruined, I turned back home.

But as I headed up our hill I couldn't stop thinking about the coyote, lying there alone, so close to the asphalt, left to rot and perhaps be struck again until it was nothing but those indistinguishable fur pancakes so common on Wisconsin roads. Rushing into the house, I summoned my husband. I'm not a wimp. I've touched plenty of dead animals and held numerous domestic pets in my arms when they had to be put down. But for some reason, I couldn't touch the coyote. "We can't just leave it there," I said to my husband. He pulled on the torn grey ski jacket he uses for dirty jobs and walked back down the hill with me. "Oh, the poor thing," I thought he murmured. "The poor, sweet thing." Then, without a word, he lifted the coyote in his arms and bent over the scraggly hedgerow and barbed wire at the edge of our farmer neighbor's field. He laid the coyote down there gently, just out of sight, in the tall grass alongside the field. "That's better," he said. "That's a greener place to rest." It seemed to me that I hadn't ever seen anything as tender as the moment when he held the coyote in his arms, cradling it against his chest.

We hear coyotes fairly frequently where we live, here in the tranquil farm country stitched together with patches of woods and prairie, about fifteen miles outside Madison. There is nothing I like better than the sound of their uncanny, ululating yip. It is primal, essential and utterly wild. Some people say it gives them a chill; when I told an especially citified friend about it, she actually shuddered. But it pleases me to hear their barks, shrieks, and howls. I love to think of them, running through the fields at night, while we lie sleeping. The sound reminds me of the West, where I lived for many years and saw coyotes often, so there is an element of homesickness it salves for me, as is the way with things that move us. But it goes deeper than that. The sound of the coyotes' cry is more than just a reminder. It is something more powerful that echoes in my bones, as if my whole body becomes a flute in their presence. When I listen to them, I vanish, lost in another creature's world. That's the most important thing. They do not even know it—and wouldn't care if they did.

Once, when my first husband and I were cross-country skiing up a snowed-in fire road in the San Gorgonio wilderness in Southern California, a mountain coyote veered out from the thick cover of lodgepole pine and ran beside us for a good three quarters of a mile, its yellow eyes blazing. It moved easily, gracefully, glancing at us occasionally, but not afraid. I don't know what prompted it to accompany us that way, as if we were all going somewhere together. Much better than we were at navigating the terrain, the coyote seemed to be playing a game, keeping the pace up with no apparent effort. Coyotes are both intelligent and playful, much like our domestic dogs. They are, in fact, said to be the smartest member of the canine family. I could almost see that coyote's grin. I've never forgotten the lamps of its eyes, turned deeply upon us, or how, when it finally moved off into the forest again, it looked back at us once over one shoulder for a moment, as if to tell us something. Then it was gone, as if it had never been there.

I saw coyotes all the time when I lived in the Pomona/Claremont area, at the far eastern edge of Los Angeles County. There, where wilderness slams up against the city in closer juxtaposition than any other place I've ever known, coyotes were and remain ubiquitous. Smart, adaptable, elusive, they have adjusted well and even thrived. Some of the highest coyote population densities ever recorded have been logged in southern California. Coyotes are strong, agile, and versatile, quick to make themselves at home in changing ecological habitats. Homeowners with the chutzpah to build in the foothills know (or should know) not to feed coyotes and to keep their small pets inside. A house cat is a meal to a coyote. A friend who lived in the foothills told me once about finding a tuft of fur and one brown paw, all that remained of her beloved cat.

But my coyote sightings were always at the edges of things. For a number of years, I ran in an undeveloped regional park, known locally as Puddingstone for the conglomerate that defined its rough terrain, in which, astonishingly for the desert, a small lake (which had been dammed) lay embedded. As I looped through the rolling hills that were alive with wild mustard and purple lupine in California's brief spring, then burnt to the golden brown that looks like velvet from a distance in summer and fall, I often saw lone coyotes trotting briskly along, going about their business. Recent press about coyote attacks notwithstanding, they are naturally wary of humans. I wasn't scared, knowing a single coyote would not hurt me. If I happened to encounter one face to face—which I did from time to time—we always passed one another respectfully, like two strangers with a mutual agreement not to mess with one another. Walking up on their toes, as coyotes do, they were silent and golden. They were a part of the landscape, like the Western meadowlark singing its heartbreakingly beautiful song (one I have never heard anywhere else), or the San Gabriel Mountains that rose just to the north, their jagged outline piercing the sky as if the world had just been made that morning. As I ran, I rested my eye first on Mt. Baldy, then on Timber, Thunder, and Telegraph peaks, comforted by their massive presence. It's hard to feel frightened with a mountain range at your side.

There was just one time when I was afraid. Running in the early morning instead of in late afternoon, as I usually did, I saw a pack of seven coyotes cross the road a half mile or so ahead. They moved sinuously and efficiently, trotting in a small, tight group that flowed together in one fluid loop, clad in every shade of the brown, gold, and grey fur that allows them to blend so well into the landscape. Unlike me, running for my physical and mental health and the dream time summoned by the human body in motion, the coyotes ran with raw purpose, nothing on their mind but safety, food, and survival. They were beautiful in the sunlight, their weave of golden brown bodies seemingly sprung from the foothills around us. They were also achingly thin. I froze, considering what to do. They paused and looked back. There were seven of them, one of me, and no one else around for several miles. I decided to turn around, retracing my steps the way I'd come. Although I didn't think they would follow, I looked behind me, to reassure myself that they were not. But they were already gone. I stopped again and scanned the hills. What was it like to vanish that way? I couldn't see them anywhere. But I felt their gaze on me, seven pairs of golden eyes watching me till I disappeared.

A good friend during my California years had a cabin in Big Santa Anita Canyon, in the San Gabriels, where we sometimes hiked together. A few old-timers who still lived in the canyon year round had taught a young resident coyote, nicknamed Snooper, to beg for food. Female coyotes can be as light as twenty pounds (as opposed to males, who weigh in at up to forty pounds), but despite her handouts, Snooper seemed especially small. Her coat was unusually pale, almost buff-colored, so that she stood out sharply, leggy and vulnerable-looking against the greenery along the stream that rushed through the steep-sided canyon. "Here, Snooper," my friend called, tossing bits of meat and cheese to her across the creek, remarking on her cuteness. Back and forth she paced, darting in for the food, and then darting away to gobble it down. It was a nervous ballet that I found painful to watch. I've fed birds my whole life and have a wildlife feeder in the backyard of my house here in Wisconsin, where I've seen foxes, skunks, raccoons, and opossum (though it's primarily ground feeding birds and wild turkeys that avail themselves there). But something about feeding Snooper didn't feel right. It was as if, to get the food, she had to step too far outside her wildness into our world, and that bothered me. She wasn't there for entertainment. And she wasn't safe. I knew my friend meant well, but I couldn't help feeling that the young coyote would be the loser in the end, shot the minute she came too close or snapped at a child.

I was turning my 1967 Volkswagen Bug around in the dream, backing up from a bank ablaze with golden poppies and purple owl's clover the likes of which I had not seen since I left California, when the coyote appeared. It was panting heavily and looked as desperate as I felt, trapped in the grid of city streets that looked like Los Angeles. I felt concerned about the coyote, but when it jumped on the roof of the car I knew something was wrong. "Roll up the windows," I shouted to my companion. But I didn't move quickly enough. Flecks of saliva showered me like rain, still warm from the coyote's mouth. Had I been cursed or baptized? Coyote is the Trickster, after all, master and mistress of change and transformation. For a number of Native American tribes, especially in the Southwest, Coyote is both creator and destroyer, a wily shape shifter whose unpredictable actions nearly always have unexpected results. A Jungian analyst I know once told me that the coyote's elusiveness makes it especially well suited to personify psychic permeability and changeability. "Coyote is there, then not there," she said, "visible and then invisible. Coyote always vanishes, just when we think we have him in our sights." The Navajos call Coyote "God's Dog." I cannot imagine a better name.

When I was coming of age in rural New York State in the late 1960s and early 1970s, a couple of the coolest kids in our school dropped out and hitchhiked to Arizona, where they lived for a while, along with their mutt, Tara. I wanted to be like Debbie, with her mane of wild blond hair and Indian print skirts that always seemed prettier than my own. I envied her Billy, with his curly red hair and androgynous ease in his body, a cascade of blue and green beads spilling down his chest. I was a good girl, in the Regents track at North Salem High School, college bound. But I had a rebel heart and wished I could be them, coming back from the wilderness with a dog that had, they claimed, mated with a coyote. I yearned to see those pups, rolling and tumbling at Billy's parents' ramshackle farmhouse, where kids said his father would offer you dope. My father, a scientist interested in animal behavior, was curious about the so-called coy dogs, too, though I could tell he had deep reservations about that kind of crossbreeding (which was rare at the time and results in a sterile litter). But somehow, I never got to see those pups. Years later, when I first saw a coyote cross the Glendora Ridge Road before me on a summer morning in the San Gabriels, I thought of the coy dogs for some reason, wondering what had become of them. Here was the real thing. The coyote turned the yellow fire of its eyes upon me, holding me in its gaze for a moment as I looked deep into its bottomless spirit. I looked away first, and the coyote melted down the hillside.

If asked, I could describe exactly (though I won't) where the pair of foxes that live on our drumlin hill have their two dens. But I have no idea where the coyotes that we hear at night bear their young (though I know they will move the pups immediately if disturbed), or how it is that they survive, living so close to humans in what is basically unfriendly territory. I haven't ever seen coyote skins hammered up on fence posts here, the way I have in New Mexico, where half my family lives. But farmers are not coyotes' friends. I know coyotes make their dens in rocky crevices, riverbanks, hollow logs, under rocks, and the dens of other animals, which they sometimes enlarge for their own purposes. I know they eat everything from grasshoppers to bird eggs to snakes to small rodents to rabbits to deer. They love fruit, and in the desert West they will eat cactus and mesquite beans. They have excellent vision, a strong sense of smell, and can run up to forty miles an hour, covering up to eight square miles in their home territory. But I cannot tell you where they live, and if I do discover their den, I will try my best to forget it. The coyotes are a mystery, their yips like the aurora borealis made audible. It is a wordless green conversation I will never understand, a keen plainsong that pierces the darkness of a winter night.

This afternoon, walking across the snowy fields near our house and into the Department of Natural Resources land beside Island Lake, my husband and I saw coyote tracks. Smaller than our collies' prints, larger than the foxes', they run in nearly the same straight line as the latter, the hind paws falling close or directly into the forepaw tracks, in one perfect line. They looked like they were balancing as they walked, and the tracks were beautiful, pressed like the shadows of flowers into the white expanse. I could have followed them forever, watching how they parted and met, criss-crossing over the ground the way their voices do at night. "They're here, aren't they?" I asked my husband in what wasn't really a question. "Even when we can't see them, they're here."

268

"They are, indeed," he replied. And we walked on, the snow blowing in our faces, our prints mixing with theirs, then vanishing, braided briefly into the larger mystery.

C. W. Truesdale

Doña Baby

1.

She wears spike heels into the jungle. It is necessary for her to lean on her husband's left arm. He is dressed in a burgundy velour leisure suit and is perhaps twenty years her senior. He is perhaps strong and rigid and rich enough to hold up her sinuous long curves, her lustrous black hair which spills out from under her sun hat and piles up in loose folds on her shoulders. No doubt he has paid dearly for her. The complex negotiations through the marriage-broker, the family pride, the honor.

She is like a puppet, but he is no ventriloquist. The last thing he dares do is to put pure Castilian Spanish into her mouth. He may be Argentinian.

He props her up in the clearing and moves gingerly away. He prepares his cameras, the tripod, a classy production number.

The Boras, a meager band who are among the last few remaining pure Indians in Peru, gather dancing around her. They offer her gifts. They ignore the rest of us. Crude berry necklaces, cloth dolls, reed flutes. They are wearing bark cloth skirts with curious hieroglyphic designs like the ones we bought yesterday in Iquitos. Except for the nursing mothers, they are all very old or very young. The teenagers, dressed in Levis, are tittering.

The Boras dance around her in a long line, like a serpent. The toothless old men beat bark drums in the background.

She has come all the way from Spain for this moment. And she knows how to smile like the Virgin. With long delicate white fingers, she reaches out for one of the babies and holds it, smiling, to her lips.

"Madonna, Madonna," they cry.

2.

Though I watch television a lot, I seldom take it seriously and am always dumbfounded when something really good shows up on it. Sometimes, I'm annoyed when this happens.

One night I was watching one of those pretentious arts anthology programs and not paying much attention, until it dawned on me that this guy was doing something very weird. I believe that his name was Fong, or Fang, though I'm probably wrong on both counts. For entirely personal reasons, I prefer "Fang."

I missed the beginning of his performance, though I could hear the familiar Satie piano music he was using, a strange choice, but, as it turned out, exactly the correct one.

His performance was—intensely—both an event and a voice-over explanation. I had the distinct intuition—perhaps from his carefully articulated and elegant movements, perhaps from the way he used the word "meditation"—that this "event" was something he had performed many, many times. Maybe it was the only real event in his life. As though each time he did it, he was preparing himself for a ritual sacrifice and at the same time doing a T.V.-type sports commentary, voice-over. It was very disconcerting. Like watching someone you love very much being made love to by a stranger.

3.

She was an older black lady, on the way home, she said, from a harrowing day at work. She seemed to fit very snugly into herself, like fingers into a glove.

It was the usual place, Phebe's, where I used to go when I was compulsively on the make, or just compulsive, as I was that night. It was full of actors and dramatists, as usual, out-of-work show people from the Off-Off-Broadway set. Even the waitresses. If I were still on my own, and in New York, no doubt I'd still be going there, to hone away at my story and polish it, until all the glittering depths of it shone like a ruby.

There are times when it feels wonderful to do that—once the rough edges have been ground away. To try it out on pure strangers. Just to see how it fits them.

She stayed a full hour by the barroom clock over the mirror, where I could watch myself talking to her and make slight adjustments of expression. At times she let herself cry and reached out her dark hand and brushed away the sweat from my brow. Other times she drew away. Her eyes grew hard and cold and I could tell she was struggling with the fear in herself. That I might try to involve her, or something even more basic, that I might hurt her brutally.

I needed to risk that. For that one hour I had to hold her, or give way wholly to the terror inside of me. Her trusting me was the warm line between ordinary humanness and Bellevue, between Art and Madness.

"I want very deeply," I said, "to send you my book."

She hesitated just a moment, then rummaged around in her bag. She gave me her neat white business card, and left.

4.

Fang is down on his knees, just in front of and a little to his left of the plain wooden desk chair. He is meticulously unwrapping the cloth roll that contains his props. The soothing

Satie music is playing in the background. He draws two long satin strips about six inches wide from the roll and explains that he is about to perform the ancient Chinese ceremony of foot-binding. The Satie fades away, and we hear instead the voices of an older woman and a child. The child is sobbing. Fang explains that it is the voice of his mother. His little sister is sobbing from the pain.

At this very moment, he anoints his own left foot and ever so slowly begins to bind it. When he has finished with both feet, he rises into a cramped, semi-upright posture, then swiftly bends down on to his knees again and removes two little pointed blood-red slippers from the cloth roll, which he places awkwardly on his feet.

I became aware of the Satie again as Fang sways over the cloth roll, like a cobra, and lifts up, firmly but gently, a plain cloth doll about a foot and a half long. He grasps her by the scruff of the neck, like a mother cat her young, and moves her across the platform in front of his chair, exactly as you have seen geishas move in Japanese films. Her movements, which are pure translations of what the mother is saying to her daughter about the lovely end and reason for such suffering, are tuned with such elegance and grace to the Satie you believe wholly in her reality. At that moment, Fang is his sister absorbed in her pain and dreaming of her lover, who is also Fang moving now, the male doll with its tiny penis in the same fashion, only more upright and vain, over the prone figure of the doll-woman. He places one hand on her calf and draws himself down until his mouth touches her feet.

You expect more. The Satie is now so erotic that nothing would surprise you.

Suddenly Fang moves. He covers them over almost roughly, as if he could not bear to watch them. As if they would do before my eyes what I wanted them to do.

Fang moves over the cloth roll again. He takes out two embroidered white satin garments and puts them on like a woman. Perhaps he is his sister, I thought, on her wedding day. I know that he is confusing me. I feel that he is doing this deliberately. He wants me to assume that these are wedding garments when in fact they are traditional Chinese mourning attire.

He bends way over now and rests his cheek on the floor. The music stops. The light fades away.

5.

Reynaldo, our guide, edges out into the clearing among the Boras. He looks beautifully up into the sun, like an eagle, and motions us to move on. We have exhausted their meager supply of trinkets and their repertoire. Tomorrow, there will be another group. And tomorrow.

Reynaldo is very quick. I am teaching him how to paddle the dugout canoes American-style. I am confident we will win the race tomorrow.

Reynaldo likes the American girls in Cuzco, where he goes on vacation. He especially likes the noisy blond ones from California, who come down to buy dope and study anthropology.

Reynaldo is half Indian. He has dark features, refined by a Portuguese mother. He has the same delicate dark luminosity you see in the children of Vietnamese women and American blacks. He moves with grace, like a Spaniard. But he smiles like an Indian. Or an angel, displaced and fallen.

Luisa Villani

The Danger Creature Chronicles

1. Accutron

The night I slept in my car, it wasn't cold. Mist filtered across a transformer, and tension wires hummed in the park-and-ride. All I had to do was wait for morning, for the YMCA to open, to shower and change my clothes, to go to work, to walk into a classroom where sixteen over-indulged and four under-privileged freshmen would tell me about their lives by means of an essay meant to introduce us. What would I tell them about my life?

Hello, my father is bipolar. He spent much of the night pacing outside my bedroom door, occasionally softly knocking, wanting to know if I was still a witch, if I would please speak to him without spells. Through all this my mother slept. Through all this his Pomeranians snored. I finally went out the bedroom window with my keys and my gym bag and my briefcase. But I wasn't cold.

Even if it had been cold, my inner heat would have warmed me. Even if the tension wires hadn't hummed, I would have hummed myself, hummed like a watch, an Accutron, with its tuning fork movement, forever sweeping the second hand on. A clockwork like that is necessary to move through the seconds of deceit.

I told my brother about it once, after my father had his first break. I flew from Pennsylvania to L.A. eight times that year, cancelled numerous classes, did not get to know my students as I should have. But my younger brother, who wouldn't do the flying, even though he lived a mere two hundred miles from the epicenter, was *grateful*. "I don't know how you finally got him seen." Nobody knew how I did it. Not even my father. That magic is for another tale. This is not a tale of magic. This is a tale of anger and how it hums in the body.

"It's important to remember the good times," my brother said. I said I did. I remembered the Oldsmobile Vista Cruiser, the magical wagon, and the trips to Disneyland, even before my brother could talk, and the carrying in from the slumber of blue leather by a man whose wrist hummed with the accuracy prized by astronauts.

That was my gem of memory, the thing I held to when that solid arm was now tracing the door frames and mumbling about tiny sentences tearing his five-bedroom house apart, how he needed to fill the rooms to keep them solid, with DVDs of John Wayne, with substantial things, with things to remember the past, like here, see this thing, *your brother gave it to me.* I opened the box. It was an Accutron watch. The card read: "From your son. I remember when you used to carry me inside and I could hear the hum of your watch. . . ."

2. The Proper Use of Spells

The terrible thing is that I understand the voices, though, I, myself, have never had the luxury of losing my mind. I assume losing one's mind is like a faith fall, a folding of the arms, the mind folds in, and all good reason collapses like a beach umbrella closing for the season. I watch it go with its tattered valise trailing the same pair of nylons for miles.

276

My father never doubted I would catch him, so he fell off his meds . . . again. As his serotonin levels fell, the danger creature in him rose like a gas bubble from the primordial ooze, and wore him like a skin.

This incantation I call the saint's patience hymn or the caring daughter ditty. It begins with the staccato knock of knuckles on a door, very reminiscent of a conductor's baton.

When danger creature rises, it wants what it wants, when it wants it, like a piece of pie at 2 a.m., so it knocks on your bedroom door. It knocks and it knocks, till you rise in your sweatpants, and you go to an all-night diner, where the brown laminate table wears a patina of tiny scratches. Everything here is dulled, the way creature likes it, fogged by something that can never be wiped away. Watch the waitress's arm. Back and forth. That rhythm. Begin your line.

Here comes the coffee, pie, french fries, and maybe a bloody steak . . . but no cigarettes. *The machine is out here, Dad.* Keep talking. Television, or weather. The spell of *be here now*. In the moment, you see the countless random impacts required to create the table's film. You see the need to change the name of the 5150 psychiatric hold to the 50/50, because those are really the odds. You see the need to keep creature listening—*these are lovely menus, don't you think?*—so you can track his movements.

You rub the talisman in your pocket—a fragment of mirror you stole from the hospital where you were born—and you move to the negotiations. Good behavior for a strawberry shake. Not crying in public for more chocolate silk. Sugar is good. Feed the starving brain. But, no, we can't get cigarettes now, *all the stores are closed.* Don't argue when he comments on the beauty school student in the corner with her books and mannequin head. She is black, and the mannequin is white, and he wants to do something about that. The spell of *you are right.* You are always right. *Wouldn't you like a witness?*

Use the urgency of the helicopter's gunmetal whir to bend him into the car; after all, this is Los Angeles and there is a need for spotlights and for mirrors and for a little smoke. *They have your brand in that machine near the hospital.* It's not so much a herding as it is a shepherding, as in *the Lord is my*, which you secretly intone all the way there.

3. A Danger Creature

When my uncle died, I thought the danger creature died with him. He was a nasty bugger too. Small and black, and nail-sharp he was, with big hairy feet. He kicked in my bedroom door one day, after I had the audacity to tell my uncle he wasn't my father.

I was sixteen. I ran down the hallway immediately, realizing what I'd done. Danger creature yelled down my back, as tears streamed down my front. My small, calm father picked up the door, leaned it against the wall, and when the danger creature was gone, he said slowly, "Why do you have to make him mad?"

We both knew better than to wave even the tiniest scrap of red, not even a daisy petal, in front of danger creature's face.

When my uncle died, very still in his bed, staring at the center light on the ceiling, concentrating so hard on that point, his eyes slowly closing, his breath slowly rasping, I thought the danger creature was dying too, and I was sad, because I was an adult, and he'd never asked for my forgiveness, but that is not the danger creature way.

Nor is it the danger creature way to die.

At first it was the inheritance my uncle left to the "good" nieces and nephew, which wound up all in my father's care. Then, a gradual unleashing. After all, you can't open the cage door all at once. Danger creature is not a circus cat. He must be embraced by his victims, so they invite the infectious bite, from which, apparently, there is no recovery. Allure fills danger creature's arsenal, like the allure of a super-deluxe luxury motor home, when gas prices have spiked, so that you give up financial sanity and buy it—outright with your new money.

But then it doesn't quite satisfy (dissatisfaction is another of creature's arrows), so you give it away, to your youngest son, who after all, never turned down any scrap from your table (because, truth be told, he already has a little danger creature lapping his heart's blood), and you buy the one you *really* wanted, the super-*super*-deluxe model, a LAND YACHT, and then, there you are, captain of the Arizona desert in your Airstream LAND YACHT, and you spend, spend, spend, as you ride, ride, ride, feeling your metal box like freedom.

4. The Witch I Would Become

I have one, thick, black hair, three inches from my wrist, on the inside white of my arm. My aunt, who always took care to notice my childhood quirks, called it my meanness hair. *That's all the meanness you have,* she said. That hair still grows, ever so slowly, and three times each year, I pluck it out, let it begin again.

It's sad to have so little meanness. As a freshman in high school, Robert Reinert offered me gold and his undying love, behind the bleachers, if I would just wear his ring. I refused both. I was kind, but I'm sure now that was just a little mean. I once found a hundred-dollar bill on the floor of a drugstore and didn't turn it in, then bought Christmas presents for my whole family. I once married a man when I didn't know what love was, but he didn't know either, so I don't think that was mean, because he was twenty years my senior.

I used to dress every morning in a tailored suit, then pretend all day I had no curves. At train stations, I nudge my way into line from the sides. I say *hello* to people on planes, then fake sleep. When my father had his last break with reality, I marked it all in silence, the Krakatoa of his rage, the Laurentian Abyss of his blame. Then, I planned for my escape.

Step-by-step, like a fog, I simply cleared.

He called months later, in a panic. "What if I need you?"

I explained I had a job, I had students, and I couldn't simply leave *in medias res*. The story is now here, where I am, and I will never give up my story again to piece you together. You see, finally I am whole, mean, and not willing to divide.

And then, finally then, he admitted I was mean, that I'd always been mean, that my living under his roof had been a scheme, to use his shelter, his table, to give nothing when I owed him everything. And there it was: an open door.

I could turn toward all that dark, argue for the dwindling light of my goodness, then watch that glint turned on me like a shining dagger, once again.

280

Or, ahead, through a brief aperture shaped like a woman, I could walk into the scorching brightness, where I would be blackened, but free.

A long pause.

You are absolutely right, I said, *I used you.*

A longer pause. Then I held the kitchen counter as something roared past me. The ground swelled with his molten anger— I simply hung up the phone. Unsteady, unborn, I walked into the light of a life which would become, the witch I would become.

5. Absolute Black

This is my theory of psychology: everyone has a danger creature, embodied approximately in the amygdala, and it is your relationship to this creature which determines your sanity, not the relationship you have with your higher self, because if you ignore your creature, deny it, cage it, or try in any way to lock it in a closet, it will eat you alive and wear you as a skin.

So I've decided to pay attention to my creature, the way one pays attention to a caracal on an African savannah as it stops lapping its reflection, lifts its head from the watering hole, and twitches its batwing ears, and, more importantly, I've decided to listen to the other creatures I see so they don't maul me, or my danger creature doesn't maul them.

Which is why, on our first spa date together, when my stepdaughter cried over her gift—"But I don't know what they will do to me"—and she had a meltdown outside the car, I looked at her diamond tears and whispered, "Be calm, little creature," and I reached for her hand slowly, as if I were holding out raw tuna to a feral cat, or as if I were negotiating with her from a rooftop. Her fear was that real.

And still, her animal eyes glistened with tears, each dark as a beetle. Eyes so black they were shiny. A black so shiny it was a mirror.

Mark Vinz

Tales from a Fourth Grade in the Fifties

1. By the Numbers

One day our teacher announced something she called a *new policy*. We couldn't just raise our hands anymore when we wanted to be excused to go to the bathroom. We had to raise fingers—one finger for making water, as she called it, and two fingers for the other thing. Most of us couldn't figure out what difference it made. A trip to the bathroom was a trip to the bathroom, after all, and if there were some reason why the teacher and everyone else had to know what we were up to, I could only chalk it up as another of those unsolvable mysteries of grownups.

For the first couple of weeks the new policy didn't seem to make much of a difference. Most of the girls never raised their hands anyway, and nobody seemed to care what number a boy had to go—nobody, that is, but this skinny, bug-eyed kid named Roger everyone kept away from because we thought he was the dumbest one in the whole class. "Teacher, teacher," he'd cry out at least once a day, "I can't remember the difference between Number One and Number Two. Which one is for taking a leak?"

Sometimes Teacher would take Roger out in the hall to talk to him, where we could see his head bobbing like a yoyo behind the panes of glass in the door. When that happened, we knew he wouldn't be raising his hand again about anything for at least a couple of days. But we also knew that soon enough he'd be at it again, and as the teacher's face got redder and redder we began to wonder just how long he could keep it up.

283

One day a week or so later, Paul Jackson, who was easily the most popular boy in class and also the best softball player, raised his hand and said the same thing, that he couldn't remember how many fingers to hold up. Then Buck Weisman asked the same question, followed by Ferdie Johnson, and then the teacher told us all to put our heads down on our desks and not to say another thing. She also told us we were going to have another new policy, starting immediately. We'd have to write her a note about what we had to do in the bathroom and then bring it up to her desk when she called on us.

The new policy worked for about two days, until Roger raised his hand and asked the teacher how many *r*'s there were in "urinate" so he could write it in his note. That was the only time we'd ever heard a teacher scream. It was when we also knew that from then on we'd have to start holding it till recess—and that Roger wasn't nearly as stupid as we'd all thought he was.

2. Vocational Education

The classroom job I wanted the most was to be paper monitor. Maybe it was because it seemed to involve such an attractive combination of power and responsibility—enough to earn me Teacher's nodding approval for a change. Or maybe it was because it would make my mother proud when I raced home after school to tell her, especially because she used to be a teacher herself. "I knew you could do it," she'd say—just as she always did.

Being paper monitor meant organizing and passing out whatever papers we needed for the day's schoolwork and then, later, collecting whatever we'd been drawing on or writing on as part of our assignments, and finally stacking all the papers neatly on the table by Teacher's desk in the order of the rows our desks were in.

284

If I was amazed when Teacher chose me for the job, most of my classmates barely seemed to notice, probably because half the kids in our classroom were already monitors. There were hall monitors, to make sure we didn't run on the way to or from lunch or recess. There were drinking fountain monitors to make sure no one got pushed or no one butted in when we were lining up. There were coatroom monitors to be sure everything got hung up neatly, and there was even a monitor of monitors—someone to be sure all the other monitors did their jobs and to report it to Teacher if they didn't.

Most of the monitors, of course, were girls. Teacher made it clear that in her experience girls were far more responsible than boys, at least in most positions—especially the ones that involved keeping order. A lot of us boys thought it had more to do with being willing to rat on your classmates. And that, as it turned out, was exactly what happened to me.

Near the end of school on my first day as a paper monitor, Lisa, the girl who was the head monitor, complained to Teacher that some of the students didn't get all the papers I was supposed to be passing out, and that the papers I had managed to collect weren't in the proper order. Soon enough, the look on Teacher's face told me that my career as a paper monitor had come to an abrupt end. It also told me to look forward to yet another rendition of her *hopeless daydreamer* speech.

By the end of the afternoon, I was back at my old job of clapping erasers, sneezing and wheezing in clouds of chalk dust. At least I got to go outside for a few minutes, and sometimes with Weird Charlie to help me, though he liked to clap the erasers against his shirt and pants and come back into the classroom looking like some kind of zombie.

Once in a while I found myself imagining working with people like Charlie when I grew up—the sort of guys I'd seen standing around on loading docks on the way downtown. At least there wouldn't be any girls like Lisa there. I was pretty sure that most of them were going to grow up to be teachers.

285

3. Word of Mouth

Rumors about the 5th grade teacher began to grow not long after we started 4th grade. Aside from being very large and old, she supposedly took great pleasure in beating naughty children in the cloakroom that ran between our classrooms. We did hear her yelling in there once in awhile, and Weird Charlie told us to listen for a thumping sound on the wall, which was the teacher banging kids' heads against it.

Mostly we had problems enough with our own teacher, who was also very large and old, and strict—not at all like our 3rd grade teacher, who even used to hug us sometimes. Our 4th grade teacher moved a desk on either side of hers in the front of the room, reserved as punishment for for talkers or other rule-breakers. I ended up sitting in one of those desks a couple of times. Most of the boys did.

The best thing to happen in 4th grade was when Teacher had to have some kind of operation and was gone most of the winter after Christmas vacation and part of the spring. We knew things were looking up when the substitute—who ended up staying with us the whole time—moved those two desks back with the others on her very first day with us. The other thing she started right away was a "free time" period when we got to read whatever we wanted to at our desks, or maybe the whole class would play a game like Twenty Questions. The more we grew attached to that always-smiling substitute, the meaner and more threatening the 5th grade teacher next door became. It almost seemed like we'd been given our substitute as a reward for what we were going to have to face in the future.

Just about the time the snow started melting seriously, I came down with a bad cold and had to miss a couple of days of school. The day I returned I could tell immediately that things had changed. That cold, gray silence was back, along with our old teacher, stricter and sterner than ever. It didn't take me long to discover she'd been though my desk. TAKE THIS HOME AT ONCE, she'd written on a slip of paper, in reference to the comic book she'd found there. It wasn't long before the two desks were back beside hers in the front of the room.

When we finally made it to the last day of class, our old teacher told us how much she appreciated how good we'd been when she was gone, and that was especially important because we'd be the last class she'd ever teach. She and the 5th grade teacher had decided to retire together and do some traveling. Most of us just sat there stunned at the news. We really didn't understand much about retirement, and while we were relieved about not having to face that scary 5th grade teacher in the fall, we also felt a little cheated, a little disappointed, and we couldn't begin to understand why.

4. The Most Important Meal

When my father was home, my parents liked to have bacon and eggs for breakfast. When he was on a trip for his job, which was most of the time, I usually had cold cereal. My mother had such a hard time getting me out of bed and ready for school, there usually wasn't time for anything else. She kept trying to get me to eat oatmeal—doctoring it up, as she called it, with milk and sugar, but it still tasted awful. Even if breakfast was the most important meal of the day, as we kept hearing in school, I'd rather go without anything than eat oatmeal.

During the unit on nutrition, we had to keep a record of every breakfast for three weeks. At first I tried to be truthful, but when there got to be too many days with just orange juice or Cheerios, I'd start adding sliced bananas or strawberries, or maybe some toast and raspberry jam. But why stop there? Some days I wrote down pancakes or scrambled eggs and ham. Teacher—the good substitute, not the crabby old regular one—was pretty impressed when she checked my record. It was all I could do to keep from adding T-bone steak or spaghetti. Maybe that was when I first figured out that teachers could be fooled just like anybody else and if what you told them made them pleased, then it wasn't really the same thing as lying, was it?

What I had forgotten about was parent-teacher conferences, which were held a couple of times a year. "Your teacher and I think you've got a pretty good imagination," was all that my mother said afterwards. It took me a while to figure out Teacher had showed her my breakfast record, and then I felt worse than if either of them had yelled at me. When I thought about it some more, I began to realize I was pretty good at making things up, that this wouldn't be the last time I'd get in trouble for it, and that I probably wasn't ever going to stop.

Julie Marie Wade

Just You Wait

"I'm drowning here,
& you're describing the water."

The water is lush & cool. The water consists of fishes with vermillion eyes & scuba divers seeking recompense for stolen treasure. The water will not wait. The water is not accustomed to waiting. The water understands (implicitly) that you are afraid. The water will forgive your tremors, your flails, but is not interested in negotiating your fears. The water speaks (explicitly) in waves. The water dashes many dreams to stone. The water harbors many stones as dreams. The water remains complicit, clouded, circumspect: equal parts wavering & unwavering. The water enjoys an occasional & well-placed play on words. The water will not laugh & cannot stop crying. The water is at once stoic & superfluous where emotions are concerned. The water regards the moon coldly. The water is a breeding ground for science fiction. The water swallows trashy romance novels & family-sized umbrellas. The water contains a silverware drawer replete with spoons. The water is specialized in ontology, epidemiology, & acrobatics. The water also knows something (implicitly) about tautology, effervescence, & ravines. The water taxes for occupancy per diem. The water simulates envelopes & epithets, unfolding & dispensing. The water rarely engages in debate concerning justice, light, the vitality of sand, the accoutrement of shells, or the significance of sailing. The water understands you do not understand. The water will not wait, after all. The water is not accustomed to waiting. The water is weak & warm. The water is controlled by invisible currents that mimic gravity but cannot replicate it. The water is different every time. The water separates (explicitly) porous driftwood from dark ruddy logs. The water composes symphonies, performs operas. The water dictates to an imaginary amanuensis on the shore. The water would like to be kind. The water is not sure how to be kind. The water swallows patchwork blankets & beach towels. The water is stricken with grief but has never learned precisely how to mourn. The water is specialized in sinking. The water remains pent, pickled, prone: equal parts willing & unwilling. The water would like you to enter. The water would like you to feel comfortable, but is not interested in generous gestures of assuage. The water is shy & struggles with salutations. The water fears itself unremarkable. The water bellows when it means to inquire. The water suggests you have had a hard day & should take off your shoes. The water has already eaten. The water exists in tenuous relation to voyeurism & seduction: those cult-followers in the ringside seats. The water hopes you will not judge the water prematurely. The water hopes you are able to stay awhile. The water would be happy to fix you a drink. The water once wrote a lyric poem called "Capsize," which was recited near a lighthouse in Bar Harbor. The water remembers when you were a child, remembers it fondly. The water keeps your pink jelly-shoes for posterity. The water is novice & ageless & lost. The water rebukes cliffs & renounces valleys. The water understands the pressure is always changing. The water wishes you would step back a little. The water is concerned with catachresis, though it has never uttered the word. The water is the strong, silent type. The water has a lava lamp in place of a heart. The water regrets it is unable to lunch today. The water desires your presence at a future event. The water blushes & rushes over your toes. *Thank you*, the water says. *Thank you for listening.*

"Or else."

Fabled ending or outcome. Epilogue of *what if? & then what? & why not?* Caprice's cornerstone. Threat's conviction. Frontispiece (or) shield. Dorsal (or) ventral. That-which-is-left-dangling. If I cast my nets wide, will I catch you? If I hunker down, shiny amphibian in the slick wetland grasses, will I strike & will someone else yield? There is this other about it, this "other" & this furtive "othering." What happens is . . . & no one knows how to answer, but we know it's wrong; we understand that we are meant to be afraid, outraged, indicted. Rubble loosens at the precipice. Ascend at your own risk. *Falling Rocks.* If I jump off a bridge, will you follow? If I leap from a tree with a frayed rope wrapped over & under my glistening naked splendor, will we collide inside the shallow water? Is collision ever a good thing? What happens is . . . & no one knows how to answer, but we know it's light & ache-filled, eyes straining to see as through fog. Your guiding hand through a white subversive darkness. Something on the other side? Dorsal? Ventral? Switch, flip, turn. There is this other about it, this "other" & this furtive "othering." We don't know what frightens us, but leave a light on in the closet please & a note inside the lunchbox that promises forgiveness or reprieve. If a tree falls in a forest, is it *indicative* of error? If I am watching from the landing of a tree house, Rima-like—bird-girl cloaked in leaves & trepidation—does my vision validate or overwrite the scene? What happens is . . . & no one knows how to answer, but we know it's cold & sweat-streaked & lascivious: what only some are entitled to feel. Caprice's cornerstone. Threat's conviction. Is the promise (always) punishment? Is the captor (ever) kind? Futures as elusive as storybook rhymes: shoes that fit because they're forced to, because they *must*. If I discover I am not "just like" my neighbor, will I be forced to resign our common garden? If I lean in close to the window that marks us separate, delineates our heterogeneous zones, am I inviting a similar voyeurism to that which I seek to extract? There is this other about it, this "other" & this furtive "othering." Frontispiece (or) shield. Dorsal (or) ventral. The chiming of a grandfather clock. The keeping of tide schedules. One eye bent on the moon. What happens is . . . & no one knows how to answer, but we know it's always with us—need or de-mand—three-way contingency or contractual two-party agreement. Two steps forward, another back. That-which-is-always-left-dangling.

"You can't marry someone when you're in love with someone else."

Though it nearly happened, like a fever sweeping the fore-head of every swooning girl. And this time, for once, I wanted to be just like all the others. I knew I could love a man. I was well-practiced in the art of obligation, & I had a curtsy or two left in me from the formative ballet class. I could keep pace with my contemporaries. I could be very good & somewhat graceful. Or I could wash my hands of the whole matter, which is why whenever I tell this story, there's always a prayer hidden somewhere for the man I tried to love & all the ways I failed. There's a joy also, & a primitive sigh: *wife* like an over-plucked string on a tired guitar: but oh how I yearned to make music! What interests me now is the way we fore-shadow our own disappointments, then learn to forget them somehow. When, as a child, I circled the *Ms.* box on my of-fering envelope, much to my mother's chagrin, & announced proudly—with George Bailey bravado: "I'm not going to get married, *ever,* to anyone, do you understand? I want to do what I want to do." But then I was born again into adoles-cence, all contested worth & cultish fascination. "Doubt," the

292

dragon said, "is the only word I trust," & perhaps I trusted also this revision of my wants, this surrender of my secret complications. Like the girls at Catholic School, whose faces I wanted to kiss or crush. Like all the dreams where I turned suddenly male, at odds with myself, for the fleeting brush of a stranger's breast. I wouldn't let the world crack open: *Twilight Zone* or worse—*The Twilight of the Golds*. How could I survive, I asked myself, in a world that wished me otherwise, or not at all? But it was still my call: courteous at times & comfortable at others, convenience of the standing date & restlessness of slow receding water. I convinced myself of stunning certainties, of soap box overturned to pretty pedestal & promise of a ring that paid for reason. My dress was very white & very straight, sequins & lace & taken in around the waist. I had not been eating much. Too many cigarettes & not enough sleep, coffee by the quart & gin-&-tonics. Until I was sitting one day on the back porch of a best friend's garden apartment, where she was very good at living alone & somewhat graceful at hiding poems she'd rather nobody saw, & I realized I wanted to hold her hand on the rollercoaster of the future & hear her voice on the intercom of my interior monologue & that I had been, all this time, standing outside myself, becoming the mute carpenter of my grandfather & the manic magician of his daughter, assembling a box with my own two hands in order to make myself of all people—the ultimate act—disappear. New frost was tender on the blades of grass. Deer crept in from subtle & dramatic distances. If this had been a fairy tale, then I knew at last the forest was listening. A few of the trees had bowed their heads, & a slow admonishing light filtered through the clouds. Illumination came gradually, then indisputably. She who I loved best, in spite & because of her femaleness, having everything to do with gender & absolutely nothing at all, confessed in a quiet voice to loving me also. "So I guess the old movie was right," despite the fact I was no Captain von Trapp & my husband-to-be no

Baroness Schraeder. And the woman who resembled least of all Fraulein Maria professed the first of our rich history of surprises: "You know," she said, "I've never even seen *The Sound of Music....*"

"Skirt the issue."

red wool pinned for safety lest unraveling take place & the plaid promise of the school girl cliché that all is as it should be & is meant to stay pleated skirts & pencil skirts ruffles & dirndls knee-length skirts & circle skirts A-lines & broom-sticks mini-skirts maxi-skirts poodle skirts embroidered with prancing cotton-headed dogs & sarongs & culottes & tennis skirts with their irresistible white cotton & tulip-cut skirts & Gibson Girl skirts & corsets & denim & every imaginable anachronism & jersey puffball skirts & flapper skirts complete with fishnet stockings & peacock skirts with fashionable plumage & petticoats suitable for square-dancing & jumpers made of velvet or corduroy & tutus made of transparent tulle & brushed twill riding skirts & diamond-cut calico skirts & Katie skirts Abbie skirts Hampton taffeta suits with matching skirt & jacket & prairie skirts & soft linen Susannah skirts & wrap skirts & cargo skirts with pockets for cigarettes & spare change & ankle-length satin skirts & trouser skirts reversible beach skirts & nylon slips barely long enough to camouflage their garters flamenco skirts & hula skirts & old-fashioned kilts & high-fashion flare & frayed-to-the-fringe leather skirts & bubble skirts & bustled-up Victorian lace skirts willow bark & chain mail skirts & every homemade assemblage of zip & shift including but not limited to the hybrid *skort* & even kayak skirts & saddle skirts & most important of all *bed skirts* which disguise not only the sin of the skin but the place where flesh is most likely to mingle no shortage of skirts & nothing that can't be covered by a simple drape & a few

stitches of pliable silk you think you won't be skirted just you
wait

"There's no hole on earth where the heart drops through without bringing something with it."

Despite its long affiliation with loss, love also accrues: steady
accumulation of boxes no longer reserved for shoes; strange
tinctures & hollow rings, powdered with sugar or stronger;
Kewpie dolls won in dart games & a dozen *Trivial Pursuits,*
series of subsequent editions. And the luggage & the pass-
ports & the key-chain souvenirs, all figurative of course: also
fashionable & futuristic & fact. You don't journey alone any-
more. There is someone else to think of, to offer the window
seat to—or perhaps she prefers the aisle. A twin bed looks
suddenly lonely, & more so the large bed, bereft of multiple
bodies. Your pillow adopts her scent; your blankets no longer
yours. The whole world pluraled, this second pulse shadow-
ing your own. Old companions less companionable: radio,
television—mere background noise. You begin to hear her
voice reciting the grocery list or answering the phone. There
is an attention to content but also to form. You form your syl-
lables with her presence in mind, tailored to the shape of her
body. You anticipate her wishes, her kisses, the warm place
she has been sitting, wrapped in one of her sweaters with
burly wood buttons & in-folded sleeves. You wonder if you
are becoming transparent, if she can always see through you
to the seed of your truest intention. Will she warm her hands
on the low fire you always keep burning, clandestine & solely
for her? Will you remain astonished by her luminous capac-
ities: for pleasure, for penance & pardon? There is *with her*
& *without her* but never *beyond.* She has altered your consti-
tution. You find her in miniature & metonym: pretty crescents

of her thumb nails, velveteen lobes of her ears. You can no longer watch *Jeopardy!* in solitude. Marlboro lights & lucky bamboo trigger visceral reminiscences. And the tatters on your map, torn together: Rapid City, South Dakota, Niagara Falls, Mount Shasta's elaborate & surreal setting sun. You remember bookcases in Nancy Drew stories, how they almost always hid the mystery stairs. She has passed through those passageways now; she has found your counterfeit copy of *Great Expectations* & tipped it just so, exposing the secret threshold. And the safe behind the picture with the traveling eyes, & the skeleton key sequestered in the flower pot, & all that spare change lining the sofa cushions. Not piracy or bribery, but a deep & unencumbered knowing. You have climbed into the hold together. You have sifted through the treasure. And each day past, & every day forward, you have crossed your hearts & murmured something about honor. You have ridden bicycles with cross-hatched baskets stuffed full to brimming with roses, all figurative of course: also tender & romantic & accurate beyond accounting. There have been no altars, nor will there be, but extraordinary kindnesses & tokens whose meanings exceed the scope of words. You have handled handkerchiefs & checkbooks & gold pocket-watches, meting out an uncertain number of hours. You have made public parables & private apologies. You have swept chimneys & taken out the ash. You have stood together on the fire escape of a condemned building. You have crossed your hearts & promised not to die.

Cecilia Woloch

Shine

I had one white dress and gave it away.
—Kathleen McGookey, *Whatever Shines*

If What We Love Turns to Glass,
How Do We Keep It Safe

I'd like to make something tender for both of us. Something, at least, to put into your hands. Something like those flowers I saw by the side of the road in the Polish countryside. Though some might call them weeds, as I might have called them once. But that summer evening, just after the storm, I walked along naming them to myself: *buttercup, thistle, poppy, homely oh lovely dandelion.* I thought them jewel-like, there in the high grass; blue mist rising off the fields. Men on bicycles wobbling home. Everything softening in the blur of twilight: woodsmoke, drizzle, sky. I thought then, as I think now: so where's the line between beauty and sorrow; where's the line between terror and joy? How the small daughter of my friends had run out the open door of the house, screaming and laughing, into the rain. How your mother—still beautiful, still—had hobbled each day down the road to the store. How all those years you watched her disappear until she disappeared for good. How my father, those same years, adrift, drifted too far in his ship of bones; then only the smell of flowers above that bed where he'd lain to die. So I take your suffering, you take mine, we take it up—shall this be a bouquet? That evening in Poland I walked for an hour, away from then back toward the church. I called to no one, and no one called to me—though the warm room was waiting, the bread. I would give you this now: the pale green dome; the meadow; the quiet house, lights coming on. How the child, in her sleep, breathed the breath of birds. How the little boat of my heart goes out.

I'd Like a Love Letter
and Too Much Light in My Eyes

I'd like a bird to fly into my left hand and sit there warming it, feather and pulse. I'd like to sleep with a big cat some-times—mountain lion or tiger or lynx. But mostly I'd like to slide into a warm bath with you now. Steam in our eyes and our hair. So I've wanted too much. So where's the crime? Never flowers or jewels or a sleek limousine, though I've had those things. I would give them back. Or I would accept them again, every gift. So I've not settled down with some pots and pans, but loved the smooth sheets of each strange new bed. I can't seem to stay in one place long enough to ever get sick of it. Listen: you call to me, I'll come. I'll pack a bag full of lingerie and meet you, breathless, wherever you are. What can I bring you that you would lick from my fingers, like sugar, with your tender, feathery tongue? How else to spend ourselves but on love? You want the red lace against my breasts. You want nothing for breakfast. I want that, too.

Really, I Couldn't Say
When My Kisses Got Closer to Your Mouth

—when that voice in my head that repeats, *You'll never be loved, you'll never be loved,* shut up. I tell you I loved, in the childhood story, how the tigers turned into butter and, in their

298

turn, got eaten up. I keep thinking about the morning I woke and you were still sleeping, still holding my hand. Your face in that halo of fairytale curls. I keep thinking about a day I spent in the mountains, the sheep like clouds. Clouds with short, clumsy legs, but clouds. A farmer stood near his tasseled horse at the plow and smiled for the pictures I took. Red tassels. Loved creature. Loved. Now the house is locked up tight, and somewhere a siren keeps going off. Some wounds don't ever heal. But I like your woundedness, your mouth. I like thinking this will all come true, if we're brave and good enough. The girl won't be eaten by the witch. The boy will find the way back home through the woods by the small coins of bread on the path, by the moon. Really, I never know where it begins. The buttery longing turned to a sweetness too sweet to bear. Almost too sweet.

Because New Love Smells Like Grass

Because messages fly between us—quick, quick—like the shadows of birds. Here, mist and blurred light, sheets of rain. There, your body pale as the snow that doesn't fall, almost luminous. Almost the sweet ghost of itself. And if I've loved before this weather all things sharpened, where's that edge? Would you describe your hands as calm? Your voice caught, nervous as a boy's. Well, I swore off swearing off the things that crave me long ago. When I was rushing for a train. When I was ridiculous with grief, my heart too heavy for its wheels. See, if you could see me now, you'd laugh, unbraid my hair. At least I hope that's what you'd do. Unwrap this black scarf from my throat. And then the rain would give us back the world within the world we made. When we leaned close, undid our names; you fed me chocolate from your palm. Now, snow. Now, sleep. Keep warm. This, too, will green again until there's no green left in it. God wants us not to turn our heads. My tongue's a wing, if you believe in it, that makes you holy, slick.

You Simply Close Your Hand
Around Whatever Shines

Dear Heart—I grow more and more fond of you. Fonder and fonder, like grass growing high and wild at the edge of a quiet pond. Of your hair, like tangled sun. Of your face, your eyes, your thoughtful hands. And whatever this is between us, we say, let's not give it any name. Which might stop its blossoming, we agree. Though it's not so much flowering as green. A green shoot to handle with tenderness now. As in: *to fondle;* as in: *to be fond*. We might skip stones on that pond's smooth surface, might gather weeds, but we'll keep our word. And jaded as we are, we can touch without irony. Kindly lie down. Your skin gives off some kind of light when you sleep, and I'm grateful for that. I would not want you hurt. We disappear from each other, come back, disappear. And those others we've called *beloved* part the curtain of high grass, a breeze.

The Silk of Longing
Is Never Worth What We Are Paid

Oh lamb. Oh lonely in your room above the childless neighbors, too. The blue of afternoon went on and on like winter, didn't it? The first lights flickering at dusk along the street to make you sad. You took the subway into town, then taxied back, your meager store of cash diminishing again. And still awake at four a.m., you wanted anything but this: the silent bed; the empty kitchen; birdsong startling the trees. Open your hand and kiss your palm. That's my kiss, as real as salt.

300

Then turn your head and kiss your shoulder, pale as snow, then, warm as milk. The day turns over when we sleep. We need our sleep. Take comfort there. I wish for you the book of childhood's secrets, love's dark stairs. I climbed them once to you; would climb again toward you now. And keep you company a while. And lie down next to you. Oh lamb.

Gary Young

I Want to Sing

> Tseng Tzu said, "I have heard the Master say
> that on no occasion does a man realize himself
> to the full, though, when pressed, he said that
> mourning for one's parents may be an exception."
> —*The Analects,* Book XIX, no. 17

My mother was a beautiful woman. She had been a beautiful child. She danced for the soldiers, then, and sang for them, and everyone clapped and cheered. When her period came, she thought she was dying. Her face broke out, and her mother screamed, how could you do this? How will we live? Who will love you now? Years later, my mother turned to me. I was twelve. We'd stopped to rest in a little town. She put her hands on my cheeks. Let me get that, she said, and she dug her nails into me, picking until I bled. That's how it starts, she said, and it wasn't the shock or the pain, it was the look on her face that made me want to cry.

*   *   *

I was home from the hospital and not expected to survive. My mother had come to visit before I died. She needed my attention; she was still weak. She had tried to take her life again. I have trouble breathing, she said, and tapped a gold coin hanging from a choker at her throat. It's to hide the scar, she said. But the coin was too small. I gave her my hand to sit; I gave her my arm to rise. When friends arrived for dinner, she danced for an hour, beautifully. Everyone agreed she had a talent.

302

*　　*　　*

Tell me a story, she says, one I haven't heard. So I tell her, it was autumn. Mother took us to see George. I'd made him lunch, but he couldn't eat; he was dying then of cancer. No, she says, a happy one. I tell her, you were three. There was a party in the old house. They dressed you like a flapper, and everybody danced. It's strange, she says, I can't remember, and you can't forget. I stole money to buy you food, I tell her. I know, she says, you told me before. I hid the food under my bed, but I couldn't bring myself to eat it.

*　　*　　*

I waited for my mother in the greenhouse. It was warm, and I could feel the presence of the air. I practiced words in my breath on the windows. I thought I was alone, but an older boy in the corner called my name. I asked, how do you know me? And he said, I'm your brother. He said our parents had sent him away, but he knew me, and watched me every day. That night my mother said, someone is playing a joke on you, but I knew she was lying. I believed him, I still believe him, an orphan, a boy I could never be.

*　　*　　*

The burning house turned our night clothes yellow. Standing at the curb, my brother batted ashes with his hand. We had a puppy, and my mother shouted, where's the dog, and then, my God, where's Cathy? I remember the sound of breaking glass, and walls too hot to touch. I remember pulling my sister from her bed, and leading her out into the world again. I didn't wonder, then, how I'd found her, or how my mother could have turned so easily to send me back into the smoke and flames. It was my house; I knew where I was. I could find my way even in the dark.

303

*   *   *

My mother cut her toenails and her cuticles every night until they bled. She'd take a little pick and peel away the skin; she'd cut the pale flesh away with shears. I couldn't stop her, and if I asked, are you finished, she always said, no. I sat on her bed and watched; my attention was all I had to give. It was all she ever wanted.

*   *   *

Terrified of another pregnancy, my mother asked the doctor to remove her uterus, and the doctor did. After the surgery, our dog made a nest of torn rags in a corner of the house. When we stroked her belly, our hands came away wet with milk. The vet said, she isn't having puppies, she's just a high-strung breed. She began to have seizures. Her body convulsed, and her small eyes jerked in her head. I'd pry her jaws apart, feed her raw eggs and whiskey, and she'd relax. She'd lick my face in gratitude. My mother used to say, that dog is almost human; she really is like one of the family.

*   *   *

The light from her room was penetrating, otherworldly, blue. I didn't recognize the smell, but I remember thinking, the air is burning. I was afraid to go in. I could see her lying on the bed. Her skin was blistered; she'd fallen asleep under the tanning lamp. That winter, she did it again. They covered her face with a salve, and she seemed to be melting. While she was away, I lifted the lamp over my head, and let it fall. When she discovered the lamp was broken, she screamed, nothing's safe, I can't keep anything for myself.

*   *   *

304

My mother entertained the troops in Vietnam. When she came back, she handed me the photograph of a soldier, and said, he was killed sneaking into camp the night I sang. You may not believe this, she said, but I've never felt as safe as I did while I was there. The Vietnamese soldier in the photograph is hanging by his wrists. A curtain of blood fans out from his neck. His hands are swollen; he was still alive when they strung him up with wire. My mother said, those boys couldn't do enough for me; they treated me like a queen in Vietnam. I still have a picture of the one who gave her his life.

*   *   *

My mother wouldn't ride, but when the horses had been turned out to pasture, she'd pour salt on our cabin floor, and dance all night for the cowboys. One summer she missed a turn driving into town, and rolled her car into a ditch. She was so happy to be hurt, to be an event. In the hospital she introduced me to a girl who'd spent two days pulling slivers of glass from her teased and bloody hair. My mother asked, did you miss me? But before I could answer, she turned to the girl and said, we have had such a time.

*   *   *

My mother had the flesh burned from her lips; she had the skin peeled from her face. She wanted to look young again. When the scabs fell away, and she couldn't bear the bright, new scars, she poisoned herself. I have so much to tell you, she said later. She said, I left my body. I knew I was dying, and I could see my body there. I floated away from it, down the hall, and through the door into the street. There were people everywhere, she said. It was beautiful. They wanted me to lead a parade. Mother, stop, I said, I was there.

305

                              *   *   *

My mother practiced yoga. She leaned forward from her
waist, pulled her legs behind her neck, and said, my vagina's
collapsed; the doctors say there's nothing they can do. In the
mental ward she met a young man from Texas. He had small,
hard muscles, and his face twitched when he showed me his
tattoos. He and my mother talked about home, and madness,
about the future and electric shock. They fell in love. When
they were released, he terrorized my mother, broke into her
house and beat her again and again. I should have had him
arrested and put away, but she was so happy, so excited, that
I didn't have the heart.

                              *   *   *

My mother loved violets. When she spent whole days in bed
for days on end, I brought her violets, and put them in a cup
on the nightstand by her head. I skipped lunch all week for
the money to buy them, and the florist would nod and say,
violets again. When I brought them home, my mother said,
you precious thing. Then she'd look at the flowers and say,
they're beautiful, but they never last.

                              *   *   *

My cousin had a dream last night about my mother. He said,
I was sobbing, and she held me, and rocked me in her arms
as I cried. She turned and looked behind us, at a room full of
people, and I asked, do they know you're here? And she said,
no, no they don't. My cousin said, I'd never dreamed of her
before, and I woke up happy; I was still crying, but I felt all
right. Then he stopped, and I asked, how is she? And he said,
great, great. She looked great.

*   *   *

I last saw my mother a week after her suicide, in a dream.
She was so shy; she was only there a moment. I'd called her
stupid. How could you be so stupid? Eight years later she's
back. What do you want, I ask her, what do you really want?
I want to sing, she says. And she sings.

AFTERWORD: SOME THOUGHTS
ON THE PROSE SEQUENCE

Robert Alexander

At first consideration, it makes sense to ask of a sequence that each part should be able to stand alone, as an integral object. Otherwise, how does such a sequence differ, say, from a short story broken up into parts?

For the sequence to be successful, it must itself function as a poem—that is, as a piece of art surrounded by the frame of silence. But who can ask of a poem that each section be complete by itself? Who can say of a sonnet: the octave must stand on its own, and the sestet as well? Instead, we ask only that the entire poem be self-reliant—and so we should ask of a sequence only that it be of a piece, entire. Some of the sequences in this book are indeed composed of integral sections, but in some other cases the sections can't be isolated, set apart as complete within themselves.

In each case, the whole is more than the sum of its parts. The multitude of ways in which interrelated sections can fit together is precisely why the prose sequence is so fascinating: so many possibilities, from the nearly-seamless narrative to the fragmented, hallucinatory reverie.

It has been suggested that these pieces contain accounts, as Cartier-Bresson says of his photographs, of "decisive moments." And indeed they do, but it may be better to think of them as *significant* moments, since *decisive* implies that they fit together in a narrative frame—but narration is only one of the possible systems of organization. In other words, the manner in which the pieces fit together creates a rudimentary montage . . . narrative, syllogistic, or following some other scheme.

One of the most important short prose sequences, historically speaking, is Ernest Hemingway's "In Our Time." This series of short sketches with a military theme, describing for the most part scenes from the Great War, first appeared in 1923 in the "Exile's Number" of the *Little Review* (edited by Ezra Pound). An expanded version of this sequence was published the following year as a chapbook by Bill Bird's Three Mountains Press in Paris, and its sections (titled "chapters") were later incorporated between the short stories of Hemingway's first commercial collection, also titled *In Our Time* (Boni & Liveright, 1925).

This sort of experimentation was rife among Modernist writers.[1] In *transition workshop*, for example—drawn from the pages of *transition* magazine—Eugene Jolas included prose sequences by James Joyce, Dylan Thomas, Jolas himself, and Harry Crosby, among others.[2] William Carlos Williams' *Kora in Hell,* published in 1920, has the subtitle *Improvisations*. It's a series of twenty-seven prose sequences (some of which first appeared in the *Little Review*), and each sequence is itself composed of three sections, plus in some cases an italicized "note." As Williams says regarding the organization,

> I have placed the following Improvisations in groups, somewhat after the A. B. A. formula, that one may support the other, clarifying or enforcing perhaps the other's intentions.
>
> The arrangement of the notes, each following its poem and separated from it by a ruled line, is borrowed from a small volume of Metastasio, *Varie Poesie Dell'Abate Pietro Metastasio*, Venice, 1795.[3]

It shouldn't be imagined, however, that the prose sequence is a twentieth century development only. William Blake's

Marriage of Heaven and Hell (first published in 1790) fits this description, as does Walt Whitman's *Memoranda during the War*, which was later incorporated into *Specimen Days* (1883).

One modern conception of sequence, or of montage, traces its lineage to cinema. In 1929, Sergei Eisenstein, the famous Russian film director, laid out a precise discussion of the significance of montage. He starts with a quote from Goethe: "In nature we never see anything isolated, but everything in connection with something else which is before it, beside it, under it, and over it."[4] As Eisenstein goes on to say, "Shot and montage are the basic elements of cinema. . . . To determine the nature of montage is to solve the specific problem of cinema."

Rather than being limited to the sort of sequential chronological narrative found in stage drama, "montage is an idea that arises from the collision of independent shots—shots even opposite to one another." Eisenstein turns then to language itself: "In another field, a concrete word (a denotation) set beside a concrete word yields an abstract concept—as in the Chinese and Japanese languages, where a material ideogram can indicate a transcendental (conceptual) result." So cinema (or in our case sequences) can follow a non-narrative structure. As Eisenstein asks, "Now why should the cinema follow the forms of theater and painting rather than the methodology of language, which allows wholly new concepts of ideas to arise from the combination of two concrete denotations of two concrete objects?" Each piece in a sequence "can evoke no more than a certain association"—and it is "the accumulation of such associations. . . . which will be an all-embracing complex of emotional feeling."

Eisenstein concludes that this process "can be formally identified with that of logical deduction" or "a kind of filmic reasoning." In other words, each sequence has its own sort of progression, which affects the reader, in the end, as a unified work of art. The possibilities inherent in this concept of a sequence are pretty much limitless, and the editors of this anthology have aimed to include a broad variety—narrative, syllogistic, or following some other scheme.

[1] Various examples of short sequences, including Hemingway's, can be found in *Family Portrait: American Prose Poetry 1900-1950,* ed. Robert Alexander (Buffalo, NY: White Pine Press, 2012).

[2] Eugene Jolas, ed., *transition workshop* (New York: Vagabond, 1949).

[3] William Carlos Williams, Prologue, *Kora in Hell: Improvisations* (Boston: Four Seas Co., 1920), 30.

[4] All quotes are from "A Dialectic Approach to Film Form," reprinted in *Film Form: Essays in Film Theory*, ed. and trans. Jay Leyda (New York: Harcourt, 1949), 1-16. Jay Leyda was himself the author of a prose sequence, "It May Have Been the Spring Evening" [etc.], which appeared in *Blues: A Magazine of New Rhythms* (vol. 1, no. 8, Spring 1930), edited by Charles Henri Ford while he was a student at the University of Mississippi.

Contributors' Notes

Robert Alexander is the founding editor of the Marie Alexander Poetry Series. His most recent book of prose poems is *What the Raven Said.*

Nin Andrews is the editor of a book of translations of the French poet Henri Michaux entitled *Someone Wants to Steal My Name*, published by Cleveland State University Press. She is also the author of six chapbooks and five full-length poetry collections. Her book, *Why God Is a Woman*, was published in 2015 by BOA Editions. "The Year Prayer Wasn't Enough," "Confederate Gil," "Mr. Simmons" first appeared in *Storyscape*; "Magic" in *Sixth Finch*; and "Hair Spray and God's Minions" in *Indiana Review.*

John Azrak is the former English Chair of a Long Island high school. He has published widely and has work forthcoming in *Poetry East, Still Point Arts Quarterly, Paddlefish, Pinyon Review*, and *Nimrod International.*

Wendy Barker's most recent collection of poetry, *One Blackbird At a Time* (winner of the John Ciardi Prize), was published by Bk Mk Press. Her poems have appeared in numerous journas and anthologies, including *Best American Poetry 2013*, and she is poet-in-residence at UT San Antonio. *Nothing between Us: The Berkeley Years* was published by Del Sol Press in 2009.

Eric Braun's fiction has appeared in *Minnesota Monthly, Third Coast Review,* and *Redivider*, among other journals. A recent McKnight Artist Fellow, Eric lives in Minneapolis where he is a freelance writer and editor and full-time nostalgist. "My Beard" originally appeared in *Redivider.*

A fourth-generation Nebraskan, **Amy Knox Brown** is Program Director and Assistant Professor of English at the College of St. Mary in Omaha. Her story collection *Three Versions of the Truth* was a finalist for the Shenandoah/Glasgow Prize for Emerging Writers, and her work has appeared in *Virginia Quarterly Review, Narrative,* and other literary magazines.

Nickole Brown's books include her debut, *Sister,* a novel-in-poems (Red Hen Press, 2007), and her latest collection, *Fanny Says* (BOA Editions, 2015). Currently, she is Editor of the Marie Alexander Poetry Series and teaches at the low-residency MFA in Creative Writing at Murray State.

Leah Browning is the author of three nonfiction books for teens and pre-teens, and her third chapbook, *In the Chair Museum,* was published by Dancing Girl Press in 2013. "Little Signs" first appeared in a slightly different form in *971 Menu.*

Cathleen Calbert is the author of three books of poetry: *Lessons in Space, Bad Judgment,* and *Sleeping with a Famous Poet.* Her work has appeared in the *New York Times* and the *Paris Review,* and she was awarded the Mary Tucker Thorp Award from Rhode Island College, where she is a professor of English.

Michael Campagnoli can be seen most mornings running somewhere along the coast of Maine with his mongrel dog, Yogi, and Anthony, his equally mongrel son. "In the Bar of the Commodore" and "The Beards" first appeared in *Rattle;* "September 16," "The Druse," "Puissant and Ready to Prove," "The Stump," "Humane Interests," "On The Esplanade," and "It Happened All The Time" in *Quiddity*; and "Song of Zokat Blatt" in *Inkwell.*

Christopher Citro's first book of poetry, *The Maintenance of the Shimmy-Shammy*, was published by Steel Toe Books in 2015. His poems appear or are forthcoming in *Prairie Schooner, Third Coast, Verse Daily,* and elsewhere, and his creative nonfiction has been published in *Colorado Review.* He received his MFA in poetry from Indiana University. "Happy Birthday to Me" was first published as an Architrave Press broadside. "Happiness, in a Way," "Something Awful, Autumn Nights," and "Be My Guest" were first published in *Used Furniture Review.*

Jennifer Kwon Dobbs was born in Wonju, Republic of Korea, and lives in St. Paul, Minnesota. She is the author of *Paper Pavilion*, recipient of the 2007 White Pine Press Poetry Prize, and *Song of a Mirror,* a finalist for the 2009 Tupelo Press Snowbound Chapbook Award; she is currently an assistant professor of creative writing affiliated with the Race and Ethnic Studies Program at St. Olaf College.

Jacqueline Doyle teaches at California State University, East Bay. Her flash prose has appeared in numerous journals, including *Vestal Review, Sweet, Monkeybicycle, The Rumpus, Café Irreal,* and *blossombones* (where "Dora" was originally published), and she earned a Notable Essay listing in *Best American Essays 2013.*

Russell Evatt's work has appeared in *Barrow Street, Cimarron Review, Lake Effect, Louisville Review,* and *Poems & Plays.* He lives and works in South Texas.

Wesley Fairman is a graduate of the low-residency MFA in Creative Writing at Murray State University; she serves as the fiction editor for *Sawmill,* a Typecast Publishing publication. Dedicated to enriching the literary arts community in Louisville, Wesley has directed the Writer's Block Festival and the InKY Reading Series.

Elisabeth Frost's books are *All of Us: Poems* (White Pine Press), *The Feminist Avant-Garde in American Poetry* (Iowa), and the chapbooks *A Theory of the Vowel* (Red Glass Books) and *Rumor (*Mermaid Tenement Books). Selected collaborations with the artist Dianne Kornberg appear in the volume *Bindle* (Ricochet Editions). She is Professor of English and Women's Studies at Fordham University.

Casey Fuller received his MFA from the Rainier Writing Workshop at Pacific Lutheran University. His work has appeared in *Crab Creek Review, The Portland Review, Two Hawks*, and others.

Molly Fuller has her MA from Ohio University and her MFA from Sarah Lawrence College. Her most recent chapbook, *All My Loves*, is forthcoming from All Nations Press. "The Neighborhood Psycho Dreams of Love" originally appeared in *Quickly*, and was reprinted in *The Neighborhood Psycho Dreams of Love* (Cutty Wren Press, 2013). "Match" originally appeared in *Crack the Spine.*

Maureen Gibbon is the author of the novels *Swimming Sweet Arrow*, *Thief* and *Paris Red.* Her prose poem collection *Magdalena* was the 2007 recipient of the Marie Alexander Prize for Poetry.

Sarah Goldstein was born in Toronto and lives in western Massachusetts. Her writing has most recently appeared in *Anti-* (online), *Denver Quarterly, Handsome,* and *Verse.* Her first book, *Fables*, was released in 2011 from Tarpaulin Sky.

Jeffrey Greene is the author of several poetry collections, a memoir, and two personalized nature books. He teaches at the American University of Paris and for the Pan-European

MFA program. "Domestic Narratives" originially appeared in *The Prose Poem Project.*

Sonia Greenfield teaches writing at University of Southern California–Dornsife, and her work can be found in the *2010 Best American Poetry.* Her book, *Boy with a Halo at the Farmer's Market,* won the 2014 Codhill Prize. "In Parts" was originally published in *The Bellevue Literary Review.*

Carol Guess is the author of thirteen books of poetry and prose, including *Tinderbox Lawn* and *Doll Studies: Forensics.* She is Professor of English at Western Washington University. "Revival of Rosemaling" originally appeared in *Sou'wester Magazine*, Volume 38, No. 1, Fall 2009; and in *Darling Endangered* (Brooklyn Arts Press, 2011).

Jessica Rae Hahn received her MFA from Emerson College. Her work has appeared in *Cerise Press* and *Seneca Review,* among other journals. She teaches visual arts and pre-kindergarten, and lives in Cincinnati with her poet fiancé.

Marie Harris was New Hampshire Poet Laureate from 1999-2004. She is the author of four books of poetry, including the prose poem memoir, *Your Sun, Manny* (2nd expanded edition,White Pine Press, 2010), and a new children's book, *The Girl Who Heard Colors* (A Nancy Paulsen Book; Penguin, 2013).

Jim Harrison is the author of thirty-five books of fiction, nonfiction, and poetry. His most recent collections include a volume of poetry, *Dead Man's Float* (Copper Canyon), in which "Hospital" appears, and the forthcoming novella collection, *The Ancient Minstrel.*

Pamela Hart is writer in residence at the Katonah Museum of Art where she manages a visual literacy arts in education program. She was awarded a National Endowment for the Arts poetry fellowship in 2013, and her chapbook, *The End of the Body* was published in 2006.

Holly Iglesias is the author of *Angles of Approach* (White Pine Press), *Souvenirs of a Shrunken World* (Kore Press) and *Boxing Inside the Box: Women's Prose Poetry* (Quale Press). Her most recent publication is the chapbook, *Fruta Bomba* (Q Ave Press), which is one section of a work in progress entitled *Sturdy Child of Terror.* She teaches in the Master of Liberal Arts Program at the University of North Carolina–Asheville. "Nothing to Declare" was first published in the chapbook, *Fruta Bomba* (Q Avenue Press, 2012).

Siel Ju can be found in Santa Monica and her poems and stories have been published or are forthcoming in *Denver Quarterly, ZYZZYVA, The Missouri Review, Hobart, Drunken Boat*, and other journals. Her chapbook of poems, *Feelings Are Chemicals in Transit*, was published by Dancing Girl Press in 2014. An earlier version of "The Locust of Desire" appeared in *ZYZZYVA*.

Elizabeth Kerlikowske is the winner of the 2013 Standing Rock Cultural Arts Chapbook Contest for *Last Hula*; another chapbook, *Suicide Notes* will be published this spring. Her works have appeared in various literary reviews and anthologies, and she teaches at Kellogg Community College in Battle Creek, Michigan. "Forever Tutu," "The Max Factor," "The Price," and "Dress Rehearsal" first appeared in *Sweet: A Literary Confection.*

Robert W. King received his Ph.D. from the University of Iowa and the Writers Workshop in 1963. He has published a creative non-fiction book, *Stepping Twice into the River: Fol-*

lowing Dakota Waters, and two books of poetry, *Old Man Laughing* (2007) and *Some of These Days* (2013).

Jenn Koiter divides her time between Delhi and Los Angeles, where she attends the MFA program at Antioch University. Her work has appeared in the *South Dakota Review, Barrelhouse, Bateau, Anti-, Copper Nickel, Rock & Sling,* and *No Tell Motel.*

Elizabeth Langemak lives in Philadelphia, Pennsylvania, where she teaches at La Salle University. Her work appears in publications such as *Shenandoah, Literary Imagination* and *Best New Poets.*

Gian Lombardo has published six collections of prose poetry, the latest of which are *Machines We Have Built* (Quale Press, 2014) and *Who Lets Go First* (Swamp Press, 2010). He teaches book and magazine publishing at Emerson College where he directs the Literary Publishing Certificate program.

Christina Manweller's work has recently been published in *Black Warrior Review, South Loop Review, Creative Nonfiction, Hotel Amerika,* and *Crannóg Literary Magazine* (Ireland), among other publications.

Debra Marquart's books include three poetry collections, a book of short stories, and a memoir, *The Horizontal World: Growing Up Wild in the Middle of Nowhere,* which was awarded the 2007 PEN USA Creative Nonfiction Award. Marquart teaches in the Stonecoast Low-Residency MFA Program at the University of Southern Maine, and she is the Director of the MFA Program in Creative Writing and Environment at Iowa State University. "Whisker Meditations," which originally was published in *Georgetown Review,* appears in *Small Buried Things: Poems* (New Rivers Press, 2015).

Kathleen McGookey's work has appeared in a variety of literary journals and anthologies. Her book, *Stay,* is just out from Press 53. She has published a book of prose poems, *Whatever Shines,* two chapbooks, and a book of translations of French poet Georges Godeau's prose poems, *We'll See.* Her next full-length collection, *At the Zoo*, is forthcoming from White Pine Press. Sections of "Nine Letters" have been published in *Columbia Poetry Review, Glassworks, The Literary Review, Miramar,* and S*ugar House Review,* and will appear in *At the Zoo.*

Monica Nawrocki lives on a remote island off the west coast of Canada with her partner and dog. She earns her living as a substitute teacher—often reading under-construction manuscripts to captive classroom audiences and impersonating someone different every day. "Vancouver Conversations" first appeared in *Sawmill.*

Pamela Painter's work has apeared in numerous anthologies, and her fourth story collection,*Ways to Spend the Night* is forthcoming from Engine Books. She teaches at Emerson College in Boston.

Irena Praitis is a professor of literature and creative writing at California State University–Fullerton. Her recent books include *Straws and Shadows* (Moon Tide Press, 2012) and *One Woman's Life* (Diversion Press, 2010).

Alizabeth Rasmussen is a freelance writer and photographer whose work has appeared in *damselfly press, Wild Violet,* and *Mused: The Bella Online Literary Review.* She blogs regularly at *Write Click* and is a blog editor for *Literary Mama.*

William Reichard is the author of four collections of poetry, most recently *Sin Eater* (2010) and *This Brightness* (2007) both from Mid-List Press. Reichard is the editor of the anthology, *American Tensions: Literature of Identity and the Search for Social Justice* (New Village Press, 2011). His fifth poetry collection, *Two Men Rowing Madly Toward Infinity,* is forthcoming from Broadstone Books.

Richard Robbins has published fiction and nonfiction in a variety of places; his poetry collections include *Radioactive City* and *Other Americas.* He currently directs the creative writing program at Minnesota State University–Mankato. Portions of "Betrayals" first appeared in the *South Dakota Review, Permafrost, Weber Studies,* and *Pebble Lake Review.*

Jim Ruland is a veteran of the U.S. Navy, author of the short story collection *Big Lonesome,* and curator of the Southern California-based reading series Vermin on the Mount, now in its tenth year. His novel *Forest of Fortune* was published by Tyrus Books in 2014. Part of "At the Orpheu Café was originally published in The Last Bookstore's *Indie Shelves Chapbook* (Winter 2012).

F. Daniel Rzicznek's most recent publication is the prose poem chapbook *Nag Champa in the Rain* (Orange Monkey Publishing, 2014). Also coeditor (with Gary L. McDowell) of *The Rose Metal Press Field Guide to Prose Poetry* (Rose Metal Press, 2010), Rzicznek teaches writing at Bowling Green State University.

Lucas Southworth's collection of short stories, *Everyone Here Has a Gun*, won AWP's Grace Paley Prize and was published by the University of Massachusetts Press in 2013. He is an assistant professor of writing at Loyola University Maryland. "A Dainty Network of Bones" was first published in *[PANK]*.

Julie Stotz-Ghosh's work has appeared in various journals and anthologies, including *Poetry Midwest, Quarter After Eight*, and *Sudden Stories: The Mammoth Book of Miniscule Fiction*. She teaches writing and literature at Kalamazoo Valley Community College.

Laura Tansley's writing has been published in *Butcher's Dog, Cosmonaut's Avenue, The Island Review* (with Amy Mackelden and Jon Owen), *Kenyon Review Online* (with Micaela Maftei), *New Writing Scotland* and *Short Fiction in Theory and Practice*. She is co-editor of *Writing Creative Non-Fiction: Determining the Form.* "The Wake She Leaves like a Whirpool" originally appeared in *[PANK]*.

Bob Thurber is the author of *Paperboy: A Dysfunctional Novel* and two collection of stories, *Nickel Fictions* and *Nothing But Trouble.* Over the years his stories have appeared in thirty-plus anthologies and received a long list of awards and citations, including the Barry Hannah Fiction Prize and the *Meridian* Editor's Prize.

Alison Townsend, Professor Emerita at the University of Wisconsin–Whitewater, is the author of two poetry collections, *The Blue Dress: Poems and Prose Poems* and *Persephone in America,* in addition to two chapbooks, *And Still the Music* and *What the Body Knows.* "Coyote Crossings" originally appeared in *Parabola 38*, no. 3 (Fall 2013), special issue on Power.

C. W. (Bill) Truesdale was the founder and publisher of New Rivers Press and a long-time supporter of hybrid forms. He passed away in 2001, shortly before New Rivers made its own transition from the Twin Cities to a new home at Minnesota State University at Moorhead. "Doña Baby" first appeared in *Stiller's Pond: New Fiction from the Upper*

Midwest, ed. Jonis Agee, Roger K. Blakely, and Susan Welch (New Rivers Press, 1988).

Luisa Villani is a former Wallis Annenberg Fellow at The University of Southern California. Her work has appeared in the *New England Review, Prairie Schooner, Third Coast, Hotel Amerika,* and many other journals.

Mark Vinz is Professor Emeritus of English at Minnesota State University Moorhead. His poems, prose poems, stories, and essays have appeared in numerous books, magazines and anthologies; he is also the co-editor (with Robert Alexander and C.W. Truesdale) of *The Party Train: A Collection of North American Prose Poetry.*

Julie Marie Wade's publications include *Wishbone: A Memoir in Fractures; Without: Poems; Small Fires: Essays*; *Postage Due: Poems & Prose Poems; Tremolo: An Essay;* and *When I Was Straight: Poems.* She is the newest member of the creative writing faculty at Florida International University. "I'm drowning here, & you're describing the water" (*As Good As It Gets*) and "There's no hole on earth where the heart drops through without bringing something with it" (James Allen Hall) were first published in *Anti-*. "Or else" was first published in *kill author.*

Cecilia Woloch, recipient of a fellowship from the National Endowment for the Arts, is the author of six collections of poetry, most recently *Carpathia,* published by BOA Editions in 2009, and *Earth,* winner of the 2014 Two Sylvias Press Prize for the chapbook, as well as a novel-in-prose-poems, *Sur la Route,* published by Quayle Press in 2015. She conducts workshops for writers throughout the United States and around the world. "Shine" appeared in *Carpathia.*

Gary Young's most recent collection of poems, *Adversary,* has just been released, and *Precious Mirror*, a book of translations from the Japanese, is forthcoming. *Even So: New and Selected Poems* was published by White Pine Press in 2012. He teaches creative writing and directs the Cowell Press at UC Santa Cruz. "I Want to Sing" originally appeared in *No Other Life* (Heyday Books, 2005).

THE MARIE ALEXANDER POETRY SERIES

Founded in 1996 by Robert Alexander, the Marie Alexander Poetry Series is dedicated to promoting the appreciation, enjoyment, and understanding of American prose poetry. Currently an imprint of White Pine Press, the series publishes one to two books annually. These are typically single-author collections of short prose pieces, sometimes interwoven with lineated sections, and an occasional anthology demonstrating the historical or international context within which American poetry exists. It is our mission to publish the very best contemporary prose poetry and to carry the rich tradition of this hybrid form on into the 21st century.

Founding Editor: Robert Alexander
Editor: Nickole Brown

Volume 20
Nothing to Declare: A Guide to the Flash Sequence
Edited by Robert Alexander, Eric Braun & Debra Marquart

Volume 19
To Some Women I Have Known
Re'Lynn Hansen

Volume 18
The Rusted City
Rochelle Hurt

Volume 17
Postage Due
Julie Marie Wade

Volume 16
Family Portrait: American Prose Poetry 1900–1950
Edited by Robert Alexander

Volume 15
All of Us
Elisabeth Frost

Volume 14
Angles of Approach
Holly Iglesias

Volume 13
Pretty
Kim Chinquee

Volume 12
Reaching Out to the World
Robert Bly

Volume 11
The House of Your Dream:
An International Collection of Prose Poetry
Edited by Robert Alexander and Dennis Maloney

Volume 10
Magdalena
Maureen Gibbon

Volume 9
The Angel of Duluth
Madelon Sprengnether

Volume 8
Light from an Eclipse
Nancy Lagomarsino

Volume 7
A Handbook for Writers
Vern Rutsala

Volume 6
The Blue Dress
Alison Townsend

Volume 5
Moments without Names: New & Selected Prose Poems
Morton Marcus

Volume 4
Whatever Shines
Kathleen McGookey

Volume 3
Northern Latitudes
Lawrence Millman

Volume 2
Your Sun, Manny
Marie Harris

Volume 1
Traffic
Jack Anderson